MICROSOFT®

Internet Explorer 6

Introductory Concepts and Techniques

Windows XP Edition

Gary B. Shelly
Thomas J. Cashman
Steven G. Forsythe

THOMSON
COURSE TECHNOLOGY

COURSE TECHNOLOGY
25 THOMSON PLACE
BOSTON MA 02210

SHELLY
CASHMAN
SERIES®

Australia • Canada • Denmark • Japan • Mexico • New Zealand • Philippines • Puerto Rico • Singapore
South Africa • Spain • United Kingdom • United States

THOMSON

COURSE TECHNOLOGY

Microsoft Internet Explorer 6:
Introductory Concepts and Techniques
Windows XP Edition

Gary B. Shelly

Thomas J. Cashman

Steven G. Forsythe

Executive Director:
Cheryl Costantini

Senior Acquisitions Editor:
Dana Merk

Senior Editor:
Alexandra Arnold

Product Manager:
Reed Cotter

Editorial Assistant:
Selena Coppock

Print Buyer:
Laura Burns

Series Consulting Editor:
Jim Quasney

Production Editor:
Aimee Poirier

Development Editor:
Ginny Harvey

Proofreader:
Kim Kosmatka

Interior Designer:
Becky Herrington

Cover Image:
GEX Publishing Services

Compositor:
GEX Publishing Services

MICROSOFT®

Internet Explorer 6

Introductory Concepts and Techniques
Windows XP Edition

Contents

Project Three

Communicating Over the Internet

Appendix A

Internet Options

Appendix B

Adding News Accounts

Preface

The Shelly Cashman Series® offers the finest textbooks in computer education. We are proud of the fact that the previous editions of this textbook have been so well received by computer educators. With each new edition, we have made significant improvements based on the software and comments made by the instructors and students. This Windows XP edition of *Microsoft Internet Explorer 6: Introductory Concepts and Techniques* continues with the innovation, quality, and reliability that you have come to expect from the Shelly Cashman Series.

In the few short years since its birth, the World Wide Web, or Web, has grown beyond all expectations. During this time, Web usage has increased from a limited number of users to more than 600 million users worldwide, accessing Web pages on any topic you can imagine. Individuals, schools, businesses, and governmental agencies all are taking advantage of this innovative way of accessing the Internet to provide information, products, services, and education electronically. Microsoft Internet Explorer 6 provides the novice as well as the experienced user a window with which to look into the Web and tap an abundance of resources.

Objectives of This Textbook

Microsoft Internet Explorer 6: Introductory Concepts and Techniques, Windows XP Edition is intended for use in a one-credit, three- to-five week course or in combination with other books in an introductory computer concepts or applications course. Specific objectives of this book are as follows:

- To teach students how to use Internet Explorer 6
- To expose students to various World Wide Web resources
- To acquaint students with the more popular search engines
- To show students how to evaluate Web pages and do research using the World Wide Web
- To teach students how to communicate with other Internet users

The Shelly Cashman Approach

Features of the Shelly Cashman Series *Microsoft Internet Explorer 6: Introductory Concepts and Techniques, Windows XP Edition* book include:

- **Step-by-Step, Screen-by-Screen Instructions:** Each of the steps required to complete a task is presented in an easy-to-understand manner. Full-color screens with call outs accompany the steps.
- **Thoroughly Tested Projects:** Unparalleled quality is assured because every screen in the book is produced by the author only after performing a step, and then each project must pass Course Technology's award-winning Quality Assurance program.
- **Other Ways Boxes:** The Other Ways boxes displayed at the end of most of the step-by-step sequences specify the other ways to do the task completed in the steps. Thus, the steps and the Other Ways box make a comprehensive reference unit.
- **More About and Q&A Features:** These marginal annotations provide background information, tips, and answers to common questions that complement the topics covered, adding depth and perspective to the learning process.

Other Ways

1. Click Start button on Windows taskbar, click Internet Explorer icon on Start menu
2. Double-click Internet Explorer icon on desktop
3. Press CTRL+ESC, press P, I

More About

The Internet

The Internet started as a government experiment for the military. The military wanted a communication technique that would connect different computers running different operating systems. From this experiment, a communication technique originated called Transmission Control Protocol/Internet Protocol, or TCP/IP.

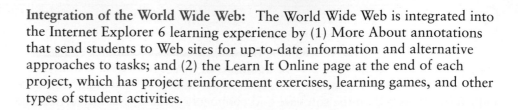

Integration of the World Wide Web: The World Wide Web is integrated into the Internet Explorer 6 learning experience by (1) More About annotations that send students to Web sites for up-to-date information and alternative approaches to tasks; and (2) the Learn It Online page at the end of each project, which has project reinforcement exercises, learning games, and other types of student activities.

Organization of This Textbook

Microsoft Internet Explorer 6: Introductory Concepts and Techniques, Windows XP Edition consists of three projects and two appendices. Each project ends with a large number of exercises to reinforce what students learn in the project. The projects and appendices are organized as follows:

Project 1 – Introduction to Internet Explorer In Project 1, students are introduced to the Internet, World Wide Web, and Internet Explorer. Topics include starting Internet Explorer; browsing the World Wide Web; refreshing a Web page; using the History list and Favorites list to display Web pages; adding Web pages to and removing Web pages from the Favorites list; saving and printing a picture, text, or Web page; copying and pasting text or pictures from a Web page into WordPad; and using Internet Explorer Help.

Project 2 – Web Research Techniques and Search Engines In Project 2, students are introduced to the eight Web page categories, techniques to search the Web using Search Companion and Search Assistant, and methods to evaluate a Web page. Topics include searching the Web using keywords or a directory; performing an advanced search; evaluating and recording relevant information about a Web source; using Search Companion to search for Web pages and change Internet search preferences; using Search Assistant to search for an e-mail address, map, landmark, definition, or picture; and using the Address bar to display a Web page, search the Web, and display folder contents.

Project 3 – Communicating Over the Internet In Project 3, students learn to read and send an e-mail message, work with Address Book, read and post an article to a newsgroup, send and receive instant messages, have online meetings, and listen to an Internet radio station. Topics include reading, replying to, and deleting an e-mail message; composing, formatting, and sending a new e-mail message; adding and deleting Address Book contacts; reading and posting a newsgroup article; subscribing and unsubscribing to a newsgroup; starting, signing in, and sending an instant message; having an online meeting; displaying the Media bar and Radio guide; and listening to an Internet radio station.

Appendix A – Internet Options Appendix A explains how to change the settings for Internet options. Settings include changing the default home page; deleting cookies and temporary Internet files; specifying a privacy setting for using the Internet; assigning a Web site to a security zone; controlling the type of content a computer can access on the Internet; setting up an Internet connection; and selecting the programs to send and receive e-mail, read and post articles to a newsgroup, and place Internet calls.

Appendix B – Adding News Accounts Appendix B contains the steps to follow to add a news account to a computer while working with newsgroups in Project 3.

End-of-Project Student Activities

A notable strength of the Shelly Cashman Series Web browser books is the extensive student activities at the end of each project. Well-structured student activities can make the difference between students merely participating in a class and students retaining the information they learn. The following activities are included in this book.

- **What You Should Know** A listing of the tasks completed within a project together with the pages on which the step-by-step, screen-by-screen explanations appear. This section provides a perfect study review for students.

- **Learn It Online** Every project features a Learn It Online page consisting of twelve exercises. These exercises utilize the Web to offer project-related reinforcement activities that will help students gain confidence in their browser abilities. They include True/False, Multiple Choice, Short Answer, Flash Cards, Practice Test, Learning Games, Tips and Tricks, Newsgroup usage, Expanding Your Horizons, Search Sleuth, Internet Explorer How-To Articles, and Getting More From the Web.

- **In the Lab** Several assignments per project require students to apply the knowledge gained in the project to solve problems on the Web.

- **Cases and Places** Up to six unique case studies including one small-group activity require students to apply their knowledge to real-world situations.

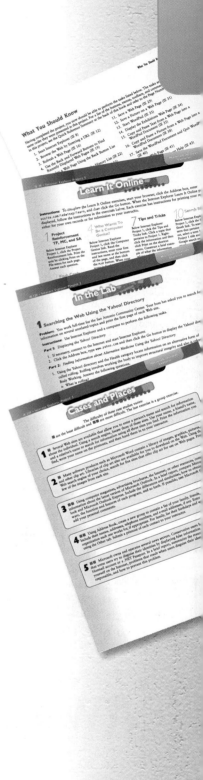

Instructor Resources

The Shelly Cashman Series is dedicated to providing you with all of the tools you need to make your class a success. Information on all supplementary materials is available through your Course Technology representative or by calling one of the following telephone numbers: Colleges and Universities, 1-800-648-7450; High Schools, 1-800-824-5179; Private Career Colleges, 1-800-347-7707; Canada, 1-800-268-2222; Corporations with IT Training Centers, 1-800-648-7450; and Government Agencies, Health-Care Organizations, and Correctional Facilities, 1-800-477-3692.

Instructor Resources CD-ROM

The Instructor Resources for this textbook include both teaching and testing aids. The contents of each item on the Instructor Resources CD-ROM (ISBN 0-619-25513-7) are described below.

INSTRUCTOR'S MANUAL The Instructor's Manual is made up of Microsoft Word files, which include detailed lesson plans with page number references, lecture notes, teaching tips, classroom activities, discussion topics, projects to assign, and transparency references. The transparencies are available through the Figure Files described below.

SYLLABUS Sample syllabi, which can be customized easily to a course, are included. The syllabi cover policies, class and lab assignments and exams, and procedural information.

FIGURE FILES Illustrations for every figure in the textbook are available in electronic form. Use this ancillary to present a slide show in lecture or to print transparencies for use in lecture with an overhead projector. If you have a personal computer and LCD device, this ancillary can be an effective tool for presenting lectures.

POWERPOINT PRESENTATIONS PowerPoint Presentations is a multimedia lecture presentation system that provides PowerPoint slides for each project. Presentations are based on project objectives. Use this presentation system to present well-organized lectures that are both interesting and knowledge based. PowerPoint Presentations provides consistent coverage at schools that use multiple lecturers.

SOLUTIONS TO EXERCISES Solutions are included for the end-of-project exercises, as well as the Project Reinforcement exercises.

TEST BANK & TEST ENGINE The ExamView test bank includes 110 questions for every project (25 multiple-choice, 50 true/false, and 35 completion) with page number references, and when appropriate, figure references. A version of the test bank you can print also is included. The test bank comes with a copy of the test engine, ExamView, the ultimate tool for your objective-based testing needs. ExamView is a state-of-the-art test builder that is easy to use. ExamView enables you to create paper-, LAN-, or Web-based tests from test banks designed specifically for your Course Technology textbook. Utilize the ultra-efficient QuickTest Wizard to create tests in less than five minutes by taking advantage of Course Technology's question banks, or customize your own exams from scratch.

ADDITIONAL ACTIVITIES FOR STUDENTS These additional activities consist of Project Reinforcement Exercises, which are true/false, multiple choice, and short answer questions that help students gain confidence in the material learned.

Online Content

Course Technology offers textbook-based content for Blackboard, WebCT, and MyCourse 2.1

BLACKBOARD AND WEBCT As the leading provider of IT content for the Blackboard and WebCT platforms, Course Technology delivers rich content that enhances your textbook to give your students a unique learning experience. Course Technology has partnered with WebCT and Blackboard to deliver our market-leading content through these state-of-the-art online learning platforms. Course Technology offers customizable content in every subject area, from computer concepts to PC repair.

MYCOURSE 2.1 MyCourse 2.1 is Course Technology's powerful online course management and content delivery system. Completely maintained and hosted by Thomson, MyCourse 2.1 delivers an online learning environment that is completely secure and provides superior performance. MyCourse 2.1 allows non-technical users to create, customize, and deliver World Wide Web-based courses; post content and assignments; manage student enrollment; administer exams; track results in the online gradebook; and more. With MyCourse 2.1, you easily can create a customized course that will enhance every learning experience.

MICROSOFT
Internet Explorer 6

Introduction to Internet Explorer

PROJECT

CASE PERSPECTIVE

As an art history major in a local community college, you have found that you can enhance your experience if you learn more about using the Internet. In fact, your art history instructor recommends you take a short college course to help you understand how to search for articles and pictures on the Internet.

You browse through your school's class schedule for the upcoming semester and find an Introduction to the Internet class offered in the Computer Information Science department. The course description emphasizes that the course is for anyone who has little or no experience using the Internet. The topics listed in the course description include connecting to the Internet using Microsoft Internet Explorer, searching the Internet for information, and saving information you find on a Web page. You decide this is the perfect course for you to learn about the Internet. So, you sign up and complete the course.

After completing the course, you decide to use your knowledge of Internet Explorer to earn money by performing Internet research for college instructors and local businesses. Instead of the usual resume/cover letter approach to obtaining a job, you decide to take out an advertisement in the local newspaper that advertises your Internet search skills.

Among the responses you receive from the advertisement is one from the manager of the Livingston Gallery. She hires you to identify the origin and authenticity of a piece of Asian art, titled *Three Leaves* that the gallery wants to purchase. You agree to search for information about the Asian art and supply the gallery with pictures and text associated with the art.

As you read through this project, you will learn how to use Internet Explorer to connect to the Internet, search the Web, and save and organize information you find on Web pages.

Introduction to Internet Explorer

PROJECT

1

You will have mastered the material in this project when you can:

- Define the Internet and the World Wide Web
- Explain a link, Uniform Resource Locator, and Hypertext Markup Language
- Describe key Internet Explorer features and the Internet Explorer window
- Enter a Uniform Resource Locator (URL)
- Browse the World Wide Web using the History list, Favorites list, or URLs
- Display Web pages using the Back list and the Back, Forward, and Home buttons

- Display recently displayed Web pages using the History list
- Add and remove a Web page from the Favorites list
- Save a picture or text from a Web page or an entire Web page on a floppy disk
- Copy and paste text or pictures from a Web page into WordPad
- Print a WordPad document and Web page
- Use Internet Explorer Help

Introduction

The Internet is the most popular and fastest growing area in computing today. Using the Internet, you can do research, get a loan, shop for services and merchandise, job hunt, buy and sell stocks, display weather maps, obtain medical advice, watch movies, listen to high-quality music, and converse with people worldwide.

Once considered mysterious, the Internet is now accessible to the general public because personal computers with user-friendly tools have reduced its complexity. The Internet, with its millions of connected computers, continues to grow with thousands of new users coming online everyday. Schools, businesses, newspapers, television stations, and government services all can be found on the Internet. Service providers are popping up all around the country providing inexpensive access to the Internet from home; but, just exactly what is the Internet?

The Internet

The **Internet** is a worldwide collection of networks (Figure 1-1), each of which is composed of a collection of smaller networks. A **network** is composed of several computers connected together to share resources and data. For example, on a college

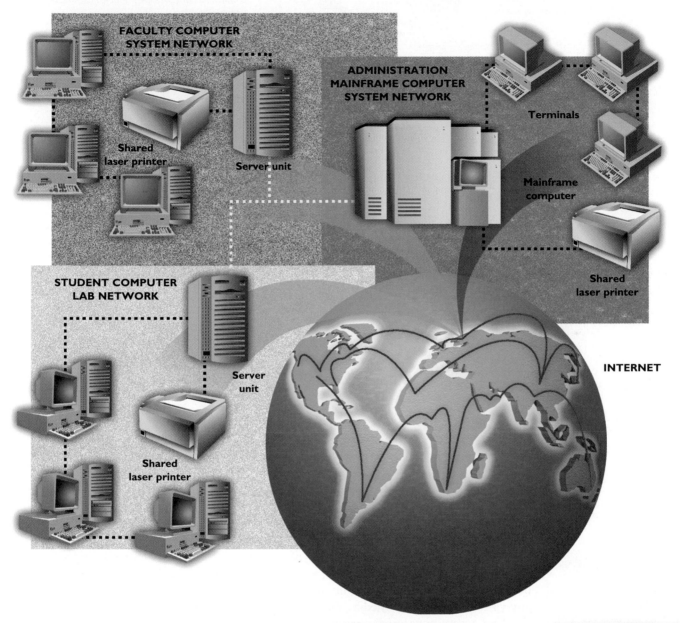

FACULTY COMPUTER
SYSTEM NETWORK

Shared
laser printer

Server unit

ADMINISTRATION
MAINFRAME COMPUTER
SYSTEM NETWORK

Terminals

Mainframe
computer

Shared
laser printer

STUDENT COMPUTER
LAB NETWORK

Server
unit

Shared
laser printer

INTERNET

FIGURE 1-1

campus, the network in the student lab can connect to the faculty computer network, which is connected to the administration network, and they all can connect to the Internet.

Networks are connected with high-, medium-, and low-speed data lines that allow data to move from one computer to another (Figure 1-2 on the next page). The Internet has high-speed data lines that connect major computers located around the world, which form the **Internet backbone**. Other, less powerful computers, such as those used by local ISPs (Internet service providers) often attach to the Internet backbone using medium-speed data lines. Finally, the connection between your computer at home and your local ISP, often called **the last mile**, employs low-speed data lines such as telephone lines. In many cases today, cable is replacing telephone lines over the last mile, which significantly improves access to information on the Internet.

More About

The Internet

The Internet started as a government experiment for the military. The military wanted a communication technique that would connect different computers running different operating systems. From this experiment, a communication technique originated called Transmission Control Protocol/Internet Protocol, or TCP/IP.

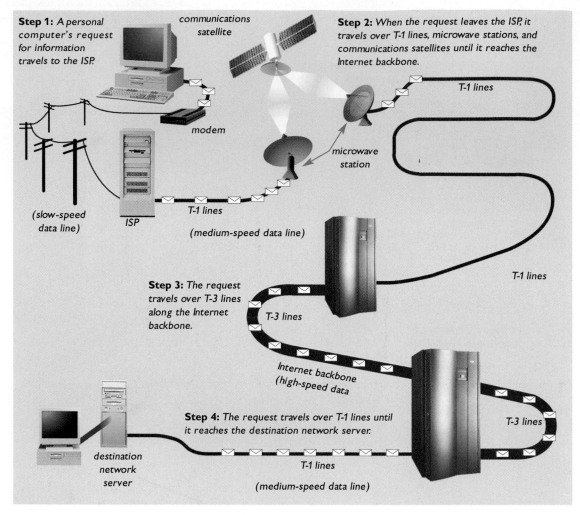

Step 1: A personal computer's request for information travels to the ISP.

communications satellite

Step 2: When the request leaves the ISP, it travels over T-1 lines, microwave stations, and communications satellites until it reaches the Internet backbone.

T-1 lines

modem

microwave station

(slow-speed data line)

ISP

T-1 lines

(medium-speed data line)

T-1 lines

Step 3: The request travels over T-3 lines along the Internet backbone.

T-3 lines

Internet backbone (high-speed data

Step 4: The request travels over T-1 lines until it reaches the destination network server.

T-3 lines

destination network server

T-1 lines

(medium-speed data line)

FIGURE 1-2

The World Wide Web

Modern computers have the capability of delivering information in a variety of ways, such as graphics, sound, video clips, animation, and, of course, regular text. On the Internet, this multimedia capability is available in a form called **hypermedia**, which is any variety of computer media, including text, graphics, video, sound, and virtual reality.

You access hypermedia using a **hyperlink**, or simply **link**, which is a special software pointer that points to the location of the computer on which the hypermedia is stored and the hypermedia itself. A link can point to hypermedia on any computer connected to the Internet that is running the proper software. Thus, clicking a link on a computer in Los Angeles could display text and graphics located in New York.

The collection of links throughout the Internet creates an interconnected network called the **World Wide Web**, which also is referred to as the **Web**, or **WWW**. Each computer within the Web containing hypermedia that you can reference with a link is called a **Web site**. Millions of Web sites around the world are accessible through the Internet.

Graphics, text, and other hypermedia available at a Web site are stored in a file called a **Web page**. Therefore, when you click a link to display a picture, read text, view a video, or listen to music, you actually are viewing a Web page.

Figure 1-3 illustrates a Web page at the Disney Online Web site. This Web page contains numerous links. For example, the seven graphics on the Web page are links. Clicking a link, such as Disney Destinations, could display a Web page from a travel agency located on the other side of the world.

FIGURE 1-3

Uniform Resource Locator (URL)

Each Web page has a unique address, called a **Uniform Resource Locator** (**URL**), which distinguishes it from all other pages on the Internet. The URL in Figure 1-3 is http://disney.go.com/home/today/index.html.

A URL often is composed of four parts (Figure 1-4). The first part is the protocol. A **protocol** is a set of rules. Most Web pages use the Hypertext Transfer Protocol. **Hypertext Transfer Protocol** (**HTTP**) describes the rules used to transmit Web pages electronically over the Internet. You enter the protocol in lowercase as http followed by a colon and two forward slashes (http://). If you do not begin a URL with a protocol, Internet Explorer will assume it is http, and automatically will append http:// to the front of the URL.

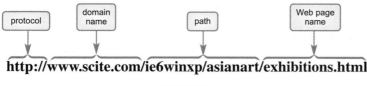

protocol	domain name	path	Web page name

http://www.scsite.com/ie6winxp/asianart/exhibitions.html

FIGURE 1-4

The second part of a URL is the domain name. The **domain name** is the Internet address of the computer on the Internet where the Web page is located. Each computer on the Internet has a unique address, called an **Internet Protocol** address, or **IP address**. The domain name identifies where to forward a request for the Web page referenced by the URL. The domain name in the URL in Figure 1-4 is www.scsite.com.

The last part of the domain name (com in Figure 1-4 on the previous page) indicates the type of organization that owns the Web site. For example, com indicates a commercial organization, usually a business or corporation. Educational institutions have edu at the end of their domain names. Government entities use gov at the end of their domain names. Table 1-1 shows some types of organizations and their extensions.

Table 1-1 Organizations and their Domain Name Extensions	
TYPES OF ORGANIZATIONS	ORIGINAL DOMAIN NAMES
Commercial organizations, businesses, and companies	.com
Educational institutions	.edu
Government agencies	.gov
Military organizations	.mil
Network providers	.net
Nonprofit organizations	.org
TYPES OF ORGANIZATIONS	NEWER DOMAIN NAMES
Accredited museums	.museum
Businesses of all sizes	.biz
Businesses, organizations, or individuals providing general information	.info
Individuals or families	.name
Certified professionals such as doctors, lawyers, and accountants	.pro
Aviation community members	.aero
Business cooperatives such as credit unions and rural electric co-ops	.coop

The optional third part of a URL is the file specification of the Web page. The **file specification** includes the file name and possibly a directory or folder name. This information is called the **path**. If no file specification of a Web page is specified in the URL, a default Web page appears. This means you can display a Web page even though you do not know its file specification. The fourth part of a URL is the **Web page name**. The Web page name identifies the currently displayed Web page.

You can find URLs that identify interesting Web sites in magazines or newspapers, on television, from friends, or even from just browsing the Web.

URLs of well-known companies and organizations usually contain the company's name and institution's name. For example, ibm.com is IBM Corporation, and umich.edu is the University of Michigan.

Hypertext Markup Language

Web page authors use a special formatting language called **Hypertext Markup Language** (**HTML**) to create Web pages. Behind all the formatted text and eye-catching graphics is plain text. Special HTML formatting codes and functions that control attributes such as font size, colors, and centering surround the text and picture references. Figure 1-5 shows part of the hypertext markup language used to create the Web page shown in Figure 1-3 on the previous page.

More About

HTML

As many as 14 HTML editing programs make it easy to create Web pages without learning HTML syntax. Editing programs include FrontPage, Hot Dog, Web-O-Rama, HomeSite, Coffee Cup, Power Web, Web Express, Cool Page, Sothink, and Dreamweaver.

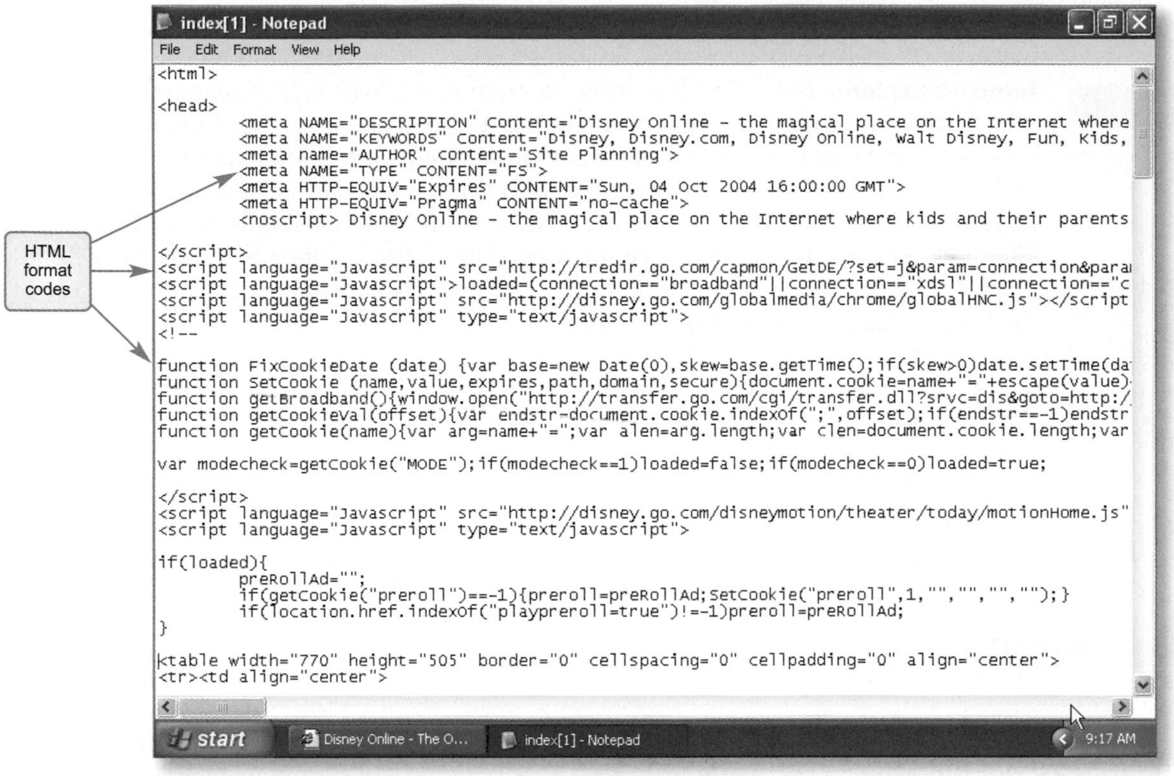

```
index[1] - Notepad                                                    _ 回 X
File  Edit  Format  View  Help
<html>

<head>
        <meta NAME="DESCRIPTION" Content="Disney Online - the magical place on the Internet where
        <meta NAME="KEYWORDS" Content="Disney, Disney.com, Disney Online, Walt Disney, Fun, Kids,
        <meta name="AUTHOR" content="Site Planning">
        <meta NAME="TYPE" CONTENT="FS">
        <meta HTTP-EQUIV="Expires" CONTENT="Sun, 04 Oct 2004 16:00:00 GMT">
        <meta HTTP-EQUIV="Pragma" CONTENT="no-cache">
        <noscript> Disney Online - the magical place on the Internet where kids and their parents
</script>
<script language="Javascript" src="http://tredir.go.com/capmon/GetDE/?set=j&param=connection&para
<script language="Javascript">loaded=(connection=="broadband"||connection=="xdsl"||connection=="c
<script language="Javascript" src="http://disney.go.com/globalmedia/chrome/globalHNC.js"></script
<script language="Javascript" type="text/javascript">
<!--

function FixCookieDate (date) {var base=new Date(0),skew=base.getTime();if(skew>0)date.setTime(da
function SetCookie (name,value,expires,path,domain,secure){document.cookie=name+"="+escape(value)
function getBroadband(){window.open("http://transfer.go.com/cgi/transfer.dll?srvc=dis&goto=http:/
function getCookieval(offset){var endstr=document.cookie.indexof(";",offset);if(endstr==-1)endstr
function getCookie(name){var arg=name+"=";var alen=arg.length;var clen=document.cookie.length;var

var modecheck=getCookie("MODE");if(modecheck==1)loaded=false;if(modecheck==0)loaded=true;

</script>
<script language="Javascript" src="http://disney.go.com/disneymotion/theater/today/motionHome.js"
<script language="Javascript" type="text/javascript">

if(loaded){
        preRollAd="";
        if(getCookie("preroll")==-1){preroll=preRollAd;SetCookie("preroll",1,"","","");}
        if(location.href.indexOf("playpreroll=true")!=-1)preroll=preRollAd;
}

<table width="770" height="505" border="0" cellspacing="0" cellpadding="0" align="center">
<tr><td align="center">

start        Disney Online - The O...    index[1] - Notepad                    9:17 AM
```

HTML format codes

FIGURE 1-5

Though it looks somewhat cryptic, HTML is similar to a computer programming language. Using HTML, you can create your own Web pages and place them on the Web for others to see. Easier-to-use Web page development software, such as Microsoft's FrontPage, is one of the many HTML authoring tools available.

Home Pages

No main menus or any particular starting points exist in the World Wide Web. Although you can reference any page on the Web when you begin, most people start with specially designated Web pages called home pages. A **home page** is the introductory page for a Web site. All other Web pages for that site usually are accessible from the home page via links. In addition, the home page is the page that is displayed when you enter a domain name with no file specification, such as disneyland.com or nbc.com.

Because it is the starting point for most Web sites, designers try to make a good first impression and display attractive eye-catching graphics, specially formatted text, and a variety of links to other pages at the Web site, as well as to other interesting and useful Web sites.

More About

Home Pages

A Web site may consist of many home pages. A computer used by faculty members or students for their hypertext documents would have many home pages: one for each person.

Internet Browsers

Just as graphical user interfaces (GUIs), such as Microsoft Windows, simplify working with a computer by using a point-and-click method, a browser, such as Internet Explorer, makes using the World Wide Web easier by removing the complexity of having to remember the syntax, or rules, of commands used to reference Web pages at Web sites. A **browser** takes the URL associated with a link or the URL entered by a user, locates the computer containing the associated Web page, and then reads the HTML codes returned to display a Web page.

What Is Internet Explorer 6?

Microsoft Internet Explorer

Internet Explorer 6 is a Web browsing program that allows you to search for and view Web pages, save pages you find for use in the future, maintain a list of the pages you visit, send and receive e-mail messages, use newsgroups, edit Web pages, and listen to radio stations. The Internet Explorer 6 application program is included with most Microsoft Windows operating system software (Windows XP, Windows 2000, and Windows 98) and Microsoft Office software (Office 2003, Office XP, and Office 2000), or you can download it from the Internet. The projects in this book illustrate the use of the Internet Explorer 6 browser.

Starting Internet Explorer

If you are stepping through this project on a computer and you want your screen to match the figures in this book, then you should change your computer's resolution to 800 × 600. For more information on how to change the resolution on your computer, see your instructor. The following steps show how to start Internet Explorer.

To Start Internet Explorer

1

• **Click the Start button on the Windows taskbar, point to All Programs on the Start menu, and then point to Internet Explorer on the All Programs submenu.**

Windows displays the Start menu and the All Programs submenu (Figure 1-6).

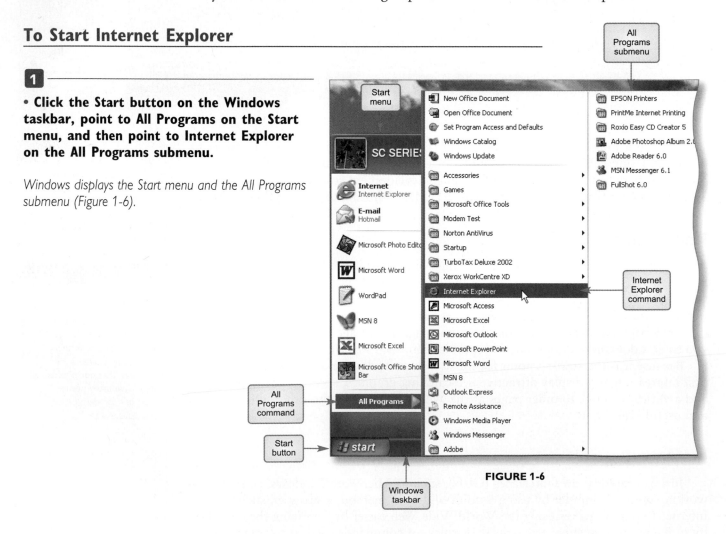

FIGURE 1-6

2

• **Click Internet Explorer.**

Internet Explorer starts. After several seconds, Internet Explorer displays the Welcome to MSN.com - Microsoft Internet Explorer window, adds the Welcome to MSN.com - Microsoft Internet Explorer button to the taskbar, displays the Welcome to MSN.com Web page title in the window title, and displays the MSN.com home page in the display area (Figure 1-7). The home page may display differently on your computer.

3

• **If the Internet Explorer window is not maximized, double-click its title bar to maximize it.**

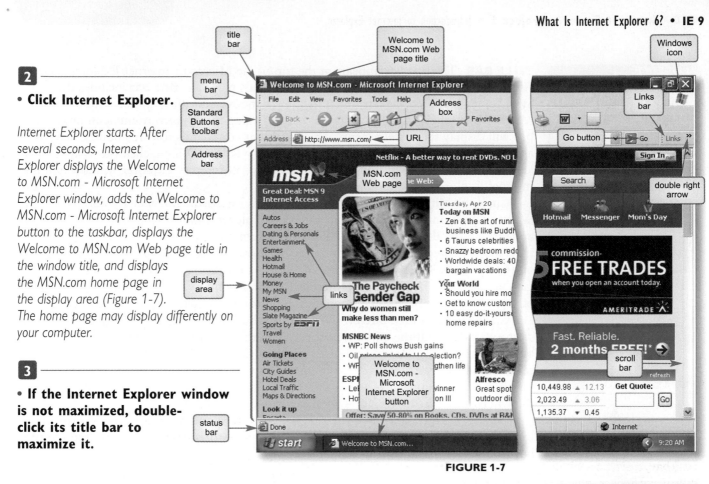

FIGURE 1-7

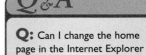

Normally, when Internet Explorer starts, the MSN.com home page is displayed. Because it is possible to change the page that initially is displayed through the Internet Options command on the Tools menu, the home page shown in Figure 1-7 may be different on your computer. For example, some schools and businesses have their own Web site home page display when starting Internet Explorer.

The Internet Explorer Window

The **Internet Explorer window** (Figure 1-7) consists of innovative features that make browsing the Internet easy. It contains a title bar, a menu bar, the Standard Buttons toolbar, an Address bar, a Links bar, a scroll bar, the status bar, and a display area where pages from the World Wide Web appear. The menu bar, Standard Buttons toolbar, Address bar, and Links bar appear at the top of the screen just below the title bar. The Address bar and Links bar appear on the same row below the Standard Buttons toolbar. The status bar appears at the bottom of the screen.

DISPLAY AREA Only a portion of most pages will be visible on the screen. You view the portion of the page displayed on the screen in the **display area** (Figure 1-7). To the right of the display area are a scroll bar, scroll arrows, and a scroll box, which you can use to move the text in the display area up and down and reveal other parts of the page.

Notice the links on the Internet Explorer home page shown in Figure 1-7. When you position the mouse pointer on one of these links, the mouse pointer changes to a pointing hand. This change in the shape of the mouse pointer identifies these elements as links. Clicking a link retrieves the Web page associated with the link and displays it in the display area.

Other Ways

1. Click Start button on Windows taskbar, click Internet Explorer icon on Start menu
2. Double-click Internet Explorer icon on desktop
3. Press CTRL+ESC, press P, I

Q & A

Q: Can I change the home page in the Internet Explorer window?

A: Yes. You can change the home page by clicking Tools on the menu bar, clicking Internet Options on the Tools menu, and clicking the Use Current, Use Default, or Use Blank button. You also can change the home page by dragging the Internet Explorer icon in the Address box to the Home button on the Standard Buttons toolbar. The Web page in the display area becomes the home page.

More About

The Display Area

You can increase the size of
the display area shown in
Figure 1-7 on page IE 9 by
moving and resizing the
Standard Buttons toolbar,
Address bar, or Links bar, or
by removing a toolbar. To
practice removing, moving, and
sizing a toolbar, perform In the
Lab Assignment 12 on page
IE 64 at the end of this project.

TITLE BAR The title bar appears at the top of the Microsoft Internet Explorer window.
As shown at the top of Figure 1-7 on the previous page, the **title bar** includes the
System menu icon on the left, the title of the window, and the Minimize, Restore (or
Maximize), and Close buttons on the right. Clicking the **System menu icon** on the title
bar will display the System menu, which contains commands to carry out the actions
associated with the Microsoft Internet Explorer window. Double-click the System menu
icon or click the Close button to close the Microsoft Internet Explorer window and quit
Internet Explorer.

Click the **Minimize button** to minimize the Microsoft Internet Explorer window.
When you minimize the Microsoft Internet Explorer window, the window no longer
appears on the desktop and the Microsoft Internet Explorer taskbar button becomes
inactive (a lighter color). The minimized window still is open but it does not appear
on the desktop. After minimizing, clicking the taskbar button on the Windows
taskbar displays the Microsoft Internet Explorer window in the previous position it
occupied on the desktop and changes the button to an active state (a darker color).

Click the **Maximize button** to maximize the Microsoft Internet Explorer window
so it expands to fill the entire desktop. When the window is maximized, the Restore
button replaces the Maximize button on the title bar. Click the **Restore button** to
return the Microsoft Internet Explorer window to the size and position it occupied
before being maximized. The Restore button changes to the Maximize button when
the Microsoft Internet Explorer window is in a restored state.

You also can double-click the title bar to restore and maximize the Microsoft
Internet Explorer window. If the window is in a restored state, you can drag the title
bar to move the window on the desktop.

More About

**Standard Buttons
Toolbar Buttons**

If the text label is not displayed
on the buttons on the Standard
Buttons toolbar, right-click the
toolbar, click Customize on the
shortcut menu, click the Text
options box arrow, click Show
text labels, and then click the
Close button. You also can
change the size of the icons on
the toolbar buttons using the
Icon options box arrow.

MENU BAR The **menu bar**, which is located below the title bar, displays menu
names (Figure 1-7). Each **menu name** represents a menu of commands you can use
to perform actions, such as saving Web pages, copying and pasting, customizing toolbars, sending and receiving e-mail, setting Internet Explorer options, quitting Internet
Explorer, and so on. To display a menu, click the menu name on the menu bar. To
select a command on a menu, click the command name or type the **shortcut keys**
shown to the right of some commands on the menu.

The **Windows icon** at the right end of the menu bar goes into motion (animates)
when Internet Explorer transfers a Web page from a Web site to the Microsoft Internet
Explorer window and stops moving when the transfer is complete. Your computer may
display another icon in place of the Windows icon.

STANDARD BUTTONS TOOLBAR The **Standard Buttons toolbar** (Figure 1-7)
contains buttons that allow you to perform often-used tasks more quickly than using
the menu bar. For example, to print the Web page in the Microsoft Internet Explorer
window, click the Print button on the Standard Buttons toolbar.

Each button on the Standard Buttons toolbar contains an icon. Four buttons contain
text labels (Back, Search, Favorites, and Media) describing the function of the button.
Table 1-2 illustrates the buttons on the Standard Buttons toolbar. The table also briefly
describes the functions of the buttons. Each of the buttons will be explained in detail as it
is used. The buttons on the Standard Buttons toolbar may be different on your computer.

By right-clicking the Standard Buttons toolbar, you can customize its buttons.
You can show or remove the text label on each button, or you can remove the entire
toolbar by clicking the appropriate toolbar name on the shortcut menu.

More About

Move Handles

In some cases, the move
handles at the left end of the
menu bar and toolbars
(Standard Buttons, Address
bar, and Links bar) do not
appear because the Lock the
Toolbars command has been
selected. To display the
move handles, right-click an
open area on any toolbar
and then click Lock Toolbars
on the shortcut menu.

ADDRESS BAR The **Address bar** (Figure 1-7) contains a move handle, toolbar title
(Address), Address box, and Go button. The **move handle** allows you to change the
size of a toolbar. If a move handle does not appear, read the More About at the bottom
of this page to learn how to display the move handle. The **Address box** holds the
Uniform Resource Locator (URL) for the page currently shown in the display area.

The URL updates automatically as you browse from page to page. If you know the URL of a Web page you want to visit, click the URL in the Address box to highlight the URL, type the new URL, and then click the Go button (or press the ENTER key) to display the corresponding page.

You can type an application name in the Address box and click the Go button to start the corresponding application, type a folder name and click the Go button to open a folder window, type a document name and click the Go button to start an application and display the document in the application window, and type a keyword or phrase (search inquiry) and click the Go button to display Web pages containing the keyword or phrase. In addition, you can click the **Address box arrow** at the right end of the Address box to display a list of previously displayed Web pages. Clicking a URL in the Address list displays the corresponding Web page.

More About

The Address Bar

To move the insertion point to the Address box when the box is empty, or to highlight the URL in the Address box, press ALT+D.

Table 1-2 Standard Buttons Toolbar Buttons and Functions	
BUTTON	**FUNCTION**
(Back)	Retrieves the previous page, (provided it was previously just viewed). To go more than one page back, click the Back button arrow, and then click a Web page title in the list.
(Forward)	Retrieves the next page. To go more than one page forward, click the Forward button arrow and then click a Web page title in the list.
(Stop)	Stops the transfer of a Web page.
(Refresh)	Requests the Web page in the display area to be retrieved from the Web site again.
(Home)	Requests the default home page to be displayed.
Search	Displays the Search Companion bar.
Favorites	Displays the Favorites bar.
Media	Displays the Media bar.
(History)	Displays the History bar.
(Mail)	Displays a menu containing commands to access e-mail messages and Internet newsgroups.
(Print)	Prints the Web page shown in the display area.
(Edit)	Edits the Web page shown in the display area.
(Discuss)	Initiates discussions.

LINKS BAR The **Links bar,** which appears to the right of the Address bar on the same row, allows you to click an icon to display a favorite Web site without first starting the Internet Explorer browser. The Address bar toolbar and Links bar are preset to display on the same row immediately below the Standard Buttons toolbar (Figure 1-7 on page IE 9). Because both of these bars cannot fit entirely on a single row, only a portion of the Links bar appears.

The Links bar contains a move handle, toolbar title (Links), and a button identified by a double right arrow. Clicking this button displays a menu containing all the buttons on the Links bar. Clicking the button a second time removes the menu. Double-clicking the move handle or toolbar title displays the entire Links bar.

When you display the entire Links bar, only a portion of the Address bar toolbar appears. Each button on the Links bar contains an icon and text label. Table 1-3 on the next page illustrates the Links bar buttons and briefly describes the functions of the buttons. Additional buttons or different buttons may appear on the Links bar on your computer. Double-clicking the move handle or toolbar title a second time displays the entire Address bar toolbar and only a portion of the Links bar.

Q&A

Q: Can I store links to Web pages on the Links bar?

A: Yes. The Links bar is a good place to store links to the Web pages you use frequently. You can add a Web page to the Links bar by dragging an icon from the Address bar or dragging a link from a Web page to the Links bar. Clicking the link on the Links bar displays the associated Web page.

Table 1-3 Links Bar Buttons and Functions	
BUTTON	FUNCTION
Customize Links	Displays tips for customizing the buttons on the Links bar.
Free HotMail	Displays the Hotmail Web site to set up and access free e-mail accounts.
Microsoft	Displays the Microsoft Windows home page.
Windows Media	Displays the WindowsMedia.com site that contains the Windows Media Guide.

More About

The Asian Arts Web Site

Notice that the URL you enter for the Asian Arts page contains the domain name (scsite.com) of the publishing company. The entire Asian Arts site has been stored on the publishing company's computer server to guarantee that the content of the Asian Arts Web site would remain the same for all students. Type asianart.com in the Address box to view the real Asian Arts site. See if you notice any differences.

Browsing the World Wide Web

The most common way to browse the World Wide Web is to obtain the URL of a Web page you want to visit and then enter it into the Address box on the Address bar. It is by visiting various Web sites that you can begin to understand the enormous appeal of the World Wide Web. The following steps show how to contact a Web site provided by Web Art Publishing in Santa Fe, New Mexico and visit the Web page titled Asian Arts, which contains information and pictures of artwork from various countries in Asia. The URL for the Asian Art page is:

```
www.scsite.com/ie6winxp/asianart.htm
```

You are not required to provide the leading http:// protocol when initially typing the URL in the Address box. Internet Explorer will insert http:// and assume the www automatically, if you do not supply it. The following steps show how to browse the Web by entering a URL.

To Browse the Web by Entering a URL

1

• **Click the Address box.**

Internet Explorer highlights the URL in the Address box and the mouse pointer changes to an I-beam (Figure 1-8).

FIGURE 1-8

2

• **Type** scsite.com/ie6winxp/ asianart.htm **in the Address box.**

The new URL appears in the Address box (Figure 1-9).

FIGURE 1-9

3

• **Click the Go button.**

The Windows icon on the menu bar goes into motion (animates) while the Asian Arts Web page is displayed and then stops moving when the Asian Arts Web page appears. The Asian Arts Web page title appears on the title bar and on the active button on the taskbar, and the URL of the Web page appears in the Address box (Figure 1-10).

FIGURE 1-10

4

• **Click the Exhibitions link.**

After a brief interval, the Exhibitions page appears (Figure 1-11). The URL of the Web page appears in the Address box and the Exhibitions Web page title appears on the title bar and on the taskbar button. A vertical scroll bar on the right side of the display area indicates the page is larger than the display area. You will have to scroll to view additional information and pictures on the page.

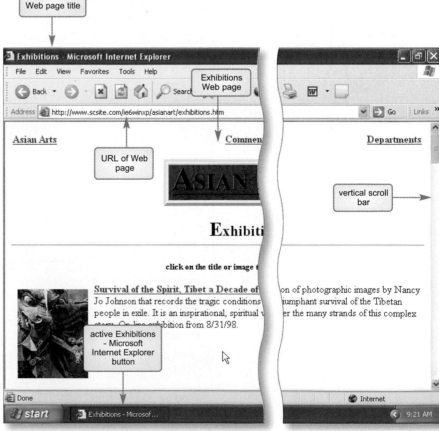

FIGURE 1-11

5

• **Scroll through the display area to display the link, The Splendors of Imperial China: Treasures from the National Palace Museum, Taipei.**

The display area scrolls and The Splendors of Imperial China: Treasures from the National Palace Museum, Taipei link appears (Figure 1-12). The picture at the right of the display area also is a link to the same page.

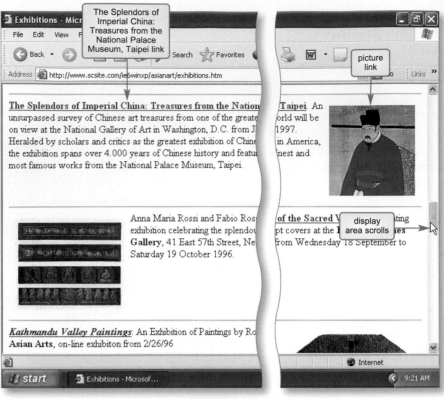

FIGURE 1-12

6

• **Click The Splendors of Imperial China: Treasures from the National Palace Museum, Taipei link.**

After a brief interval, The Splendors of Imperial China Web page appears (Figure 1-13). The URL of the Web page appears in the Address box and the Web page title is displayed on the title bar and on the taskbar button (Figure 1-13). The Web page contains pictures and descriptions of the Chinese art located in the National Place Museum in Taipei, China.

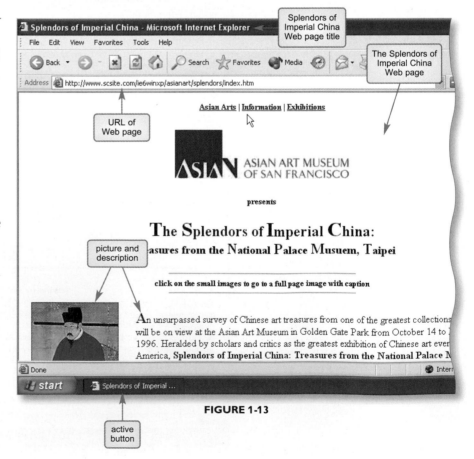

FIGURE 1-13

7

• **Scroll through the display area to view the three pictures numbered 8, 9, and 10.**

The display area scrolls to display the pictures of a stem cup, various leaves and flowers, and a globe vase (Figure 1-14). The title, Three leaves from Landscapes and Flowers, appears below the center picture.

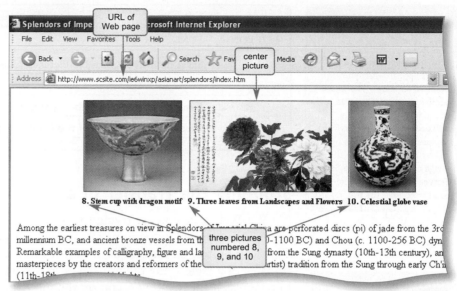

FIGURE 1-14

8

• **Click the center picture (numbered 9).**

• **Point to the larger version of the Three Leaves from Landscapes and Flowers picture.**

The Splendors of Imperial China - Image 9 Web page containing a larger version of the Three Leaves from Landscapes and Flowers picture appears (Figure 1-15). Pointing to the picture displays the Image toolbar in the upper-left corner of the image.

FIGURE 1-15

The preceding steps illustrate how simple it is to browse the World Wide Web. Displaying a Web page associated with a link is as easy as clicking a text or picture link.

Step 2 on page IE 12 involved typing a URL. If you type the wrong letter and notice the error before clicking the Go button, use the BACKSPACE key to erase all the characters back to and including the one that is wrong. If the error is easier to retype than correct, click the URL and retype it.

Pointing to an image on a Web page displays the Image toolbar in the upper-left corner of the image (Figure 1-15). The **Image toolbar** allows you to save, print, or e-mail images you find on the Web and display the contents of the My Pictures folder. The **My Pictures folder** is a central location for the storage of images you find on the Web. Each button on the Image toolbar contains an icon. Table 1-4 on the next page illustrates the buttons on the Image toolbar and briefly describes their function.

Other Ways

1. On File menu click Open, type URL in Open box, click OK button
2. Press CTRL+O, type URL in Open box, click OK button
3. Press ALT+F, press O, type URL in Open box, press OK button

More About

Image Toolbar

The Image toolbar does not always appear when you point to an image. The Image toolbar appears if the size of the image is at least 130 pixels by 130 pixels. If the toolbar does not appear, right-click anywhere on the image and then click the Save Picture As button on the toolbar to save the image.

Table 1-4 Image Toolbar

BUTTON	FUNCTION
	Saves an image to the My Pictures folder unless another location is specified.
	Prints an image.
	E-mails an image using the default e-mail program.
	Displays the contents of the My Pictures folder.

Stopping the Transfer of a Page

If a Web page you are trying to view is taking too long to transfer or if you clicked the wrong link, you may decide not to wait for the page to finish transferring. The Stop button on the Standard Buttons toolbar (Figure 1-16) allows you to stop the transfer of a page while the transfer is in progress. You will know the transfer is still in progress if the Windows icon on the menu bar stops moving. Stopping the transfer of a Web page will leave a partially transferred Web page in the display area. Pictures or text displaying before the Stop button is clicked remain visible in the display area and any links can be clicked to display the associated Web pages.

More About

Stopping the Transfer of an Image

In addition to clicking the Stop button on the Standard Buttons toolbar to stop the transfer of an image, you also can click the Stop command on the View menu, press the ESC key, or press ALT+V and then press the P key.

Refreshing a Web Page

If you decide you want to refresh the Web page, you can reload the Web page using the **Refresh button** on the Standard Buttons toolbar (Figure 1-16). This is particularly useful with Web pages that dynamically change every few minutes, such as stock quotes, weather, and the news. The following step shows how to refresh the Splendors of Imperial China - Image 9 Web page.

To Refresh a Web Page

1

• **Click the Refresh button on the Standard Buttons toolbar.**

Internet Explorer initiates a new transfer of the Web page from the computer where it is located to your computer. The Windows icon goes into motion while the transfer progresses, the window title changes momentarily, and a message appears on the status bar providing information about the progress of the transfer. The Splendors of China - Image 9 Web page reappears in the display area (Figure 1-16).

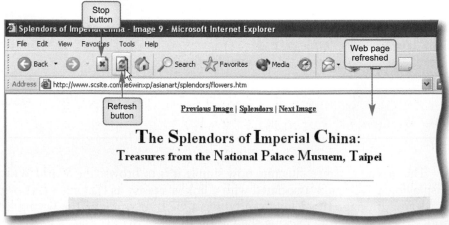

FIGURE 1-16

Other Ways

1. On View menu click Refresh
2. Click URL in Address bar, click Go button
3. Press ALT+V, press R
4. Press F5

In the event that the connection to the Web site where the page is located malfunctions and the page transfer does not finish, you can use the Refresh button to request the page again.

Finding a Previously Displayed Web Page

As you display different Web pages, Internet Explorer keeps track of the pages you visit, so you can quickly find those pages in the future. Internet Explorer stores the Web pages you visit in the **Temporary Internet Files folder** on the hard disk. When you display a previously displayed Web page, the page is displayed quickly because Internet Explorer is able to retrieve the page from the Temporary Internet Files folder on the hard disk instead of from a Web site on the Internet.

One method to find a previously displayed Web page is to use the Back button list and Forward button list on the Standard Buttons toolbar (Figure 1-17a on the next page). Each time a Web page appears in the display area, the title of the previously displayed page is added to the Back button list. Clicking the **Back button arrow** displays the **Back button list** that allows you to display a previously displayed page from the list (Figure 1-17a). Although not shown in Figure 1-17a, clicking the **Forward button arrow** when the Forward button is active displays the **Forward button list** that also allows you to display a previously displayed page from the list. Each time you end an Internet session by quitting Internet Explorer, the entries on the Back button list and Forward button list are cleared.

A second method allows you to display the **Go To list** containing all the names of all Web pages in the order they were displayed during the current session (Figure 1-17b on the next page). A check mark preceding a name in the list identifies the page currently displayed in the display area. To view the Go To list, click View on the menu bar and point to Go To on the View menu. Clicking a name in the Go To list displays the associated Web page in the display area.

A third method to display a previously displayed Web page is to use the History list (Figure 1-17c on the next page). Each time you display a Web page, Internet Explorer saves the URL for that Web page and adds a link (Web page title) to the History list. The **History list** contains links for Web sites and pages visited in previous days and weeks. Clicking the History button on the Standard Buttons toolbar displays the History list.

A fourth method uses the Address box arrow to display previously displayed Web pages. Clicking the **Address box arrow** displays the **Address box list** containing a list of previously visited Web pages (Figure 1-17d on the next page).

Finding a Recently Displayed Web Page Using the Back and Forward Buttons

When you start Internet Explorer, the Back and Forward buttons and their arrows appear dimmed and are unavailable (see Figure 1-7 on page IE 9). When you visit the first Web page after starting Internet Explorer, the Back button is no longer dimmed and is available for use. Pointing to the button changes the button to a three-dimensional button, indicating the button is active.

The steps on page IE 19 show how to use the Back and Forward buttons to find previously displayed Web pages.

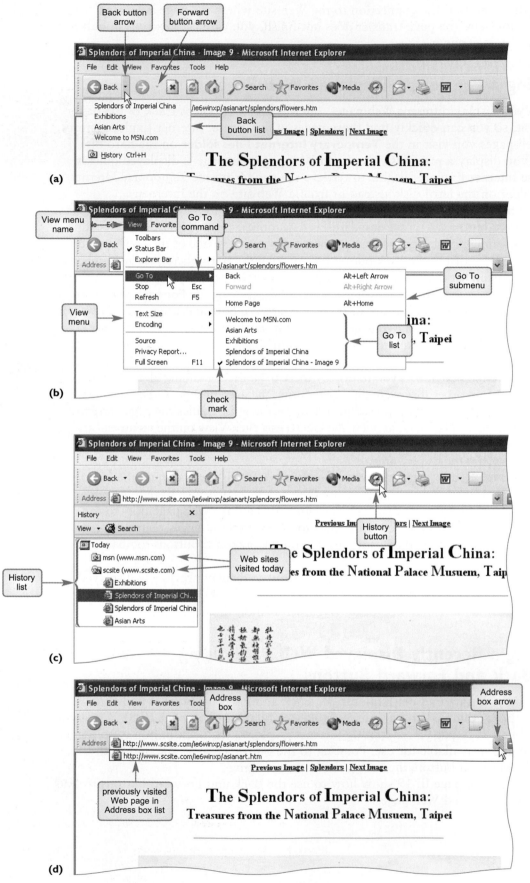

FIGURE 1-17

To Use the Back and Forward Buttons to Find Recently Displayed Web Pages

1

• **Click the Back button on the Standard Buttons toolbar.**

A ScreenTip appears momentarily when you point to the Back button and then the Splendors of Imperial China Web page is displayed (Figure 1-18). The Back button is three-dimensional, Forward button is active, and The Splendors of Imperial China Web page is not the last Web page visited in this session.

FIGURE 1-18

2

• **Click the Back button again.**

The Exhibitions Web page appears (Figure 1-19).

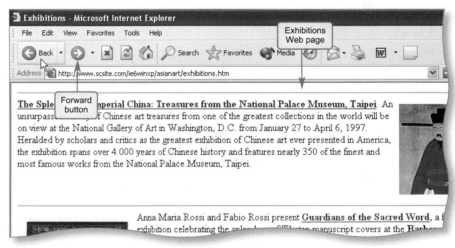

FIGURE 1-19

3

• **Click the Forward button on the Standard Buttons toolbar.**

The Splendors of Imperial China Web page appears again (Figure 1-20).

FIGURE 1-20

4

• **Click the Forward button again.**

The Splendors of Imperial China - Image 9 Web page appears (Figure 1-21). The Forward button is now inactive, which indicates there are no additional pages to which you can move forward.

FIGURE 1-21

You can continue to page backward until you reach the beginning of the Back button list. At that time, the Back button becomes inactive, which indicates that no additional pages to which you can move back are contained in the list. You can, however, move forward by clicking the Forward button.

You can see that traversing the list of pages is easy using the Back and Forward buttons. Because many pages may be displayed before the one you want to view, this method can be time-consuming.

Displaying a Web Page Using the Back Button List

It is possible to skip to any previously visited page by clicking its title in the Back button list. Thus, you can find a recently visited page without displaying an intermediate page, as shown in the following steps.

To Display a Web Page Using the Back Button List

1

• **Click the Back button arrow on the Standard Buttons toolbar.**

The Back button list displays a list of titles of Web pages you visited during this session beginning with the most recent (Figure 1-22). Your list may be different.

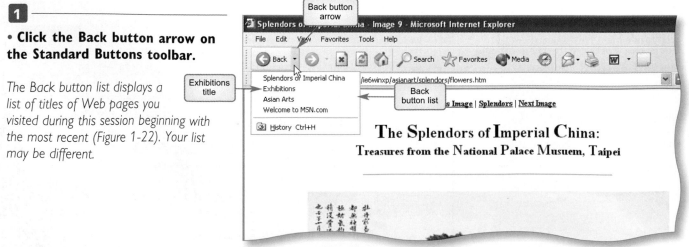

FIGURE 1-22

2

• **Click Exhibitions on the Back button list.**

Internet Explorer displays the Exhibitions Web page (Figure 1-23). Both the Back and Forward buttons are active, indicating there are Web pages to which you can move backward or forward.

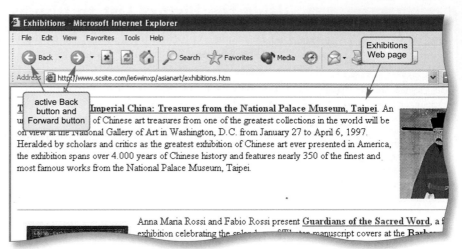

FIGURE 1-23

If you have a small list of pages you have visited, or the Web page you wish to view is only one or two pages away, using the Back and Forward buttons to traverse the lists probably is faster than displaying the Back button list and selecting the correct title. If you have visited a large number of pages, however, the list will be long, and it may be easier to use the Back button list to select the exact page.

Finding Information Using an Explorer Bar

Finding information is easier when you use an Explorer Bar. An **Explorer Bar** allows you to personalize the Microsoft Internet Explorer window so that information you use most frequently is easy to locate. Five Explorer Bars (Search, Favorites, Media, History, and Folders) are available. To display the Explorer Bar submenu that contains the five Explorer Bar commands, click View on the menu bar and then point to Explorer Bar. Table 1-5 identifies the commands on the Explorer Bar submenu and briefly describes the function of each command.

Table 1-5 Commands on the Explorer Bar Submenu	
COMMANDS	**FUNCTION**
Search	Displays the Search bar that allows you to search the Web.
Favorites	Displays the Favorites bar containing the favorites list.
Media	Displays the Media bar that allows you to play media files (music, video, etc.) and access the WindowsMedia.com Web site.
History	Displays the History bar containing a list of previously visited Web pages.
Folders	Displays the Explorer Bar containing a list of the folders on the hard drive.

When you click a command on the Explorer Bar submenu, an Explorer Bar displays along the left side of the Microsoft Internet Explorer window (Figure 1-24 on the next page). Some buttons on the Standard Buttons toolbar (Search, Favorites, Media, and History) also display an Explorer Bar. The Explorer Bars containing the History and Favorites lists are demonstrated on the following pages.

More About

The History List

You can clear the History list by clicking Tools on the menu bar, clicking Internet Options, clicking the Clear History button in the Internet Options dialog box, clicking the Yes button, and then clicking the OK button. Clearing the History List also clears the Address box list.

Using the History List to Display Web Pages

Internet Explorer maintains another list of Web pages visited called the History list. The **History list** is an alphabetical list of Web pages visited over a period of days or weeks (over many sessions). You can use this list to display Web pages you may have accessed during that time. Clicking the History button on the Standard Buttons toolbar displays the Explorer Bar containing the History list.

When the Explorer Bar is visible, the display area contains two panes. The left pane contains the Explorer Bar and the right pane contains the current Web page. The Explorer Bar will remain on the screen until you close it. To find a recently visited Web page using the History list, first display the entire History list, and then click the desired Web page title, as shown on the following pages.

To Display a Web Page Using the History List

1

• **Click the History button on the Standard Buttons toolbar.**

The History list appears in the Explorer Bar in the left pane and the current Web page is displayed in the right pane (Figure 1-24). Indented below the Today icon in the History list are the msn and scsite folders. Indented below the scsite folder are the Web pages you viewed in the scsite Web site and the title of the Web page that displays in the right pane (Exhibitions) is highlighted.

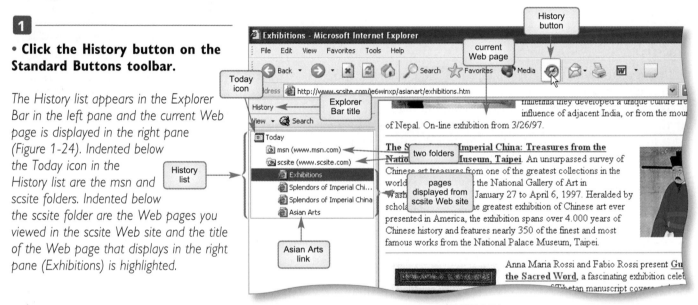

FIGURE 1-24

2

• **Click Asian Arts in the History list.**

The Asian Arts Web page appears (Figure 1-25). A pointing hand icon points to the highlighted Asian Arts title (white text) in the History list and the Web page title on the title bar and URL in the Address box change.

3

• **Click the Close button on the Explorer Bar.**

The Explorer Bar closes.

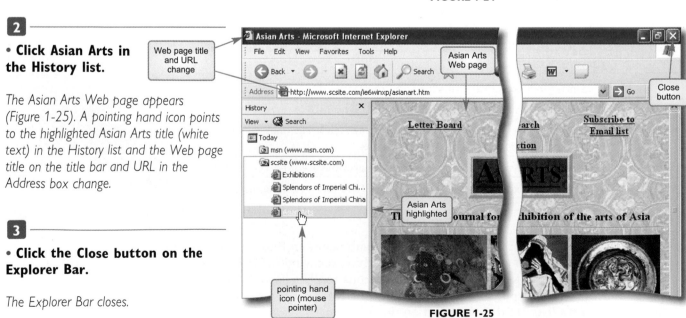

FIGURE 1-25

If you have a small History list or the page you want is only one or two pages away, you can display a Web page more quickly using the Back and Forward buttons than displaying the Explorer Bar and then selecting individual pages. If you have visited a large number of Web pages, however, the History list will be long, and you may find it easier to use the History list in the Explorer Bar to find the precise page to display.

History lists are useful for returning to a Web page you have visited recently. You can set the number of days Internet Explorer keeps the URLs in the History list by using the Internet Options command on the Tools menu. Because the History list occasionally is cleared, you should not use the History list to store the URLs of favorite or frequently visited pages permanently.

You can see from the previous figures that URLs can be long and cryptic. It is easy to make a mistake while entering such URLs. Fortunately, Internet Explorer has the capability of keeping track of favorite Web pages. You can store the URLs of favorite Web pages permanently in an area appropriately called the Favorites list.

Keeping Track of Favorite Web Pages

The Favorites feature of Internet Explorer allows you to save the URLs of favorite Web pages. A **favorite** consists of the title of the Web page and the URL of that page. The title of the Web page is added to the Favorites menu. The following steps show how to add the Asian Arts Web page to the Favorites list.

To Add a Web Page to the Favorites List

1

• **Click the Favorites button on the Standard Buttons toolbar.**

The Add button, Organize button, and Favorites list appear on the Explorer Bar (Figure 1-26). The Add button adds the title of the page and the URL in the Address box to the Favorites list. Additional or different folders and favorites may display in the Favorites list on your computer.

Other Ways

1. On View menu point to Explorer Bar, click History on Explorer Bar submenu
2. Press CTRL+H
3. Press ALT+V, press E, H

More About

Favorites

Internet Explorer allows you to change the title that identifies a favorite. Click the Favorites button on the Standard Buttons toolbar, click Organize in the Favorites list, right-click a favorite in the Organize favorites list and then click Rename. You also can rearrange the order of your favorites by dragging a favorite to another location on the favorites list and then releasing it.

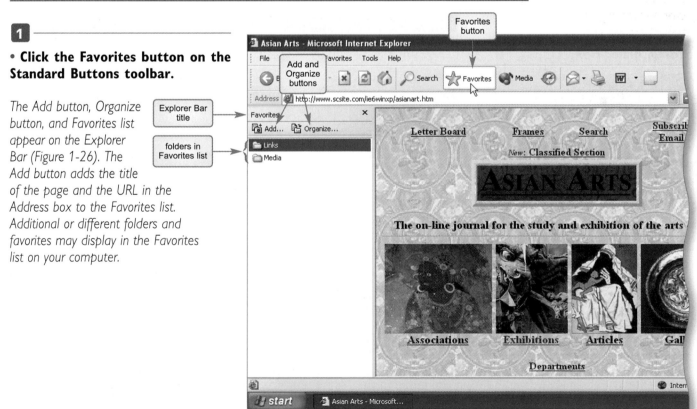

FIGURE 1-26

2

• **Click the Add button above the Favorites list.**

Internet Explorer displays the Add Favorite dialog box (Figure 1-27). The Name text box contains the title of the Asian Arts Web page and the Address box on the Address bar contains the URL.

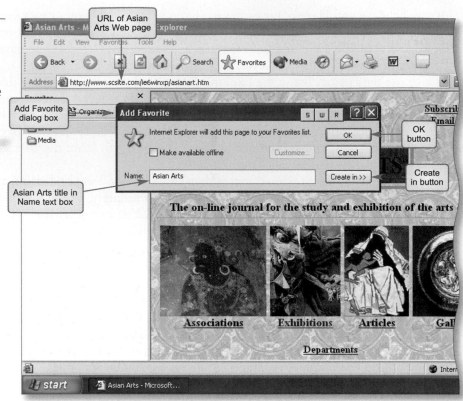

FIGURE 1-27

3

• **Click the OK button in the Add Favorite dialog box.**

The Asian Arts favorite appears in the Favorites list (Figure 1-28).

4

• **Click the Close button on the Explorer Bar.**

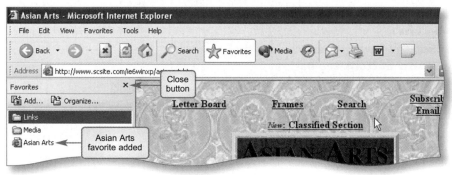

FIGURE 1-28

The Explorer Bar containing the Favorites list closes.

Other Ways

1. On Favorites menu click Add to Favorites, click OK button
2. Drag Internet Explorer icon in Address box to Favorites button on Standard Buttons toolbar
3. Press ALT+A, press A, press ENTER
4. With Explorer Bar closed, press CTRL+D

In Figure 1-26 on the previous page, clicking the Organize button allows you to manage the Favorites list. The folders in the Favorites list display below the Add and Organize buttons.

In Figure 1-27, clicking the Create in button expands the Add Favorite dialog box, displays a hierarchy of the folders in the Favorites list, and allows you to select a folder in which to store a favorite. You also can change the name of a favorite by highlighting the name in the Name text box and typing the new name.

Using the Home Button to Display a Web Page

At anytime, you can display the home page in the display area using the Home button on the Standard Buttons toolbar. The following steps show how to display the Internet Explorer home page (MSN home page).

To Display the Home Page Using the Home Button

1

• **Click the Home button on the Standard Buttons toolbar.**

The MSN home page appears in the Welcome to MSN.com - Microsoft Internet Explorer window and the URL for the home page is displayed in the Address box (Figure 1-29).

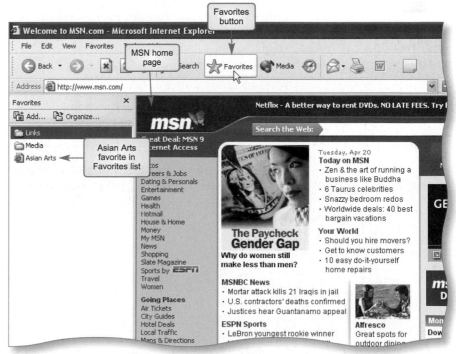

Home button

URL of home page

MSN home page

FIGURE 1-29

Displaying a Web Page Using the Favorites List

The Favorites list is used to display favorite or frequently accessed Web pages quickly, without having to navigate through several unwanted pages. Using a favorite to display a Web page is similar to using the History list to display a Web page. The following steps show how to use the Favorites list to display the Asian Arts Web page.

To Display a Web Page Using the Favorites List

1

• **Click the Favorites button on the Standard Buttons toolbar.**

The Favorites list appears (Figure 1-30). The newly added favorite (Asian Arts) is the only favorite in the list in the left pane and the MSN home page continues to display in the right pane.

Favorites button

MSN home page

Asian Arts favorite in Favorites list

FIGURE 1-30

2

• **Click Asian Arts in the Favorites list.**

The Asian Arts Web page again is visible in the right pane and the Asian Arts URL appears in the Address box (Figure 1-31). A pointing hand icon points to the highlighted Asian Arts title (white text) in the Favorites list.

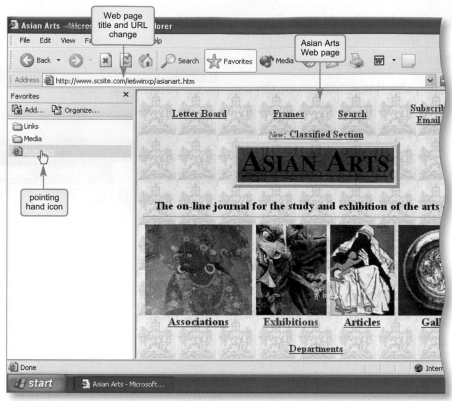

FIGURE 1-31

Other Ways

1. On Favorites menu click favorite
2. Press ALT+A, click favorite
3. Press CTRL+I, click favorite

Additional favorites are displayed in the Favorites list in Figure 1-31. Among the favorites are the Links folder that contains entries corresponding to the buttons on the Links bar and the Media folder that contains a list of interesting media sources (news, sports, music, and so on). Below the two folders is the Asian Arts favorite. Other folders and favorites may display in the Favorites list on your computer.

You have learned how to add a URL to the Favorites list and how to retrieve a Web page using the Favorites list. As you gain experience and continue to browse the World Wide Web and add pages to the Favorites list, it is likely that in time you will want to remove unwanted favorites from the list.

Removing Favorites

Several reasons are valid for wanting to remove a favorite. With the World Wide Web changing everyday, the URL that worked today may not work tomorrow. Perhaps you just do not want a particular favorite in the list anymore, or maybe the list is getting too big to be meaningful. The following steps show how to remove a favorite from the Favorites list.

To Remove a Web Page from the Favorites List

1

• **Right-click Asian Arts in the Favorites list.**

A shortcut menu containing the Delete command appears (Figure 1-32).

FIGURE 1-32

2

• **Click Delete on the shortcut menu.**

Internet Explorer displays the Confirm File Delete dialog box (Figure 1-33). A question asks if you are sure you want to send the Asian Arts favorite to the Recycle Bin.

FIGURE 1-33

3

• **Click the Yes button in the Confirm File Delete dialog box.**

The Confirm File Delete dialog box closes, the Deleting dialog box displays momentarily, and the Asian Arts favorite is removed from the Favorites list (Figure 1-34).

4

• **Click the Close button in the Explorer Bar.**

The Explorer Bar closes.

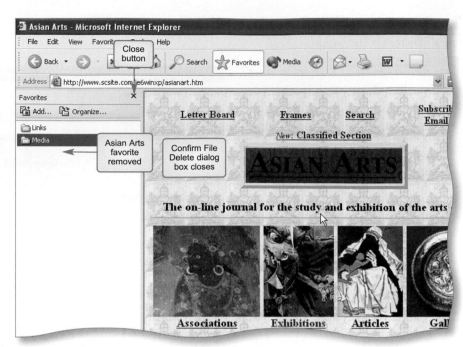

FIGURE 1-34

Other Ways

1. On Favorites menu click Organize Favorites, click favorite, click Delete button, click Yes button
2. Click Organize button in Explorer Bar, click favorite, click Delete button, click Yes button

Using the commands on the shortcut menu can help you manage favorites. Internet Explorer also provides advanced features for handling favorites. For example, you can create folders that allow you to organize the Favorites list into categories. In Figure 1-30 on page IE 25, Internet Explorer created two folders (Links and Media) that help you organize favorites. You can create additional folders using the Organize Favorites button on the Favorites bar.

You have learned to create, use, and remove favorites. Saving URLs in the Favorites list is not the only way to save information you obtain using Internet Explorer. Some of the more interesting text and pictures you locate while displaying Web pages also are worth saving.

Saving Information Obtained with Internet Explorer

Many different types of Web pages are accessible on the World Wide Web. Because these pages can help accumulate information about areas of interest, you may wish to save the information you discover for future reference. The different types of Web pages and the different ways you may want to use them require different methods of saving. Internet Explorer allows you to save an entire Web page, individual pictures, or selected pieces of text. The following pages illustrate how to save an entire Web page, how to save a single picture, and how to save text.

Saving a Web Page

One method of saving information on a Web page is to save the entire Web page. The following steps show how to save the Asian Arts Web page on a floppy disk in drive A.

To Save a Web Page

1

• **With a formatted floppy disk in drive A, click File on the menu bar.**

The File menu appears (Figure 1-35). The Save As command is displayed on the File menu.

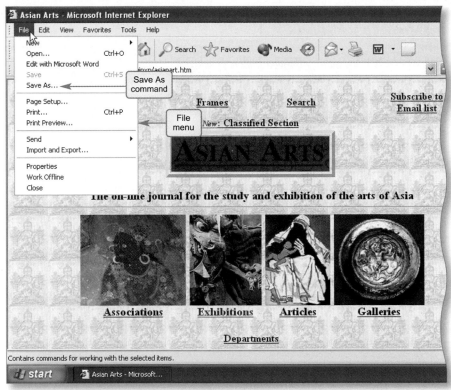

FIGURE 1-35

2

• **Click Save As on the File menu.**

Internet Explorer displays the Save Web Page dialog box. The Save in box contains the My Documents entry and the File name text box contains the highlighted Web page title, Asian Arts (Figure 1-36). You can change the file name in the File name box by typing a new file name from the keyboard. The My Documents entry in the Save in box may be different on your computer.

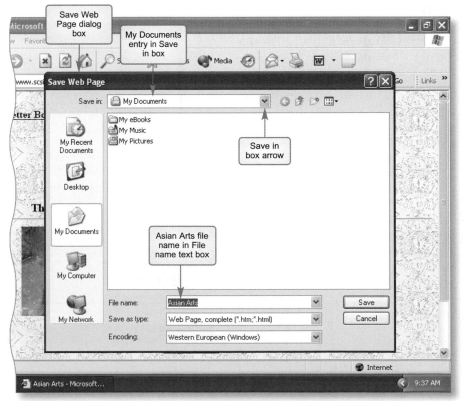

FIGURE 1-36

3

• **Click the Save in box arrow in the Save in box.**

The Save in list contains various components of the computer with the My Documents entry highlighted (Figure 1-37).

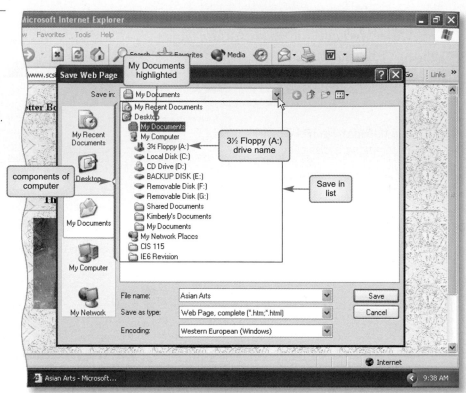

FIGURE 1-37

4

• **If necessary, click 3½ Floppy (A:) in the Save in list.**

The highlighted 3½ Floppy (A:) drive name appears in the Save in box (Figure 1-38). The entry in the Save as type box, Web Page, complete (.htm;*.html), determines how the Web page is saved.*

• **Click the Save button in the Save Web Page dialog box.**

The Save Web Page dialog box closes and a smaller Save Web Page dialog box appears while the Asian Arts Web page is saved using the file name, Asian Arts.htm, on the floppy disk in drive A.

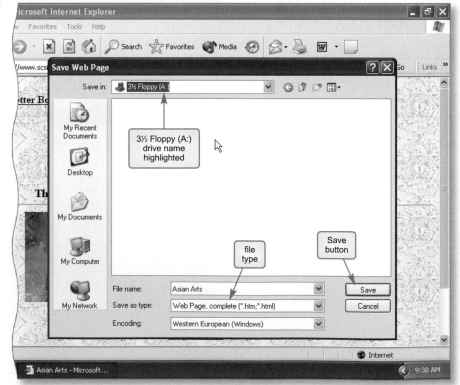

FIGURE 1-38

Other Ways

1. Press ALT+F, press A

Internet Explorer saves the instructions to display the saved Web page in the Asian Arts.htm file on drive A using HTML codes (see Figure 1-5 on page IE 7), creates the Asian Arts_files folder on the 3½ Floppy (A:) disk, and saves the pictures from the Web page in the folder on drive A. You can view the saved Web page in the Internet Explorer window by double-clicking the Asian Arts.htm file and view a list of saved pictures by double-clicking the Asian Arts_files folder.

Saving a Picture on a Web Page

A second method of saving information is to save a picture located on a Web page. In the following steps, the Galleries picture located on the Asian Arts Web page is saved on the floppy disk in drive A using the **Joint Photographic Experts Group** (**JPEG**) format. The JPEG file format is a method of encoding pictures on a computer. When you save a picture as a JPEG file, Internet Explorer can display it. The following steps show how to save the Galleries picture on a floppy disk in drive A in the JPEG format using the file name galleries.jpg.

To Save a Picture on a Web Page

1

• **Right-click the Galleries picture on the Asian Arts Web site.**

A shortcut menu, containing the Save Picture As command, appears (Figure 1-39).

FIGURE 1-39

• Click Save Picture As on the shortcut menu.

• Click the Save in box arrow in the Save Picture dialog box.

• Click 3½ Floppy (A:) in the Save in box.

The Save Picture dialog box appears (Figure 1-40). The Save in box contains the 3½ Floppy (A:) drive name, the File name text box contains the image06 file name, and the Save as type text box contains the JPEG (*.jpg) file type. The Asian Arts_files folder contains the saved Asian Arts Web page.

• Click the Save button in the Save Picture dialog box.

The picture is saved using the image06.jpg file name on the floppy disk in drive A and the Save Picture dialog box closes.

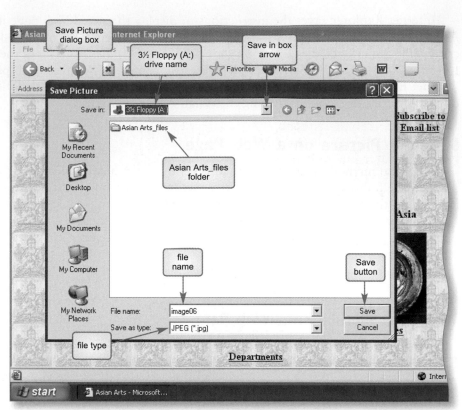

FIGURE 1-40

Other Ways

1. Right-click image, click Save Target As, click 3½ Floppy (A:) in Save in list, click Save button

Q&A

Q: Should I store all my pictures in the My Pictures folder?

A: Yes. You can use folders to organize your pictures and you easily can back up the folders in the My Pictures folder to another storage device for safekeeping. Three other folders (My Documents, My Videos, and My Media) are available to store documents, videos, and media files.

Copying and Pasting Using the Clipboard

A third method of saving information, called the **copy and paste method**, allows you to copy an entire Web page, or portions thereof, and insert the information in any Windows document. The **Clipboard**, which is a temporary storage area in main memory, temporarily holds the information being copied. The portion of the Web page you select is **copied** from the Web page to the Clipboard and then **pasted** from the Clipboard into the document. Information you copy to the Clipboard remains there until you add more information or clear it.

The following pages demonstrate how to copy text and pictures from the Exhibitions Web page into a WordPad document using the Clipboard. **WordPad** is a word processing program that is supplied with Microsoft Windows.

Starting WordPad

Before copying information from the Web page in Internet Explorer to the Clipboard, WordPad must be running. The following steps illustrate how to start WordPad.

To Start WordPad

1

• **Click the Start button on the Windows taskbar, point to All Programs on the Start menu, point to Accessories on the All Programs submenu, and then point to WordPad on the Accessories submenu.**

The Start menu, All Programs submenu, and Accessories submenu are displayed (Figure 1-41).

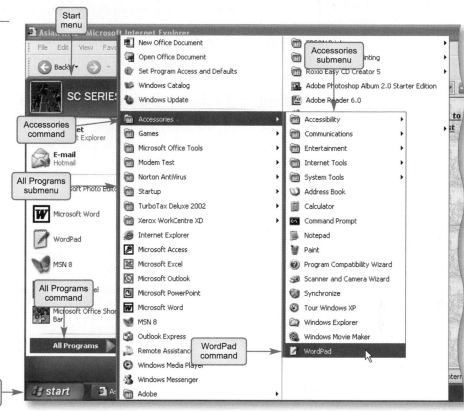

FIGURE 1-41

2

• **Click WordPad.**

Windows starts WordPad, opens the active Document - WordPad window on top of the inactive Asian Arts - Microsoft Internet Explorer window, and displays the Document - WordPad button on the taskbar (Figure 1-42). An empty WordPad document, into which the text can be pasted, is displayed in the Document - WordPad window. An insertion point and the I-beam mouse pointer appear in the empty document.

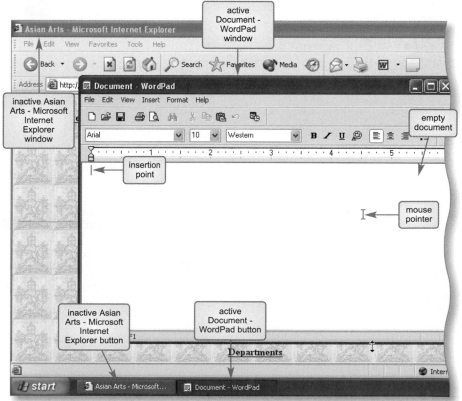

FIGURE 1-42

The Document - WordPad window appears on top of the Asian Arts - Microsoft Internet Explorer window. The Document - WordPad window is the active window. The **active window** is the window currently being used. A dark blue title bar and a dark blue taskbar button identify the active window. The Asian Arts - Microsoft Internet Explorer window is the inactive window. A light blue title bar and a light blue taskbar button identify the **inactive window**.

Using a Taskbar Button to Display an Inactive Window

Currently, the active Document - WordPad window displays on top of the inactive Asian Arts - Microsoft Internet Explorer window. After starting WordPad and before copying text from a Web page to the Clipboard, display the Asian Arts - Microsoft Internet Explorer window and then display the Exhibitions Web page. The following steps show how to display the Exhibitions Web page.

To Display the Exhibitions Web Page

1

• **Click the Asian Arts - Microsoft Internet Explorer button on the taskbar.**

The active Asian Arts - Microsoft Internet Explorer window is displayed on top of the inactive Document - WordPad window (Figure 1-43). Although not visible, the inactive window is still open, as evidenced by the taskbar button. The display area contains the Asian Arts Web page.

FIGURE 1-43

2

• **Click the Exhibitions link on the Asian Arts Web page.**

The Exhibitions Web page appears (Figure 1-44). The window title and taskbar button name change.

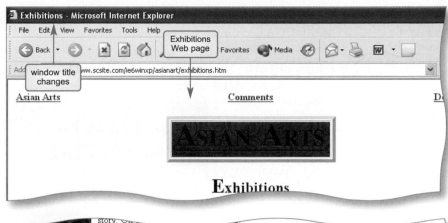

FIGURE 1-44

Other Ways

1. Press ALT+TAB, hold down ALT, press TAB to select
2. If visible, click window title bar

With the Document - WordPad window open and the text you wish to copy contained on the Exhibitions Web page, the next steps are to scroll the display area to display the text to be copied, copy the text from the Exhibitions Web page to the Clipboard, and then paste the text into the WordPad document.

Copying Text from a Web Page and Pasting It into a WordPad Document

The following steps show how to copy the text about the Splendors of Imperial China to the Clipboard, switch to WordPad, and paste the text on the Clipboard into the WordPad document.

To Copy and Paste Text from a Web Page into a WordPad Document

1

• **Scroll the Exhibitions Web page to display The Splendors of Imperial China: Treasures from the National Palace Museum, Taipei link.**

• **Position the mouse pointer (I-beam) at the beginning of the text that follows the link text.**

The Splendors of Imperial China: Treasures from the National Palace Museum, Taipei link appears (Figure 1-45).

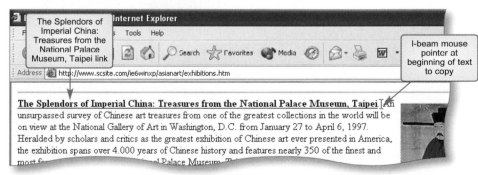

FIGURE 1-45

2

- **Drag to select the text that follows the link text.**
- **Right-click the highlighted text.**

Internet Explorer highlights the selected text and displays a shortcut menu (Figure 1-46).

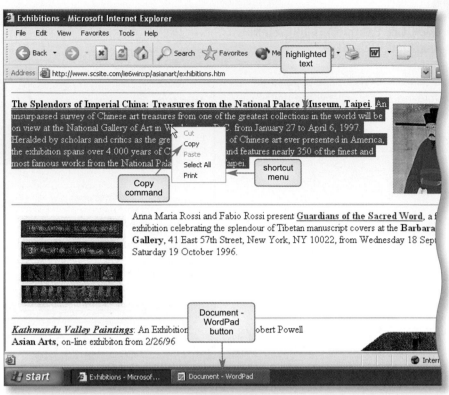

FIGURE 1-46

3

- **Click Copy on the shortcut menu.**

Internet Explorer closes the shortcut menu and copies the selected text to the Clipboard.

4

- **Click the Document - WordPad button on the Windows taskbar, and then right-click the empty text area in the Document - WordPad window.**

Internet Explorer displays the Document - WordPad window and a shortcut menu (Figure 1-47).

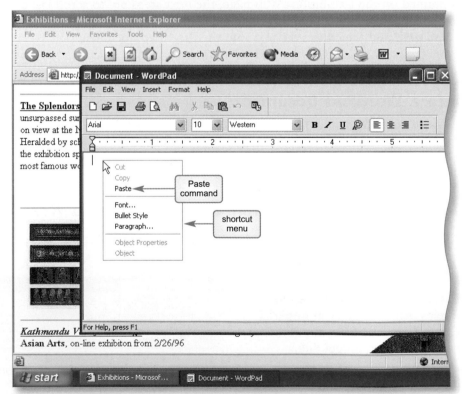

FIGURE 1-47

5

• **Click Paste on the shortcut menu.**

Internet Explorer closes the shortcut menu and pastes the contents of the Clipboard into the Document - WordPad window (Figure 1-48).

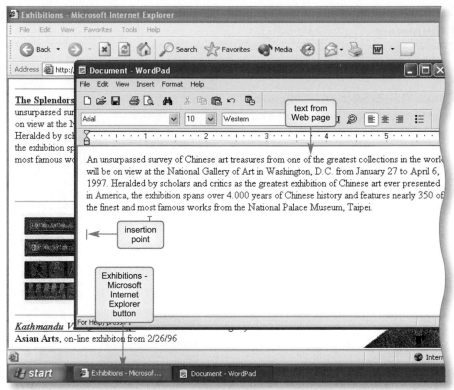

FIGURE 1-48

The text portion of the copy and paste operation is complete. The WordPad document contains a paragraph of text retrieved from a Web page.

Copying a Picture from a Web Page and Pasting It into WordPad

The steps to copy a picture from a Web page are similar to those used to copy and paste text. The steps on the next page show how to copy and then paste a picture from a Web page into a WordPad document.

To Copy and Paste a Picture from a Web Page into a WordPad Document

1

• **Click the Exhibitions - Microsoft Internet Explorer button on the Windows taskbar.**

• **Click outside the selected text to deselect the text.**

• **Right-click the picture to the right of the text.**

The Exhibitions - Microsoft Internet Explorer window is displayed, the selected text in the window is deselected, and a shortcut menu appears (Figure 1-49).

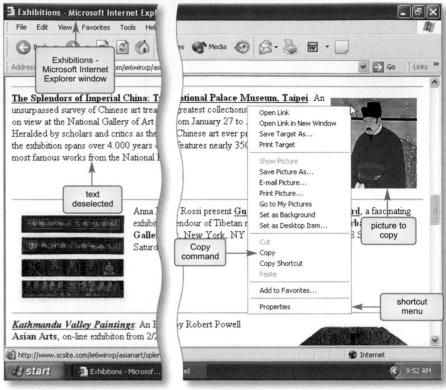

FIGURE 1-49

2

• **Click Copy on the shortcut menu.**

Internet Explorer closes the shortcut menu and copies the picture to the Clipboard.

3

• **Click the Document - WordPad button on the taskbar.**

• **Right-click an area below the insertion point in the Document - WordPad window.**

The Document - WordPad window and a shortcut menu appear (Figure 1-50). The Paste command is displayed on the shortcut menu.

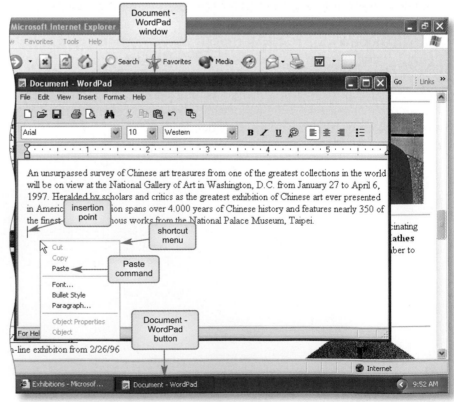

FIGURE 1-50

4

• **Click Paste on the shortcut menu.**

Internet Explorer pastes the contents of the Clipboard in the Document - WordPad window at the location of the insertion point (Figure 1-51). After pasting the picture, you can resize the picture by dragging the corners or borders of the picture in toward the center of the picture to make it smaller or outward from the center to make it larger.

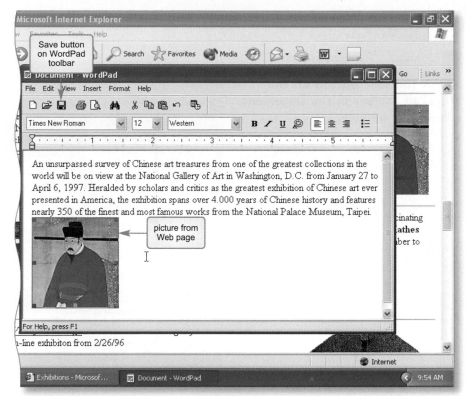

FIGURE 1-51

The copy and paste operations are complete. The WordPad window contains text and a picture retrieved from the Exhibitions Web page. The tools provided with WordPad can be used to manipulate the picture and text.

Saving the WordPad Document and Quitting WordPad

When you are finished with the WordPad document, you can save it on a floppy disk for later use and then quit WordPad. The steps on the next page illustrate how to save the WordPad document using the Splendors of Imperial China file name and quit WordPad.

More About

WordPad

WordPad can save a file as a Microsoft Word document, RTF or Rich Text Format, or as a plain text file.

To Save the WordPad Document and Quit WordPad

1

• **Click the Save button on the WordPad toolbar in the Document - WordPad window.**

WordPad displays the Save As dialog box (Figure 1-52). The Save in box contains the My Documents entry and the File name box contains the highlighted Document entry.

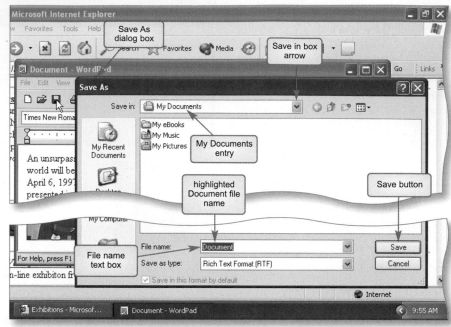

FIGURE 1-52

2

• **Click the Save in box arrow in the Save in box.**

• **Click 3½ Floppy (A:) in the Save in list.**

• **Type** Splendors of Imperial China **in the File name text box.**

The 3½ Floppy (A:) drive name appears in the Save in box, the Splendors of Imperial China file name is displayed in the File name text box, and the Rich Text Format (RTF) file type in the Save as type box determines how the document is saved (Figure 1-53).

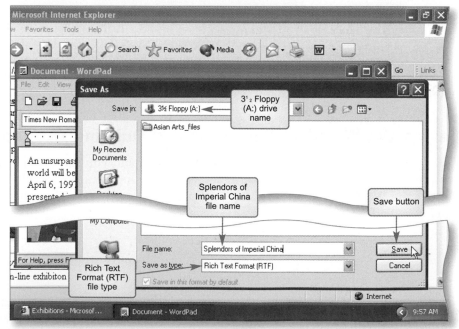

FIGURE 1-53

3

• **Click the Save button in the Save As dialog box.**

The Save As dialog box closes and WordPad saves the Splendors of Imperial China document on the floppy disk in drive A.

4

• **Click the Close button on the Splendors of Imperial China - WordPad title bar to quit WordPad.**

The WordPad window closes and the Internet Explorer window is visible on the desktop.

Computer users commonly search for and save text and pictures found on the World Wide Web to a disk for use in the future.

Printing a Web Page in Internet Explorer

As you visit Web sites, you may want to print some of the pages you view. A printed version of a Web page is called a **hard copy** or **printout**. You might want a printout for several reasons. First, to present the Web page to someone who does not have access to a computer, it must be in printed form. Second, persons other than those who prepare them often keep Web pages for reference. In some cases, Web pages are printed and kept in binders for use by others.

Internet Explorer's printing capability allows you to print both the text and picture portions of a Web page. In the following steps, you will print the Exhibitions Web Page and four pieces of paper will print on the printer (Figure 1-55 on the next page). The following steps show how to print the Exhibitions Web page.

To Print a Web Page

1

• **Ready the printer according to the printer instructions.**

• **Click the Print button on the Standard Buttons toolbar (Figure 1-54).**

2

• **When the printer stops printing the document, retrieve the printouts, which should look like Figure 1-55.**

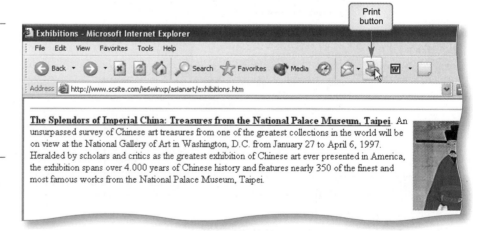

FIGURE 1-54

The URL of the Web page prints as a footer in the lower-left corner of each page (Figure 1-55). The Web page title appears in the upper-left corner of each page, the page number and total number of pages in the Web site appear in the upper-right corner of each page, and the date is displayed in the lower-right corner.

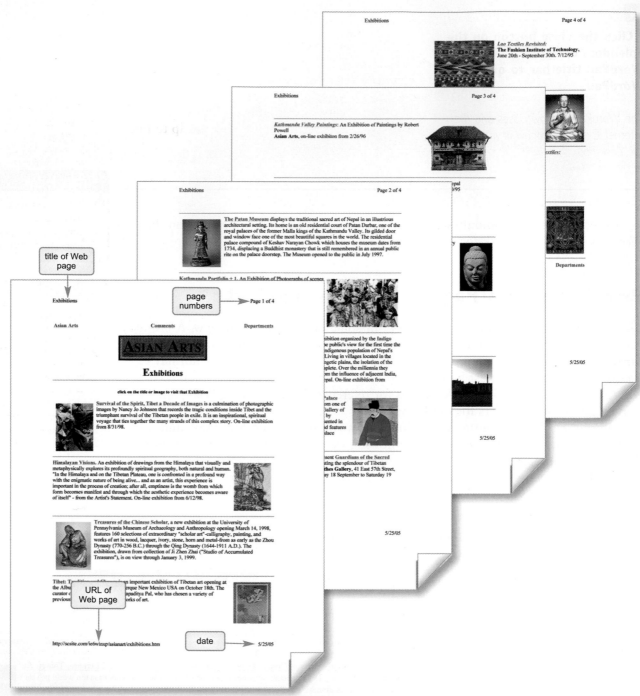

FIGURE 1-55

Other Ways

1. On File menu click PRINT, click Print button
2. Press CTRL+P, click Print button

You also can click Print on the File menu to print a Web page. When you do this, a Print dialog box displays. The printing options available in the Print dialog box allow you to print the entire document, print selected pages of a document, print to a disk file, print multiple copies, change the printer properties, and cancel the print request.

Internet Explorer Help

Internet Explorer is a program with many features and options. Although you will master some of these features and options quickly, it is not necessary for you to remember everything about each one of them. Reference materials and other forms of assistance are available within **Internet Explorer Help**. You can display these materials and learn how to use the multitude of features available with Internet Explorer. The following steps illustrate how to use the Internet Explorer Help to find more information about Uniform Resource Locators (URLs).

More About

Printing

You can choose to print a table containing a list of all links on the Web page you are printing or all documents with links on the Web page. Click the Options tab in the Print dialog box and then click the Print all linked documents check box or Print table of links check box to print the documents or table.

To Access Internet Explorer Help

1

• **Click Help on the menu bar.**

The Help menu appears (Figure 1-56). Several commands are available to provide helpful information about Internet Explorer.

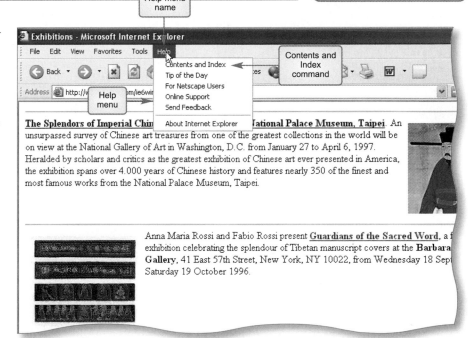

FIGURE 1-56

2

• **Click Contents and Index on the Help menu.**

The Microsoft Internet Explorer window contains the Help toolbar and two panes (Figure 1-57). The navigation pane contains four tabs (Contents, Index, Search, and Favorites) and the display pane contains Help information. The Contents sheet contains topics organized into categories, the Index sheet contains an index of Help topics, the Search sheet allows you to search for specific Help topics, and the Favorites sheet contains a list of favorite Web sites.

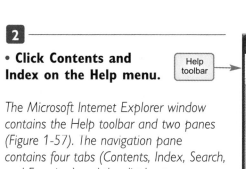
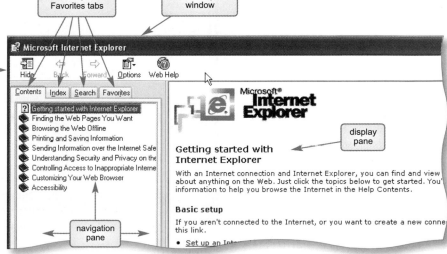

FIGURE 1-57

3

• **Click the Index tab in the navigation pane.**

The Index sheet appears in the navigation pane (Figure 1-58). The Index sheet contains a text box and a list of Help topics.

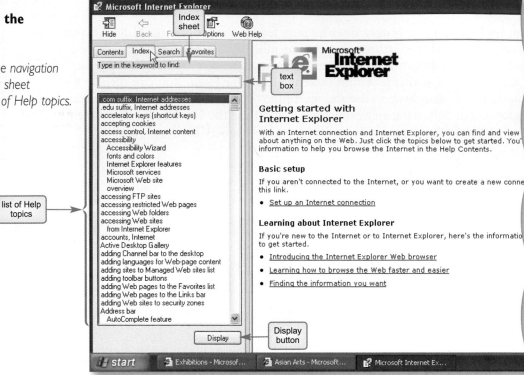

FIGURE 1-58

4

• **Type url in the text box in the navigation pane.**

When you type the letters url, the list automatically scrolls and the first entry beginning with the characters, u-r-l, is highlighted (Figure 1-59). To see additional entries in the list, use the scroll bar at the right of the list. To highlight an entry in the list, click the entry. To view the entry, double-click the entry.

FIGURE 1-59

5

• **Double-click about Internet addresses in the list of Help topics.**

The Understanding Internet addresses screen appears in the display pane (Figure 1-60). Additional information about Internet addresses can be found by clicking the Related Topics link at the bottom of the screen.

6

• **When you are finished viewing the information, click the Close button on the right side of the title bar to close the Microsoft Internet Explorer window.**

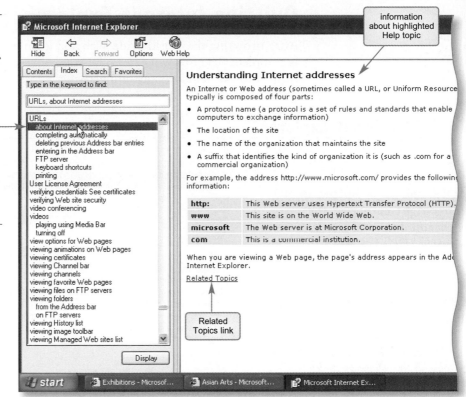

FIGURE 1-60

In Figure 1-57 on page IE 43, buttons on the Help toolbar in the Microsoft Internet Explorer window allow you to perform activities such as hiding the navigation pane, navigating among previously displayed Help topics, changing Internet options, and obtaining Help from the Microsoft Product Support Services Web site. In Figure 1-58, clicking the Display button at the bottom of the navigation pane displays information in the display pane about the highlighted Help topic in the navigation pane.

The Help menu in Figure 1-56 on page IE 43 contains several other commands, which are summarized in Table 1-6.

Other Ways

1. Press ALT+H, press C
2. Press F1

Table 1-6 Commands on the Help Menu	
MENU COMMAND	**FUNCTION**
Contents and Index	Displays Contents, Index, Search, and Favorites tabs.
Tip of the Day	Displays the tip of the day at the bottom of the Microsoft Internet Explorer window. Click the Close button to remove tip.
For Netscape Users	Displays tips for Netscape browser users.
Online Support	Displays Microsoft Product Support Services Web site.
Send Feedback	Displays Contact Us Web site to obtain technical support, ask a question, report a bug, or send comments.
About Internet Explorer	Displays version, cipher strength, product ID, license information, copyright, and acknowledgements about Internet Explorer.

Quitting Internet Explorer

After browsing the World Wide Web and learning how to manage Web pages, Project 1 is complete. The following steps illustrate how to quit Internet Explorer and return control to the Windows operating system.

To Quit Internet Explorer

1

• **Click the Close button in the upper-right corner of the Microsoft Internet Explorer window (Figure 1-61).**

2

• **Remove the floppy disk from drive A.**

The Microsoft Internet Explorer window closes and the Windows desktop is displayed.

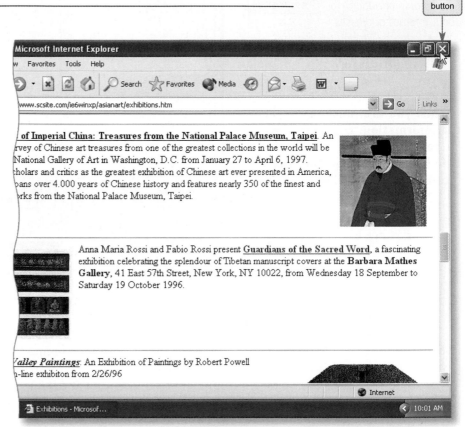

FIGURE 1-61

> **Other Ways**
>
> 1. Double-click System menu icon at left end of title bar
> 2. On File menu click Close
> 3. Press ALT+F, press C

Project Summary

Project 1 introduced you to the Internet and World Wide Web. You learned how to start Internet Explorer and use the History list, Favorites list, buttons on the Standard Buttons toolbar, and a URL to browse the World Wide Web. The project illustrated how to add and remove Web pages on the Favorites list; copy and paste text from a Web page into a WordPad document; save and print the document; and save text, a picture, and an entire Web page on disk. In addition, you learned how to use the Index sheet in Internet Explorer Help to obtain help about Internet Explorer.

What You Should Know

Having completed the project, you now should be able to perform the tasks listed below. The tasks are listed in the same order they were presented in this project. For a list of the buttons, menus, toolbars, and commands introduced in this project, see the Quick Reference Summary at the back of this book and refer to the Page Number column.

1. Start Internet Explorer (IE 8)
2. Browse the Web by Entering a URL (IE 12)
3. Refresh a Web Page (IE 16)
4. Use the Back and Forward Buttons to Find Recently Displayed Web Pages (IE 19)
5. Display a Web Page Using the Back Button List (IE 20)
6. Display a Web Page Using the History List (IE 22)
7. Add a Web Page to the Favorites List (IE 23)
8. Display the Home Page Using the Home Button (IE 25)
9. Display a Web Page Using the Favorites List (IE 25)
10. Remove a Web Page from the Favorites List (IE 27)
11. Save a Web Page (IE 29)
12. Save a Picture on a Web Page (IE 31)
13. Start WordPad (IE 33)
14. Display the Exhibitions Web Page (IE 34)
15. Copy and Paste Text from a Web Page into a WordPad Document (IE 35)
16. Copy and Paste a Picture from a Web Page into a WordPad Document (IE 38)
17. Save the WordPad Document and Quit WordPad (IE 40)
18. Print a Web Page (IE 41)
19. Access Internet Explorer Help (IE 43)
20. Quit Internet Explorer (IE 46)

Learn It Online

Instructions: To complete the Learn It Online exercises, start your browser, click the Address box, enter scsite.com/ie6winxp/learn, and then click the Go button. When the Internet Explorer Learn It Online page is displayed, follow the instructions in the exercises below. Each exercise has instructions for printing your results, either for your own records or for submission to your instructor.

1 Project Reinforcement TF, MC, and SA

Below Internet Explorer Project 1, click the Project Reinforcement link. Print the quiz by clicking Print on the File menu for each page. Answer each question.

2 Flash Cards

Below Internet Explorer Project 1, click the Flash Cards link and read the instructions. Type 20 (or a number specified by your instructor) in the Number of playing cards text box, type your name in the Enter your name text box, and then click the Flip Card button. When the flash card is displayed, read the question and then click the ANSWER box arrow to select an answer. Flip through Flash Cards. If your score is 15 (75%) correct or greater, click Print on the File menu to print your results. If your score is less than 15 (75%) correct, then redo this exercise by clicking the Replay button.

3 Practice Test

Below Internet Explorer Project 1, click the Practice Test link. Answer each question, enter your first and last name at the bottom of the page, and then click the Grade Test button. When the graded practice test is displayed on your screen, click Print on the File menu to print a hard copy. Continue to take practice tests until you score 80% or better.

4 Who Wants To Be a Computer Genius?

Below Internet Explorer Project 1, click the Computer Genius link. Read the instructions, enter your first and last name at the bottom of the page, and then click the PLAY button. When your score is displayed, click the PRINT RESULTS link to print a hard copy.

5 Wheel of Terms

Below Internet Explorer Project 1, click the Wheel of Terms link. Read the instructions, and then enter your first and last name and your school name. Click the PLAY button. When your score is displayed, right-click the scores and then click Print on the shortcut menu to print a hard copy.

6 Crossword Puzzle Challenge

Below Internet Explorer Project 1, click the Crossword Puzzle Challenge link. Read the instructions, and then enter your first and last name. Click the SUBMIT button. Work the crossword puzzle. When you are finished, click the Submit button. When the crossword puzzle is displayed, click the Print Puzzle button to print a hard copy.

7 Tips and Tricks

Below Internet Explorer Project 1, click the Tips and Tricks link. Click a topic that pertains to Project 1. Right-click the information and then click Print on the shortcut menu. Construct a brief example of what the information relates to in Internet Explorer to confirm you understand how to use the tip or trick.

8 Newsgroups

Below Internet Explorer Project 1, click the Newsgroups link. Click a topic that pertains to Project 1. Print three comments.

9 Expanding Your Horizons

Below Internet Explorer Project 1, click the Expanding Your Horizons link. Click a topic that pertains to Project 1. Print the information. Construct a brief example of what the information relates to in Internet Explorer to confirm you understand the contents of the article.

10 Search Sleuth

Below Internet Explorer Project 1, click the Search Sleuth link. To search for a term that pertains to this project, select a term below the Project 1 title and then use the Google search engine at google.com (or any major search engine) to display and print two Web pages that present information on the term.

11 Internet Explorer How-To Articles

Below Internet Explorer Project 1, click the Internet Explorer How-To Articles link. When your browser displays the Internet Explorer How-to Articles Web page, scroll down and click one of the links that covers one or more of the objectives listed at the beginning of the project on page IE 1. Print the first page of the how-to article before stepping through it.

12 Getting More From the Web

Below Internet Explorer Project 1, click the Getting More from the Web link. When your browser displays the Getting More from the Web with Internet Explorer 6 Web page, click one of the Top Stories or Featured Contents links. Print the first page.

In the Lab

1 Browsing the World Wide Web Using URLs and Links

Problem: You work part-time for *The Orange County Register*, one of California's largest newspapers. Your editor has asked you to search for information on several informational Web sites and print the first page of each Web site.

Instructions: Perform the following tasks.

Part 1: Using the Address Bar to Find a Web Page

1. If necessary, connect to the Internet and start Internet Explorer.
2. Click the Address box, type www.fbi.gov in the box, and then click the Go button to display the Federal Bureau of Investigation's home page (Figure 1-62).

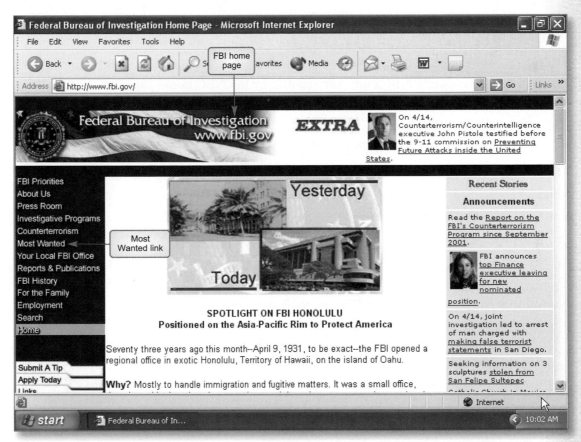

FIGURE 1-62

3. Using links in the FBI Web site, find the Web page that contains the list of the ten most wanted fugitives.
4. Click the Print button on the Standard Buttons toolbar to print the Web page.
5. Use the Back button on the Standard Buttons toolbar to display the FBI home page.
6. Click the Print button on the Standard Buttons toolbar to print the Web page.
7. Click the Address box, type www.nbc.com in the box, and then click the Go button to display the NBC home page.

(continued)

Browsing the World Wide Web Using URLs and Links *(continued)*

8. Using links in the NBC Web site, find the Web page that lists the guest stars on the Tonight Show.
9. Click the Print button on the Standard Buttons toolbar to print the Web page.
10. Click the Address box, type `www.usatoday.com` in the box, and then click the Go button to display the USA TODAY home page.
11. Using links in the USA TODAY Web site, find the Web page that contains the United States weather map.
12. Click the Print button on the Standard Buttons toolbar to print the Web page.
13. Click the Address box, type `www.cbs.com` in the Address box, and then click the Go button to display the CBS home page.
14. Using links in the CBS Web site, find the Web page that contains David Letterman's Top Ten List.
15. Click the Print button on the Standard Buttons toolbar to print the Web page.

Part 2: Using the History Button to Find a Web Page

1. Click the Home button on the Standard Buttons toolbar to display your default home page.
2. Click the History button on the Standard Buttons toolbar, click the nbc (www.nbc.com) folder name in the History list, and then click the NBC.com entry to display the NBC home page.
3. Click the Print button on the Standard Buttons toolbar to print the Web page.
4. Click the Close button on the Explorer bar.

Part 3: Using the Back Button Arrow to Find a Web Page

1. Click the Back button arrow and then click the CBS home page entry on the menu to display the CBS home page.
2. Click the Print button on the Standard Buttons toolbar to print the Web page.

Part 4: Using the Address Box Arrow to Find a Web Page

1. Click the Address box arrow and then click http://www.usatoday.com in the Address list to display the USA TODAY home page.
2. Click the Print button on the Standard Buttons toolbar to print the Web page.
3. Click the Close button in the Microsoft Internet Explorer window.
4. Discard the second page and subsequent pages of each Web site you printed. Organize the printed Web pages so that the home page is first and the Web page associated with the home page is second. Hand in the eight printed pages to your instructor.

2 Working with the History List

Instructions: Perform the following tasks.

Problem: Your instructor would like you to practice browsing the Internet for Web sites and then adding them to the History list. As proof of completing this assignment, you should print the first page of each Web site you visit.

In the Lab

Part 1: *Clearing the History List*

1. If necessary, connect to the Internet and start Internet Explorer.
2. Click Tools on the menu bar and then click Internet Options to display the Internet Options dialog box (Figure 1-63).

FIGURE 1-63

3. Click the Clear History button and then click the Yes button in the Internet Options dialog box.
4. Click the OK button in the Internet Options dialog box.

Part 2: *Browsing the World Wide Web*

1. Click the Address box, type www.mtv.com in the Address box, and then click the Go button to display the MTV.com home page.
2. Click the Address box, type www.umich.edu in the Address box, and then click the Go button to display the University of Michigan home page.
3. Click the Address box, type www.geocaching.com in the Address box, and then click the Go button to display the Geocaching home page.
4. Click the Address box, type www.espn.com in the Address box, and then click the Go button to display the ESPN home page.
5. Print the Web page.

(continued)

In the Lab

Working with the History List (continued)

Part 3: *Using the History List to Print a Web Page*

1. Click the History button on the Standard Buttons toolbar to display the History list (Figure 1-64).

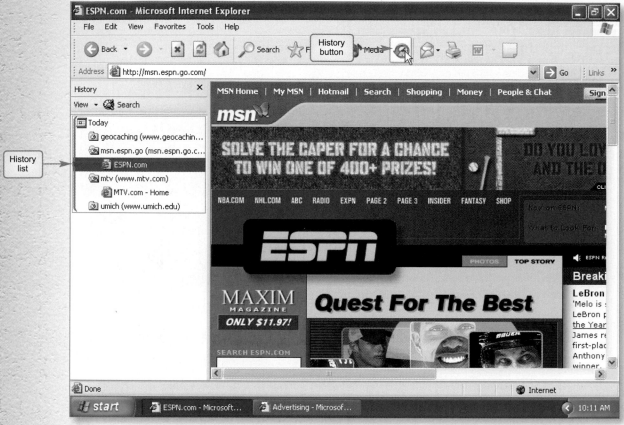

FIGURE 1-64

2. Click the umich (www.umich.edu) folder in the History list and then click the University of Michigan link. Print the Web page.
3. Click the mtv (www.mtv.com) folder in the History list and then click the MTV.com - home link. Print the Web page.
4. Click the espn.go (msn.espn.go.com) folder in the History list and then click the ESPN.com link. Print the Web page.
5. Delete the geocaching (www.geocaching.com) folder by right-clicking the folder, clicking Delete on the shortcut menu, and then clicking the Yes button in the WARNING dialog box.
6. Click the Close button on the Explorer Bar.

Part 4: *Clearing the History List*

1. Click Tools on the menu bar and then click Internet Options to display the Internet Options dialog box.
2. Click the Clear History button and then click the Yes button in the Internet Options dialog box.
3. Click the OK button in the Internet Options dialog box.
4. Click the Close button in the ESPN.com - Microsoft Internet Explorer window.
5. Hand in the printed Web pages to your instructor.

3 Working with the Favorites List

Problem: Your instructor would like you to practice browsing the Internet for Web sites and adding them to the Favorites list. As proof of completing this assignment, print out the first page of each Web site you visit.

Instructions: Perform the following tasks.

Part 1: *Creating a Folder in the Favorites List*

1. If necessary, connect to the Internet and start Internet Explorer.
2. Click the Favorites button on the Standard Buttons toolbar and then click Organize in the Favorites bar to display the Organize Favorites dialog box (Figure 1-65).

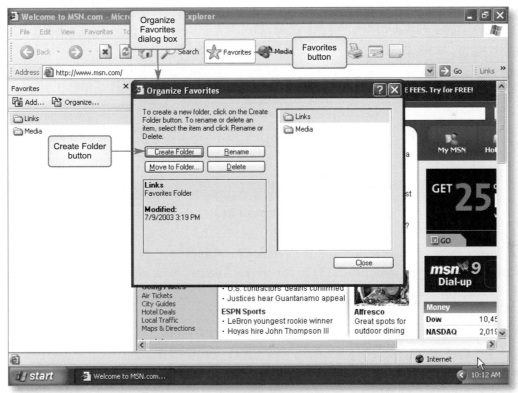

FIGURE 1-65

3. Click the Create Folder button in the Organize Favorites dialog box to create a folder titled New Folder, type your first and last name as the folder name, and then press the ENTER key.
4. Click the Close button to close the Organize Favorites dialog box.

Part 2: *Adding Favorites to Your Folder*

1. Click the Address box, type www.hemingwayhome.com in the Address box, and then click the Go button to display The Ernest Hemingway Home and Museum home page.
2. Add the Ernest Hemingway Home and Museum favorite to the your folder by clicking the Add button in the Favorites list and, if necessary, click the Create in button in the Add Favorite dialog box to display the Create in box (Figure 1-66 on the next page).

(continued)

Working with the Favorites List *(continued)*

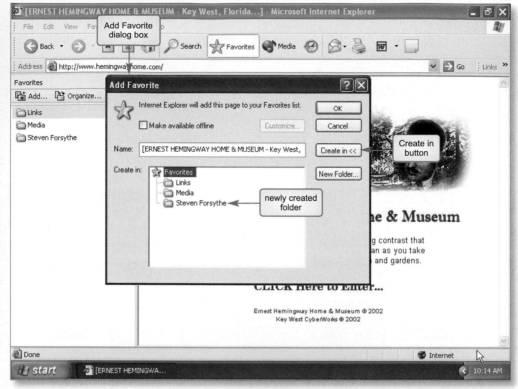

FIGURE 1-66

3. Click your folder in the Create in list and then click the OK button.
4. Click the Address box, type `www.priceline.com` in the Address box, and then click the Go button to display the Priceline.com home page.
5. Add this Web page to your folder.
6. Click the Close button on the Explorer Bar.
7. Click the Home button on the Standard Buttons toolbar to display your default home page.

Part 3: *Displaying and Printing a Favorite from Your Folder*

1. Click the Favorites button on the Standard Buttons toolbar to display the Favorites list.
2. Click your folder in the Favorites list and then click ERNEST HEMINGWAY HOME AND MUSEUM.
3. Print the Web page.
4. Click Priceline.com in the Favorites list.
5. Print the Web page.

In the Lab

Part 4: *Deleting a Folder in the Favorites List*

1. Click Organize in the Favorites list.
2. Click your folder name, click the Delete button, and then click the Yes button in the Confirm Folder Delete dialog box.
3. Click the Close button in the Organize Favorites dialog box.
4. Verify you have deleted your folder.
5. Click the Close button on the Explorer Bar.
6. Click the Close button in the Microsoft Internet Explorer window.
7. Hand in the two printed pages to your instructor.

4 Saving a Web Page on a Floppy Disk

Problem: You work part-time at E*TRADE, one of the nation's largest online stockbrokers. Your supervisor asks you to research the current stock prices of several stocks. In the process, you are expected to find the stock prices, print Web pages containing the stock prices, and save the Web pages on a floppy disk.

Instructions: Perform the following tasks.

1. If necessary, connect to the Internet and start Internet Explorer.
2. Click the Address box, type http://finance.yahoo.com/?u in the Address box and then click the Go button to display the Yahoo! Finance Web page (Figure 1-67).

FIGURE 1-67

(continued)

In the Lab

Saving a Web Page on a Floppy Disk *(continued)*

3. Enter the IBM stock symbol in the text box on the Web page and then click the Go button to retrieve the current IBM stock price. Print the Web page that displays and then save the Web page on a floppy disk. Click the Back button to display the Yahoo! Finance Web page.

4. Enter INTC, MSFT, TE, TOY, WEN, WY in the text box on the Web page and then click the Go button to retrieve the stock prices of the six stocks. Print the Web page that displays and then save the Web page on a floppy disk.

5. Click the Close button in the Microsoft Internet Explorer window.

6. Hand in the printed Web pages to your instructor.

5 Printing and Saving the Current U.S. Weather Map

Problem: You are interested in finding a current United States weather map to use on a road trip starting in Santa Barbara, California, and ending in Martha's Vineyard, Massachusetts. You want to print the map and save the map on a floppy disk.

Instructions: Perform the following tasks.

1. If necessary, connect to the Internet and start Internet Explorer.

2. Type www.weather.com in the Address box and then click the Go button to display the weather.com home page.

3. Scroll the home page to display the U.S. weather map. Click the click to enlarge link on the weather.com home page to display an enlarged weather map for the United States (Figure 1-68).

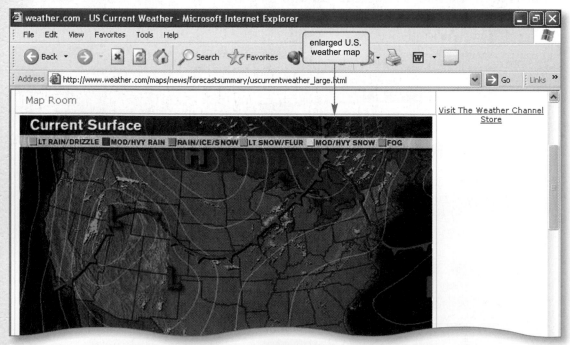

FIGURE 1-68

In the Lab

4. Right-click the weather map, click Print Picture on the shortcut menu, and then click the Print button in the Print dialog box to print the weather map.
5. Right-click the weather map and click Save Picture As on the shortcut menu to display the Save Picture dialog box. Click the Save in box arrow, click 3½ Floppy (A:), click the File name text box, type U.S. Weather map, and then click the Save button to save the picture on a floppy disk.
6. Click the Close button to close the Microsoft Internet Explorer window.
7. Hand in the printed weather map to your instructor.

6 Copying and Pasting a Picture and Text

Problem: To complete an assignment in history class, you must locate the Biography.com Web site and select an individual whose biography is on the Web site. When you find the biography of an individual you like, copy his or her picture and the text of the biography into WordPad, and then print the WordPad document.

Instructions: Perform the following tasks.

Part 1: *Retrieving a Web Page*

1. If necessary, connect to the Internet and start Internet Explorer.
2. Type www.biography.com in the Address box and then click the Go button to display the home page of the Biography.com Web site (Figure 1-69).

FIGURE 1-69

(continued)

In the Lab

Copying and Pasting a Picture and Text *(continued)*

3. Using the links on the Web site, search for the biography of an individual in which you are interested.

   a. Female suggestions - Mother Teresa, Martha Stewart, Eleanor Roosevelt, Ann-Margret, Bella Abzug, Julie Andrews, Susan B. Anthony, Hannah Arendt, Jennifer Aniston, Aretha Franklin

   b. Male suggestions - Pierce Brosnan, Martin Luther King, Mel Gibson, Hank Aaron, Charles Babbage, James Baldwin, Elvis Presley, Thomas Edison, Henry Ford, Steven Forsythe

Part 2: *Copying a Picture and Text to Microsoft WordPad*

1. If a picture of the individual is available, copy the picture to the Clipboard.
2. Start Microsoft WordPad.
3. Paste the picture on the Clipboard into the WordPad document, click anywhere off the picture, and then press the ENTER key.
4. Click the Biography.com - Microsoft Internet Explorer button on the taskbar.
5. Click the link that contains the biography.
6. Copy the biography text to the Clipboard.
7. Click the Document - WordPad button on the taskbar.
8. Paste the text on the Clipboard into the WordPad document.
9. Save the WordPad document on a floppy disk using the file name, Biography Assignment.
10. Print the WordPad document.
11. Click the Close button to close the Biography.com window.
12. Click the Close button to close the WordPad and Microsoft Internet Explorer windows.
13. Hand in the WordPad document to your instructor.

7 Copying, Pasting, and Saving a Picture

Problem: You are currently taking a political science class and must find the names and pictures of both senators from your state. Copy the names and pictures into WordPad and then print the WordPad document.

Instructions: Perform the following tasks.

1. If necessary, connect to the Internet and start Internet Explorer.
2. Click the Address box, type www.senate.gov in the Address box, and then click the Go button to display the U. S. Senate Web page (Figure 1-70).
3. Using links on the Web page, find a picture of one of the two senators who represent the state in which you live.
4. Start Microsoft WordPad.
5. Copy and paste the picture from the Web page into a blank WordPad document, click anywhere off the picture, and then press the ENTER key.
6. Find a picture of the other senator who represents the state in which you live.
7. Copy and paste the picture from the Web page into the WordPad document, click anywhere off the picture, and then press the ENTER key.

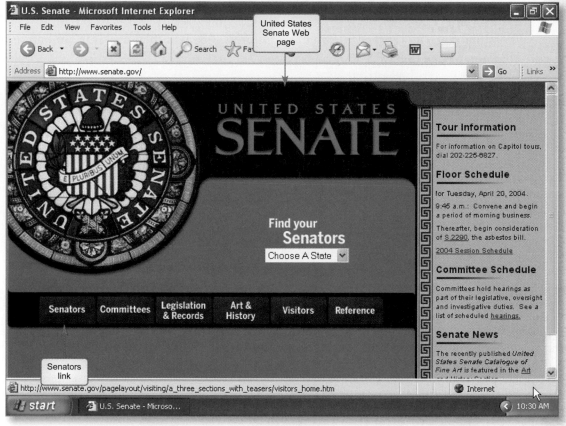

FIGURE 1-70

8. Save the document on a floppy disk using an appropriate file name.
9. Print the document.
10. Click the Close button on the WordPad window, click the Yes button in the WordPad dialog box.
11. Click the Close button on the Microsoft Internet Explorer window.
12. Hand in the document to your instructor.

8 Planning a Trip on the Web

Problem: You are planning a trip from Chicago to Las Vegas exactly one month from today. You plan to stay in Las Vegas seven days, including travel days. You want to use Expedia.com to summarize flights, hotels, car rentals, areas of interest, and directions from your hotel to the Hoover Dam museum in Boulder City, Nevada.

Instructions: Perform the following tasks.

Part 1: *Summarizing Flight Information*

1. If necessary, connect to the Internet and start Internet Explorer.

(continued)

Planning a Trip on the Web *(continued)*

2. Click the Address box, type www.expedia.com in the Address box, and then click the Go button to display the Expedia.com home page (Figure 1-71).

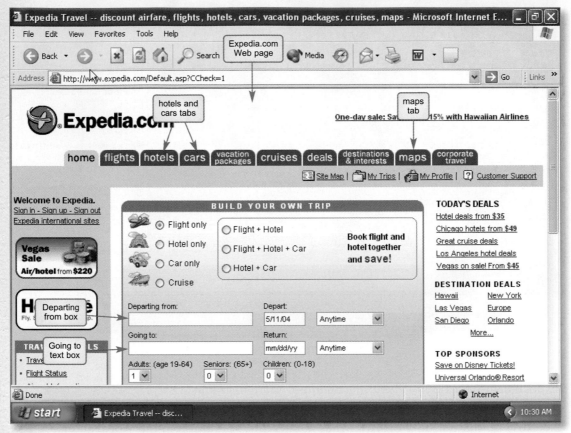

FIGURE 1-71

3. Type Chicago in the Departing from box; type Las Vegas in the Going to box; select 2 in the Adults box; select the date and time (i.e., July 7 noon) in the Depart box; and seven days from the date of departure, including the date of departure (i.e., July 13 noon) in the Return box. Click the Search for flight button.

4. When the Roundtrip search page displays, select Chicago, IL (ORD-O'Hare) in the Leaving from list. Click the Continue searching for flights now link. Scroll through the flight information and then print it.

Part 2: *Summarizing Hotel Information*

1. With the Expedia.com page displaying, click the hotels tab at the top of the page.

2. If necessary, click the Las Vegas option button or type Las Vegas in the Other city box. If necessary, enter the same dates and number of adults as described in Step 3 of Part 1. Click the Search button.

3. When the Search results page displays, scroll through the page and find the Hard Rock Hotel and Casino. If it is not on the page displayed, then request the next group of hotels by clicking the Next button. Print the page that includes the Bellagio hotel.

In the Lab

Part 3: *Summarizing Car Rental Information*

1. With the Expedia.com page displaying, click the cars tab at the top of the page.
2. Type `Las Vegas McCarran International Airport` in the Pick-up location box and then select Midsize in the Car class list. Click the Search button. Print the page.

Part 4: *Maps and Directions*

1. With the Expedia.com page displaying, click the maps tab. Click the Get Driving Directions link.
2. When the Get Driving Directions page is displayed in the Where do you want to start area, type `Las Vegas McCarran International Airport` in the Place name box. In the Where do you want to end area, type `Hoover dam` in the Place name box. If necessary, select Quickest in the Route type list and select `Miles` in the Units list. Click the Get driving directions link.
3. When the Get Driving Directions page redisplays with messages regarding multiple matches, select Bellagio Hotel/Casino, Las Vegas, Nevada in the Place name box. Scroll down and click the Get driving directions link. Print the map and directions.

9 Comparing Prices Online

Problem: You are interested in purchasing a Palm handheld device, an HP ink-jet printer, and a Canon digital camera. A friend suggested that you look on the Web for the lowest prices even though you are not yet ready to buy online. You decide to use the Web to compare prices and obtain company telephone numbers so you can contact the company with the best price and make the purchases using the telephone.

Instructions: Perform the following tasks.

1. If necessary, connect to the Internet and start Internet Explorer.
2. Click the Address box, type `www.computershopper.com`, and then press the ENTER key to display the CNET SHOPPER.COM page (Figure 1-72).

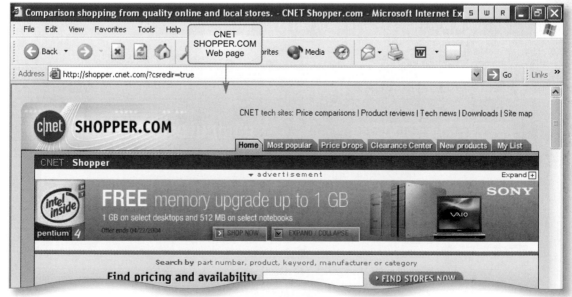

FIGURE 1-72

(continued)

In the Lab

Comparing Prices Online *(continued)*

3. Click the Palm OS link. When the next page displays, click the Palm Tungsten C (or Palm) link. Print the Search Results page. Return to the previous Web page and click Palm Tungsten T3 (or another Palm) to display the list of merchants. Click the merchant icon of the line item that has the lowest price to obtain the telephone number. Print the page.

4. Use the Back button or type www.computershopper.com in the Address box to display the CNET COMPUTER SHOPPER.COM home page. Click the Digital Cameras link. When the next page displays, click the Canon (or another brand) link. Print the Search Results page. Scroll down and click a digital camera model to display the list of merchants. Click the company info link of the line item that has the lowest price to obtain the telephone number. Print the page.

5. Use the Back button or type www.computershopper.com in the Address box to display the CNET COMPUTER SHOPPER.COM home page. Click the Printers link. When the next page displays, click the Hewlett-Packard (or another brand) link. Print the Search Results page. Scroll down and click a laser jet model to display the list of merchants. Click the company info link of the line item that has the lowest price to obtain the telephone number. Print the page.

10 Job Hunting on the Web

Problem: You are job hunting and your area of expertise is e-commerce. Instead of using the newspaper to find a job, you decide to search for jobs on the Internet. You decide to visit three Web sites in hopes of finding the perfect job.

Instructions: Perform the following tasks.

1. If necessary, connect to the Internet and start Internet Explorer.
2. Click the Address box, type www.computerjobs.com, and then press the ENTER key to display the computerjobs.com home page (Figure 1-73).

FIGURE 1-73

In the Lab

3. When the computerjobs.com home page displays, type `e-commerce` in the keyword search text box and then press the ENTER key. When the first page of the e-commerce listings displays, print it.

4. Type `www.monster.com` in the Address box and then press the ENTER key.

5. When the Monster home page appears, click the Search Jobs link. If you are asked to sign up for a Monster account, click "Not todayt, thanks" and then click the Next button. Type `e-commerce` in the Enter Key Words box and then press the ENTER key. When the first page of the e-commerce listings displays, print it.

6. Type `www.careerbuilder.com` in the Address box and then press the ENTER key.

7. When the careerbuilder.com page displays, type `e-commerce` in the Enter Keyword(s) box, and then click the ENTER key. When the first page of the e-commerce listings displays, print it.

11 Finding a Person on the Web

Problem: You are concerned about what personal information is available on the Web. You decide to search the Web for any personal information. In addition, you would like to locate antique dealers near your hometown.

Instructions: Perform the following tasks.

Part 1: *Finding a Person*

1. If necessary, connect to the Internet and start Internet Explorer.

2. Click the Address box, type `www.switchboard.com`, and then press the ENTER key.

3. When the Switchboard.com home page displays (Figure 1-74), click the Find a Person option button and type your last name in the Last Name box and your state in the State box. Leave the remaining boxes empty. Click the SEARCH button. If necessary, locate the page with your name on it by using the NEXT PAGE link. Print the page with your name on it. If you cannot find your name, print the page on which your name should have displayed.

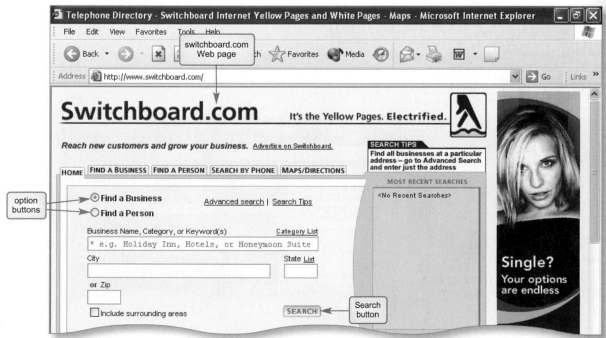

FIGURE 1-74

(continued)

In the Lab

Finding a Person on the Web (continued)

Part 2: *Finding a Business*

1. With the home page of the Switchboard.com Web site displaying, click the Find a Business option button.
2. Locate antique dealers near your hometown. You must enter a city and state. Print the page with the list of antique shops.

12 Working with Toolbars

Problem: Toolbars, toolbars, toolbars. What's the big deal? You don't understand what the big deal is, so you decide to learn more about toolbars. You want to know how to hide a toolbar, move and resize a toolbar, customize a toolbar, and use the Address bar to search for information on the Web.

Instructions: Perform the following tasks.

Part 1: *Hiding a Toolbar*

1. If necessary, connect to the Internet and start Internet Explorer.
2. If a move handle does not display at the left side of the Address bar, right-click a blank area of the Address bar, and click the Lock the Toolbars command to remove the check mark to the left of the command.
3. Right-click a blank area on the Standard Buttons toolbar to display a shortcut menu.
4. Click Links on the shortcut menu to remove the Links bar from the Microsoft Internet Explorer window.

Part 2: *Moving and Resizing a Toolbar*

1. Point to the Address title at the left end of the Address bar.
2. Move the Address bar onto the Standard Buttons toolbar by dragging the Address bar toward the Standard Buttons toolbar (Figure 1-75).

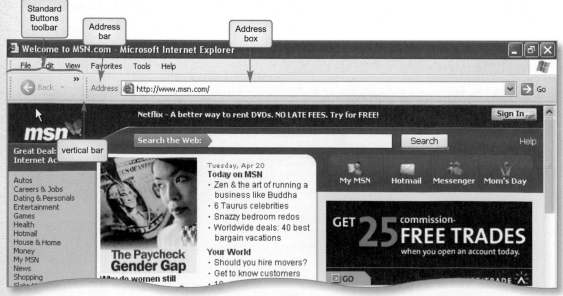

FIGURE 1-75

In the Lab

3. Point to the move handle at the left end of the Address bar.

4. Resize the Address bar by dragging the move handle on the Address bar to the right until only the Address title and Go button display on the Address bar.

5. Point to the Address title at the left end of the Address bar.

6. Move the Address bar back to its original position below the Standard Buttons toolbar by dragging the Address bar toward the bottom of the window.

Part 3: *Search for Information on the Internet Using the Address Bar*

1. Type "national weather" in the Address box.

2. Click the Go button to display a list of national weather related links in the display area.

3. Click any link to display its Web page.

Part 4: *Customizing the Standard Buttons Toolbar*

1. Right-click a blank area of the Standard Buttons toolbar and then click Customize on the shortcut menu to display the Customize Toolbar dialog box (Figure 1-76).

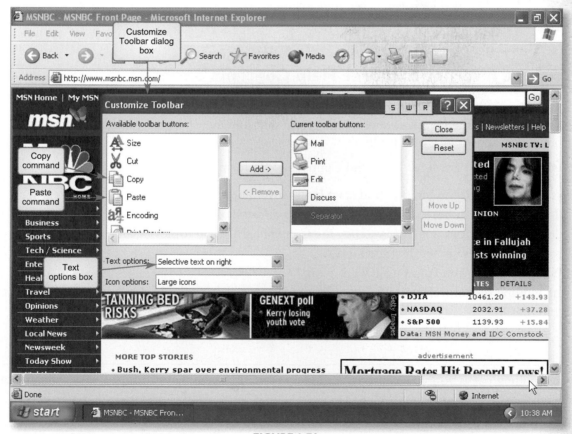

FIGURE 1-76

(continued)

In the Lab

Working with Toolbars *(continued)*

2. Click Copy in the Available toolbar buttons list.
3. Click the Add button to add the Copy entry to the Current toolbar buttons list and display the Copy button on the Standard Buttons toolbar.
4. Click Paste in the Available toolbar buttons list.
5. Click the Add button to add the Paste entry to the Current toolbar buttons list and display the Paste button on the Standard Buttons toolbar.
6. Click the Text Options box arrow and then click No text labels in the list.
7. Click the Close button in the Customize Toolbar dialog box. The Copy and Paste buttons display without text labels on the Standard Buttons toolbar.

Part 5: *Returning the Toolbar to Its Original Configuration*

1. Right-click a blank area of the Standard Buttons toolbar, click Customize, and then click the Reset button.
2. Click the Close button in the Customize Toolbars dialog box.
3. Right-click a blank area of the Standard Buttons toolbar and then click Links.
4. Click the Close button in the Microsoft Internet Explorer window.

13 Using the Internet Explorer Help Contents Sheet

Problem: Not knowing much about the Contents sheet in Internet Explorer Help, you decide to learn more about the organization of the Contents sheet, how to use the Contents sheet to search for information on the Web, and change the appearance of a toolbar.

Instructions: Use Internet Explorer Help and Contents to perform the following tasks.

1. If necessary, connect to the Internet and start Internet Explorer.
2. Click Help on the menu bar and then click Contents and Index.
3. If the Contents sheet does not display, click the Contents tab. Help topics in the Contents sheet are organized into the categories shown in Figure 1-77.
4. Click the Finding the Web Pages You Want book.
5. Click the Finding the information you want on the Internet Help topic. List two ways to find information on the Internet.

_____

_____

6. Click the Finding pages you've recently visited Help topic. List two ways to find Web sites and pages you just visited.

_____

_____

In the Lab

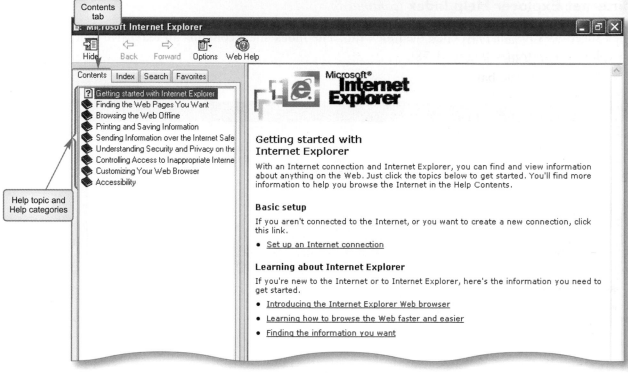

FIGURE 1-77

7. Click the Customizing Your Web Browser book. Click the Changing the appearance of the Windows toolbar. List three ways to change the appearance of a toolbar.

_____

_____

_____

8. Click the Close button in the Microsoft Internet Explorer window.
9. Click the Close button in the Microsoft Internet Explorer window.
10. Hand in the answers to the questions to your instructor.

14 Using the Internet Explorer Help Index

Problem: Not knowing much about the Index sheet in Internet Explorer Help, you decide to learn more about the Index sheet by using the sheet to search for the following topics: cookies, certificates, content advisor, and shortcut keys.

Instructions: Use Internet Explorer Help to perform the following tasks.

1. If necessary, connect to the Internet and start Internet Explorer.
2. Click Help on the menu bar and then click Contents and Index.

(continued)

Using the Internet Explorer Help Index *(continued)*

3. If the Index sheet does not display, click the Index tab. The Index sheet contains an extensive index of Internet Explorer Help topics (Figure 1-78).

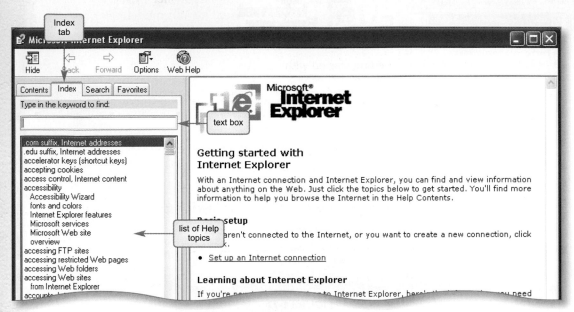

FIGURE 1-78

4. Type cookies in the text box, double-click the about cookies topic, and then answer the following questions.
    a. What is a cookie? _____
    b. What does a cookie contain? _____

5. Select the text in the text box, type autocomplete in the box, double-click the overview Help topic, and then answer the following questions.
    a. What does the AutoComplete feature save? _____
    b. What does AutoComplete do? _____

6. Select the text in the text box, type certificates in the box, double-click the obtaining a personal certificate Help topic, and then answer the following questions.
    a. List two types of certificates. _____
    b. What is a digital ID? _____

7. Select the text in the text box, type content advisor in the box, double-click the controlling access to the Internet Help topic, and then answer the following question.
    a. What is the purpose of Content Advisor? _____

8. Select the text in the text box, type shortcut keys in the box, click the Display button, and then answer the following questions.
    a. What is the shortcut key to go to the next Web page? _____
    b. What is the shortcut key to refresh the current Web page? _____
    c. What is the shortcut key to stop downloading a Web page? _____

9. Click the Close button in the Microsoft Internet Explorer window.

10. Click the Close button in the Microsoft Internet Explorer window.

11. Hand in the answers to the questions to your instructor.

Cases and Places

The difficulty of these case studies varies:
■ are the least difficult and ■■ are more difficult. The last exercise is a group exercise.

1 ■ Your old car broke down and you are in the market for a new one. Type the URL autos.msn.com to display the MSN Autos home page. Select your favorite make and model and then click the Go button to search for a new car. Check the availability and prices for two additional models of the same make. Print three pages with some results.

2 ■ Your uncle would like to invest in the stock market. He has asked you to find fundamental stock information about Microsoft Corporation (MSFT), NetFlix (NFLX), XM Satellite Radio (XMSR), Fuelcell Energy Inc. (FCEL), and TiVo Inc. (TIVO). Use the Yahoo! Web site (finance.yahoo.com) to obtain today's stock price, dividend rate, daily volume, 52-week high, 52-week low, and the P/E (price earnings ratio). To display this information, enter the stock symbol and click the Get button. When the stock price displays, click the Detailed link to display the desired information. Print the detailed results for each stock. In addition, when the detailed information displays for TiVo Inc., scroll down and click the first topic under Recent News. Print the page.

3 ■ You are planning a vacation to Cancun, Mexico. You want to leave exactly one month from today and plan to stay seven days, including the travel days. Check with Northwest Airlines (nwa.com), Continental Airlines (continental.com), Delta Airlines (delta.com), and Southwest airlines (southwest.com) for travel specials to Cancun. Print any Web pages containing travel specials and then summarize the information you find in a brief report.

4 ■■ You have decided to purchase a computer online. You plan to spend between $800 and $1,200 for a computer with a monitor and a printer. Visit three online computer stores, such as Compaq (compaq.com), Dell (dell.com), and Gateway (gateway.com). On each site, find a computer that sells for the amount you plan to spend. For each site, print the page that indicates the computer and price. Compare the three computers. Which one is the best buy? Why?

5 ■■ Although Internet Explorer may be the most widely used browser program, it is not the only browser program in use today. Using the Internet, computer magazines and newspapers, or other resources, prepare a brief report about three other Web browsers in use today. Describe their features, differences, and similarities.

Cases and Places

6 ■■ **Working Together** Have each member of your group visit a daily newspaper Web site, such as the New York Times (nytimes.com), Chicago Tribune (chicagotribune.com), Los Angeles Times (latimes.com), Miami Herald (miamiherald.com), and a local newspaper's Web site. Print at least one page from each newspaper site. Compare the latest headline news. Navigate through each site. How are the newspaper sites similar and dissimilar? Which newspaper has the best Web site? Why? Present your findings to the class.

Web Research Techniques and Search Engines

PROJECT

2

CASE PERSPECTIVE

After taking a short college course to better understand how to search for information on the Internet, you feel confident you can find the appropriate resources on the World Wide Web to use for an upcoming English class research paper. The topic you chose for the paper is the discovery of the Perseid meteor shower.

You decide the first step in researching the meteor shower should be to search the Web for authoritative Web sites. You recall from taking an Internet class that Web sites are classified into nine different categories and three basic types of search tools.

While talking to your English instructor, he emphasizes that it is very important to evaluate each Web site for its reliability, significance, and content. From the bottom drawer of his file cabinet, he retrieves a document titled, Web Resource Evaluation Worksheet, to simplify the process of evaluating Web sites.

Next, you talk to the instructor of the Internet course you just completed. She had several good ideas about searching the Web for specific topics and reminds you that you should be as specific as possible while performing a search. From a bookshelf in the back of the room, she retrieves a book titled, *The Value of Boolean Expressions and Internet Searching*, for you to read. As you were leaving, she reminds you that using WordPad is an easy way to create a working bibliography.

With the information gathered from your instructors and the knowledge from your Internet class, you are confident you can find valid Web sites and perform the research necessary to write the discovery of the Perseid meteor shower research paper.

As you read through this project, you will learn how to locate information on the World Wide Web and evaluate the information for its usefulness as a Web resource.

Web Research Techniques and Search Engines

PROJECT

2

Objectives

You will have mastered the material in this project when you can:

- Describe the nine general categories of Web sites
- List the criteria for evaluating a Web resource
- Describe the three basic types of search tools
- Search the Web using either a directory or keywords
- Search the Web using Search Companion and Search Assistant
- Customize and refine a search

- Describe the techniques used for successful keyword searches
- Describe how to create a working bibliography
- Compile a list of works cited for Web resources
- Search the Web for mailing addresses, maps, definitions, and pictures
- Use the Keyword system and the Address bar to search the Web

Introduction

Research is an important tool for success in an academic career. Writing papers, preparing speeches, and doing homework assignments are all activities that rely heavily on research. When researching, you are trying to find information to support an idea or position, to prove a point, or to learn about a topic or concept. Traditionally, research was accomplished using books, papers, periodicals, and other materials found in libraries. The World Wide Web provides a new and useful resource for supplementing the traditional print materials found in the library. Recent estimates place the number of Web pages at more than three trillion, up from just a few million pages in 1994.

While the Web is a valuable resource, you should not rely solely on the Web for research information. Web sites change quite frequently, which means Web pages may become unavailable. In addition, the information found on Web pages is not always up-to-date, accurate, or verifiable.

This project demonstrates successful techniques for locating information on the Web and then evaluating the information for its usefulness as a source.

Types of Web Resources

Web sites are organized by content into nine categories: advocacy, blog, business/marketing, educational, entertainment, informational, news, personal, and portal. In addition, the Web provides other resources whereby you can access useful information when doing research. The next several sections describe the types of Web sites and other resources.

Advocacy Web Sites

An **advocacy Web site** contains content that describes a cause, opinion, or idea (Figure 2-1a on the next page). The purpose of the advocacy Web page is to convince the reader of the validity of a cause, opinion, or idea. These Web sites usually present views on a particular group or association. Sponsors of advocacy Web sites include the American Association of Retired Persons (AARP), the Democratic National Committee, the Republican National Committee, the Society for the Prevention of Cruelty to Animals, and the American Civil Liberties Union.

Blog Web Sites

A **blog Web site**, short for Web log, uses a regularly updated journal format to reflect the interests, opinions, and personalities of the author and sometimes Web site visitors (Figure 2-1b). A blog has an informal style (similar to a diary) that consists of a single individual's ideas or a collection of ideas and thoughts among visitors.

Business/Marketing Web Sites

A **business/marketing Web site** contains content that tries to promote or sell products or services (Figure 2-1c on the next page). Nearly every business maintains a business/marketing Web site. Dell Inc., 21st Century Insurance Company, General Motors Corporation, Kraft Foods Inc., and Walt Disney Company all have business/marketing Web sites. Many of these companies also allow you to purchase their products or services online.

Educational Web Sites

An **educational Web site** offers exciting, challenging avenues for formal and informal teaching and learning (Figure 2-1d on the next page). On the Web, you can learn how to sail a boat or how to cook a meal. For a more structured learning experience, companies provide online training to employees, and colleges offer online classes and degrees. Instructors often use the Web to enhance classroom teaching by publishing course materials, grades, and other pertinent class information.

Entertainment Web Sites

An **entertainment Web site** offers an interactive and engaging environment (Figure 2-1e on the next page). Popular entertainment Web sites offer music, videos, sports, games, ongoing Web episodes, sweepstakes, chats, and more. Sophisticated entertainment Web sites often partner with other technologies. For example, you can cast your vote about a topic on a television show.

More About

Advocacy Web Pages

Other advocacy Web pages include the Maine Democratic Party, and National Rifle Association. For more information about advocacy Web pages, visit the Internet Explorer 6 More About Web page (scsite.com/ie6winxp/more) and click Advocacy Web Pages.

More About

Business/Marketing Web Pages

Other business/marketing Web pages include Chevron and DuPont. For more information about business/marketing Web pages, visit the Internet Explorer 6 More About Web page (scsite.com/ie6winxp/more) and click Business/Marketing Web Pages.

More About

Educational Web Pages

Other educational Web pages include Scuba.com and Rockler.com. For more information about educational Web pages, visit the Internet Explorer 6 More About Web page (scsite.com/ie6winxp/more) and click Educational Web Pages.

More About

Entertainment Web Pages

Other entertainment Web pages include Nascar.com and NBC. For more information about entertainment Web pages, visit the Internet Explorer 6 More About Web page (scsite.com/ie6winxp/more) and click Entertainment Web Pages.

Figure 2-1a (advocacy)

Figure 2-1b (blog)

Figure 2-1c (business/marketing)

Figure 2-1d (educational)

Figure 2-1e (entertainment)

Figure 2-1f (informational)

Figure 2-1g (news)

Figure 2-1h (personal)

Figure 2-1i (portal)

FIGURE 2-1

Informational Web Sites

An **informational Web site** contains factual information (Figure 2-1f). Many United States government agencies have informational Web sites providing information such as census data, tax codes, and the congressional budget. Other organizations provide information such as public transportation schedules and published research findings.

News Web Sites

A **news Web site** contains newsworthy material including stories and articles relating to current events, life, money, sports, and the weather (Figure 2-1g). Many magazines and newspapers sponsor Web sites that provide summaries of printed articles, as well as articles not included in the printed versions. Newspapers and television and radio stations are some of the media that maintain news Web sites.

Personal Web Sites

A private individual or family not usually associated with any organization may maintain a **personal Web site** or just a single Web page (Figure 2-1h). People publish personal Web pages for a variety of reasons. Some are job hunting. Others simply want to share life experiences with the world.

Portal Web Sites

A **portal Web site** offers a variety of Internet services from a single, convenient location (Figure 2-1i). Most portals offer the following free services: search engine and/or subject directory; news; sports and weather; Web publishing services; reference tools such as yellow pages, stock quotes, and maps; shopping malls and auctions; and e-mail and other forms of online communication.

Many portals have Web communities. A **Web community** is a Web site that joins a specific group of people with similar interests or relationships. These communities may offer online photo albums, chat rooms, and other service to facilitate communications among members.

Table 2-1 Popular Portals and Their URLs

PORTAL	URL	PORTAL	URL
AltaVista	altavista.com	HotBot	hotbot.com
America Online	aol.com	LookSmart	looksmart.com
Euroseek.com	euroseek.com	Lycos	lycos.com
Excite	excite.com	Microsoft Network	msn.com
Go.com	go.com	Netscape	netscape.com
Google	google.com	Yahoo!	yahoo.com

Other Web Resources

A number of other resources where you will find useful information are available on the Web. File transfer protocol (FTP), newsgroups, and for-profit database services all contain information and files that you can use for research purposes.

Papers, documents, manuals, and complete ready-to-execute programs are available using FTP. **File transfer protocol** (**FTP**) is an Internet standard that permits file uploading and downloading (transferring) with other computers on the Internet. Uploading is the opposite of downloading; that is **uploading** is the process of transferring documents, graphics, and other objects from your computer to another computer on the Internet.

Gopher started out as a document retrieval system to assist people in getting help for computing problems. Today, it has become a directory-based method of retrieving files. Many government agencies have organized gopher sites to provide information and distribute documents and forms.

A **newsgroup** is an online area in which users have written discussions about a particular subject. To participate in a discussion, a user sends a message to the newsgroup, and other users in the newsgroup read and reply to the message. Some major topic areas include news, recreation, society, business, science, and computers.

A number of **database services**, such as Dow Jones and LexisNexis (Figure 2-2), have been developed. These services, for a small fee, allow you to perform searches for information. Some schools subscribe to these database services and make the searching services available to the faculty, staff, and students. Ask a librarian how to access these database services.

FIGURE 2-2

Summary of Types of Web Resources

Determining the exact category into which a Web resource falls is sometimes difficult because of the overlap of information on the page. You will find advertising on news Web pages. Personal Web pages may be advocating some cause or opinion. A business/marketing Web page may contain factual information that is verifiable from other sources. In spite of this overlapping, identifying the general category in which the Web page falls can help you evaluate the usefulness of the Web page as a source of information for a research paper.

Evaluating a Web Resource

Once a promising Web page is found, you should evaluate it for its reliability, significance, and content. Remember, anyone can put a page on the Web, and Web pages do not have to be reviewed for accuracy or verified by editors. You have an obligation to ensure the information and other materials you use are accurate, attributable, and verifiable.

Just as criteria exist for evaluating printed materials, criteria also exist for evaluating Web pages. These criteria include authorship, accuracy of information, currency of information, and topic and scope of coverage. Table 2-2 shows the information you should look for within each criterion when evaluating Web resources.

More About

Evaluating Resources

Although a single evaluating tool does not exist, several colleges/universities have Web sites that contain information about evaluating Web sites. These sites include Cornell University, Western Illinois University, and Michigan State University. For more information about evaluating Web resources, visit the Internet Explorer 6 More About Web page (scsite.com/ie6winxp/more) and click Evaluating Resources.

Table 2-2 Criteria for Evaluating Web Pages	
CRITERION	**INFORMATION TO EVALUATE**
Authorship	• Is the name of the person or organization publishing the page legitimate? • Does a link exist to a page that describes the goals of the organization? • Does the page include a statement of official approval from the parent organization? • Does a copyright notice appear? • What are the author's qualifications? • Are any opinions and biases clearly stated? • Does the page contain advertising? If so, is it differentiated from content? • Is the information provided as a public service?
Accuracy of Information	• Are any sources used and are they listed on the page? • Does the page contain links to other Web sites that verify the information on the page? • Are data and statistics clearly displayed and easy to read? • Is the page grammatically correct?
Currency of Information	• When was the page written? • When was the page placed on the Web? • When was the page last updated? • Does the page include dates associated with the information on the Web page?
Topic and Scope of Coverage	• What is the purpose of the Web page? • Does the page declare a topic? • Does the page succeed in describing or discussing the declared topic? • Are points clear, well-stated, and supported? • Does the page contain links to related resources? • Is the page under construction?

You may want to create an evaluation worksheet to use as an aid in consistently evaluating the Web pages you find as potential resources. Figure 2-3 shows a sample evaluation worksheet template created from the criteria listed in Table 2-2 on the previous page. You can make copies of this worksheet, or create a new worksheet to use each time you find a possible research source.

Web Resource Evaluation Worksheet

Web Page Title:

Web Page URL:

Type of Web Resource

    Advocacy Business/Marketing Educational Entertainment Informational News Personal Portal

    Reasons?

Authorship

    What are the author's qualifications?

    Is there a sponsoring organization? Does the page link to the organization?

    Are any opinions and biases clearly stated?

    Does the page contain a copyright notice?

Accuracy of Information

    What sources verify the information on the Web page? Does the page link to those sources?

    Is the page grammatically correct?

Currency of Information

    What date was the page placed on the Web?

    What date was the page last updated?

    What date did you visit the page?

Topic and Scope

    What is the purpose of the page?

    Does the page succeed in describing and discussing the topic?

    Are points clear, well-stated, and supported?

    Does the page include links to other related pages?

FIGURE 2-3

Finding a valuable resource among the trillions of Web pages available on the World Wide Web, however, can be quite a challenge. The most efficient way to find a probable resource from among all those pages is to use the special search tools created specifically for use on the Web. They will guide you to the information you are seeking.

Web Search Resources

The World Wide Web includes trillions of Web pages, and bibliographic control does not exist. To find information for a term paper, learn more about a topic of interest, or display the home page of a governmental agency, you must know either the URL of the Web page with the information you are after or you must use a search tool. A **search tool** is a software program that helps you find Web pages containing the desired information. Search tools fall into three general categories.

- Subject directory
- Search engine
- Keyword system

The first type of search tool, called a **subject directory**, uses a directory to organize related Web resources. Figure 2-4 shows a directory (Yahoo! directory) that is organized into broad categories. You must decide into which category the search topic falls and then click the corresponding link. When you click the link, another page of links is displayed that contains more specific categories from which to choose. You continue following the links until you find the information you are seeking.

FIGURE 2-4

Because directories allow you to choose from a list of categories, you do not have to provide any keywords to find information. You may have to spend considerable time traveling through several levels of categories, however, only to discover that no pages on the topic are available.

A second type of search tool, called a **search engine**, retrieves and displays a list of links to Web pages based on a query. A **query** is a **keyword** or **search term** (a word, set of words, or phrase) you enter to tell the search engine the topic about which you want information. The search engine uses the keyword to search an index of Web resources in its database. Some of the more popular search engines are MSN Search, Yahoo!, Google, Ask Jeeves, AltaVista, and Excite.

Figure 2-5 on the next page shows a typical **keyword search form** (Google Advanced Search) used to enter keywords to search the Web. You provide one or more relevant keywords about the topic, and the search engine will return links that point directly to Web pages that contain those keywords.

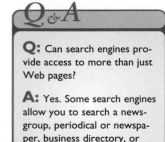

Q: Can search engines provide access to more than just Web pages?

A: Yes. Some search engines allow you to search a newsgroup, periodical or newspaper, business directory, or personal directory.

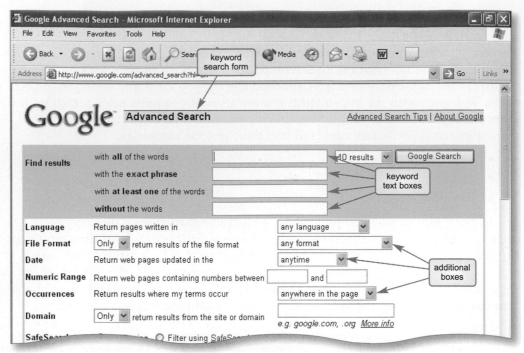

FIGURE 2-5

The index used by a search engine is created using several techniques. An automated program, called a **robot** or **spider**, travels around the Web, automatically following links and adding entries to the index. Individuals also can request that their Web pages be added to a directory or index.

All the popular portal Web sites listed in Table 2-1 on page IE 75 have both a search engine and a subject directory. Most portals also include specialized search tools that display maps and directions (Expedia), provide information about businesses (Yellow Pages), and help find people (People Finder).

The third type of search tool, a Keyword system, is part of the Internet Explorer browser. A **Keyword system** allows you to enter a name or word in the Address box to display a corresponding Web page. The Keyword system is shown in detail in Figure 2-58 through Figure 2-66 on pages IE 119-124 in this project.

Why study different search tools? Just as it is impossible for a card catalog to contain an entry for every book in the world, it is impossible for each search tool to catalog every Web page on the World Wide Web. In addition, different search tools on the Web perform different types of searches. Some search for keywords in the title of a Web page, while others scan links for the keywords. Still others search the entire text of Web pages. Because of the different searching techniques, the results of a search vary surprisingly.

When developing Internet Explorer, Microsoft realized the importance of using search tools and made several search tools accessible via the Search button on the Standard Buttons toolbar. To practice doing research on the Web, assume you are majoring in Astronomy and want to find information on the discovery of the Perseid meteor shower. The following sections show how to start Internet Explorer and use the Yahoo! directory to search for information on the discovery of the Perseid meteor shower.

Starting Internet Explorer

The following step illustrates how to start Internet Explorer using the procedure you used at the beginning of Project 1 on pages IE 8 and IE 9.

To Start Internet Explorer

1

• **Click the Start button on the Windows taskbar, point to All Programs on the Start menu, and then click Internet Explorer on the All Programs submenu.**

The Welcome to MSN.com - Microsoft Internet Explorer window with the MSN home page appears (Figure 2-6). This home page may be different on your computer.

FIGURE 2-6

Searching the Web Using a Directory

Yahoo! is famous for its directory. Starting with general categories and becoming increasingly more specific as links are selected, the Yahoo! directory provides a menu-like interface for searching the Web. Because the Yahoo! directory uses a series of menus to organize links to Web pages, you can perform searches without entering keywords. The step on the next page illustrates how to display the Yahoo! home page.

To Display the Yahoo! Home Page

1

• **Click the Address box, type** www.yahoo.com **as the URL, and then click the Go button.**

Internet Explorer displays the URL for the Yahoo! home page (http://www.yahoo.com/) in the Address box and displays the Yahoo! home page (Figure 2-7).

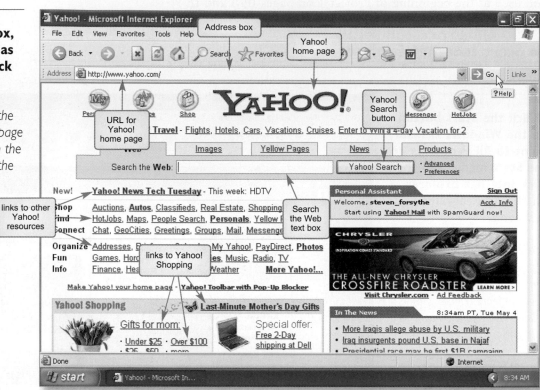

FIGURE 2-7

When you type a URL in the Address box and then click the Go button, **AutoComplete** remembers the URL you typed. As a result, when you type the URL for the Yahoo! home page in the Address box in Figure 2-7, AutoComplete may display a list of previously entered URLs in a box below the Address box. If this happens, you can select a URL from the list in the Address box by clicking the URL, or you can continue to type the URL from the keyboard.

The Search the Web text box and Yahoo! Search button below the Yahoo! title allow you to perform a keyword search. Several links appear below the text box. Scrolling the Web page displays the Yahoo! directory (Figure 2-8). Web pages in the Yahoo! directory are organized into the broad categories. You must decide into which category the search topic falls and then select the corresponding link. When you select a general link, another page of links is displayed with more specific topics from which to choose. You continue following the links until you find the information you are seeking.

Because astronomy is part of the major category, Science, this category is appropriate to start the search. The steps in Figure 2-8 through Figure 2-14 on pages IE 83-86 illustrate how to navigate through the Yahoo! directory to retrieve information about the discovery of the Perseid meteor shower.

To Search Using the Yahoo! Directory

1

• **Scroll the display area to display the Science link.**

The Science link appears in the Yahoo! directory (Figure 2-8).

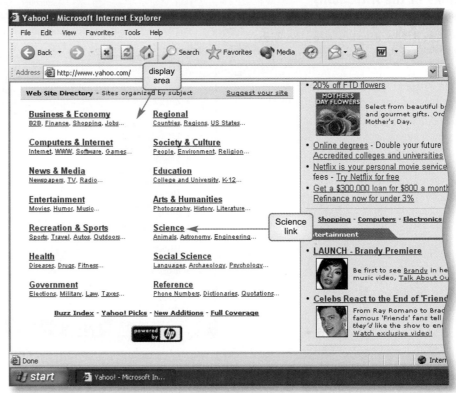

FIGURE 2-8

2

• **Click Science to view the links in the Science category.**

The Yahoo! Directory Science Web page appears (Figure 2-9). The number in parentheses next to a subcategory indicates how many Web page listings you will find if you click the subcategory. For example, the Astronomy subcategory contains 2,854 listings. The word NEW! to the right of a link indicates the link recently has been updated with new Web pages. The number of Web page listings and/or search results on your computer may be different.

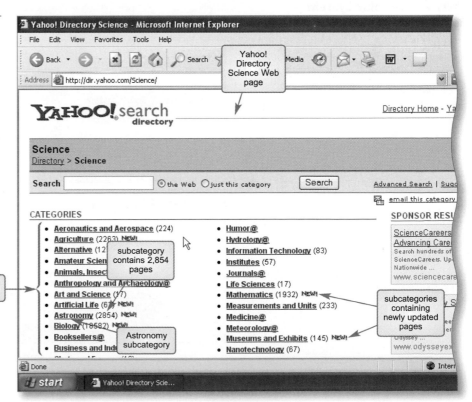

FIGURE 2-9

3

• **Click Astronomy to view the links in the Astronomy subcategory.**

• **Scroll the display area to view the Solar System subcategory.**

The Yahoo! Directory Science > Astronomy Web page appears (Figure 2-10). The Solar System subcategory contains 924 listings. An @ symbol next to a link indicates a link to another Yahoo! subcategory.

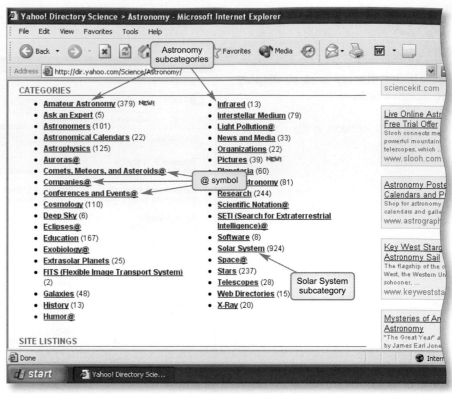

FIGURE 2-10

4

• **Click Solar System to view the links in the Solar System subcategory.**

The Yahoo! Directory Astronomy > Solar System Web page appears (Figure 2-11). The Comets, Meteors, and Asteroids subcategory contains 199 listings.

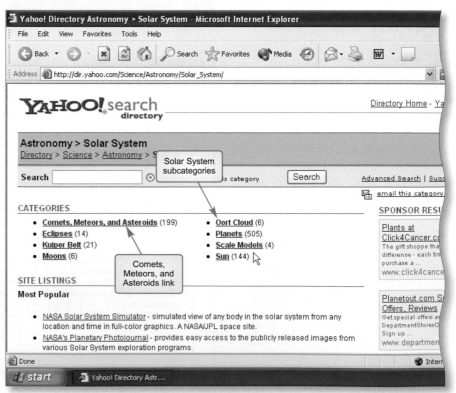

FIGURE 2-11

5

• **Click Comets, Meteors, and Asteroids to view the links in the Comets, Meteors, and Asteroids subcategory.**

The Yahoo! Directory Solar System > Comets, Meteors, and Asteroids Web page appears (Figure 2-12). The Perseid Meteor Shower subcategory contains nine listings.

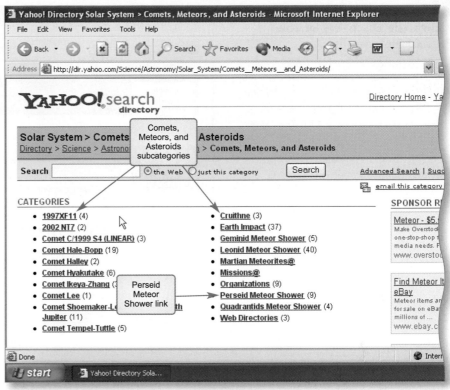

FIGURE 2-12

6

• **Click Perseid Meteor Shower to view the listings in the Perseid Meteor Shower subcategory.**

The Yahoo! Directory Perseid Meteor Shower Web page appears (Figure 2-13). The Discovery of the Perseid Meteors link is displayed at the top of the list.

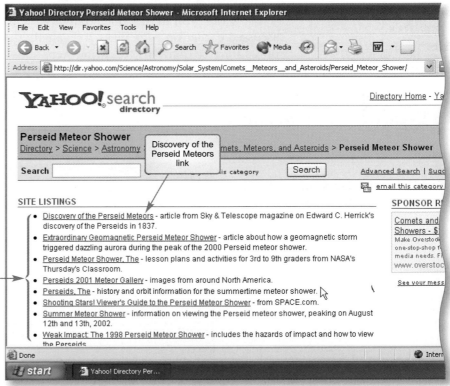

FIGURE 2-13

7

• **Click the Discovery of the Perseid Meteors link.**

The Sky and Telescope - The Discovery of the Perseid Meteors Web page containing The Discovery of the Perseid Meteors article appears (Figure 2-14). The Web page contains the Web page URL, link to the sponsoring organization, Web page title, and author name.

FIGURE 2-14

Evaluating Web Resources

Now that you have a potentially useful Web page, you should apply the criteria discussed earlier on page IE xx to evaluate the Web page to see if it can be used as a source for research. The following steps show how to use the sample worksheet template as shown in Figure 2-3 on page IE 78 to evaluate the Sky and Telescope page.

To Evaluate a Web Resource

1

• **Scroll the display area to display the bottom of the Web page.**

The bottom of the Web page, containing the 1, 2, 3, and 4 page numbers, appears (Figure 2-15).

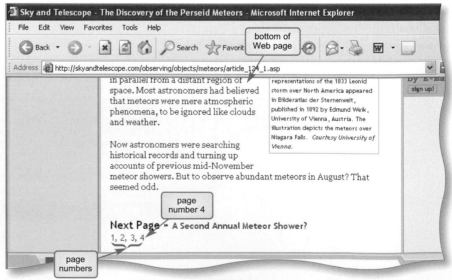

FIGURE 2-15

2

• **Click 4 at the bottom of the Web page to display page 4 in the article.**

• **Scroll the display area to display the bottom of the Web page.**

The bottom of page 4 contains the author qualifications, author acknowledgements, and copyright notice (Figure 2-16).

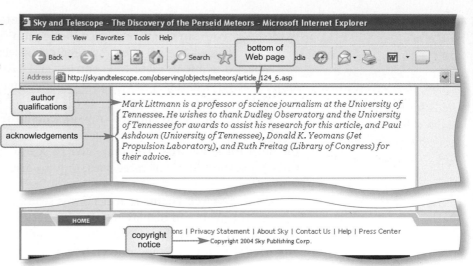

FIGURE 2-16

The information gathered so far is summarized on the worksheet illustrated in Figure 2-17. Based on the current worksheet criteria, The Discovery of the Perseid Meteors page is an exceptionally strong resource.

> **More About**
>
> ## Evaluating a Web Resource
>
> Many Web pages do not have the necessary criteria for being a research source. You will find that you discard many promising Web pages simply because you cannot find the necessary evaluation criteria.

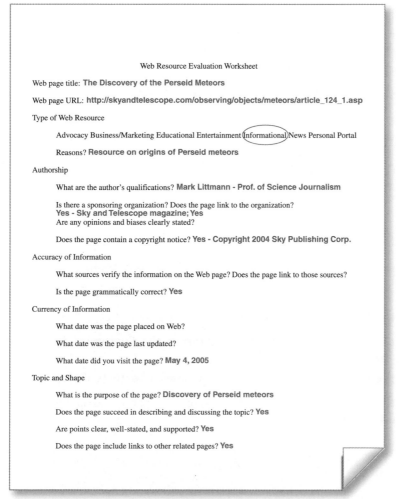

FIGURE 2-17

Instead of manually recording evaluation information on a printed copy of the worksheet, you can create an electronic version of the worksheet using a word processor. Then, for each Web resource you select, you can open a new copy of the worksheet document, record the entries, and save the document using a document name that reflects the Web resource being evaluated. Use one worksheet document per Web resource.

The previous steps showed how to search the World Wide Web using a directory (in this case, Yahoo!). By selecting from a list of categories, such directories eliminate the need for keywords. You may have to spend considerable time, however, traveling through several levels of categories, only to discover that no information on the topic is available.

Using a search engine that performs searches based upon keywords, you can explore the Web and display links to Web pages without having to maneuver through any intermediate pages. You provide one or more relevant words, or **keywords**, about the topic in which you are interested, and the search engine returns links that point directly to pages containing those keywords.

Searching the Web

Internet Explorer allows you to search the Web using either Search Companion or Search Assistant. Search Companion allows you to search for Web pages, search for files and folders on the computer, change Internet search preferences, and learn more about Search Companion. In addition, Internet Explorer allows you to search using Search Assistant. Search Assistant allows you to search for Web pages, mailing and e-mail addresses, business information, maps, definitions and encyclopedia articles, and pictures. Search Assistant also may be referred to as **Classic Internet Search**.

Displaying the Search Companion Pane

In the next section, you will use Search Companion to search the Web. In order to use Search Companion, the Search Companion pane must appear in the display area of the Microsoft Internet Explorer window. In some cases, the Search pane associated with Search Assistant may appear instead of the Search Companion pane. The following steps illustrate how to verify that the Search Companion pane appears.

To Display the Search Companion Pane

1 **Click the Search button on the Standard Buttons toolbar.**

2 **If the Search Companion pane appears, go to Step 8.**

3 **Click the Customize button on the Search pane.**

4 **Click the Use Search Companion button in the Customize Search Settings dialog box.**

5 **Click the OK button in the Customize Search Settings dialog box.**

6 **Click the Close button in the Microsoft Internet Explorer window to close Internet Explorer.**

7 **Click the Start button on the Windows taskbar, point to All Programs on the Start menu, and then click Internet Explorer on the All Programs submenu.**

8 **Click the Close button in the Search pane or the Search Companion pane.**

The Search Companion pane is displayed in the Microsoft Internet Explorer window and then closed.

Performing Step 3 through Step 8 displays the Search Companion pane and causes the display areas in Figure 2-18 below and Figure 2-19 on the next page to display the MSN home page instead of The Discovery of the Perseid Meteors article shown in Figure 2-18.

The following sections illustrate how to search the Web using Search Companion and Search Assistant.

Searching the Web Using Search Companion

An easy method to search the Web is to use Search Companion. **Search Companion** allows you to search for Web pages on the Internet, files and folders on the computer, and printers and other computers on a network. This method allows you to search the Web by typing a word, phrase, statement, or question in a text box in the Search Companion balloon and then clicking the Search button.

For instance, you can enter a statement (Give me a list of the planets in the solar system.) or a question (How many planets are in the solar system?). A search engine searches for and displays a list of links to Web pages that pertain to the words, phrase, statement, or question. In this case, the default search engine is **MSN Search**. However, the default search engine may be different on your computer.

The following steps illustrate how to search for Web pages containing information about the dates of the 2003 Perseid meteor shower.

To Search for Web Pages Using Search Companion

1

• **Click the Search button on the Standard Buttons toolbar.**

The Search Companion pane, containing the Search Companion balloon, appears (Figure 2-18). The text box in the balloon contains instructions to type your query and press the ENTER key.

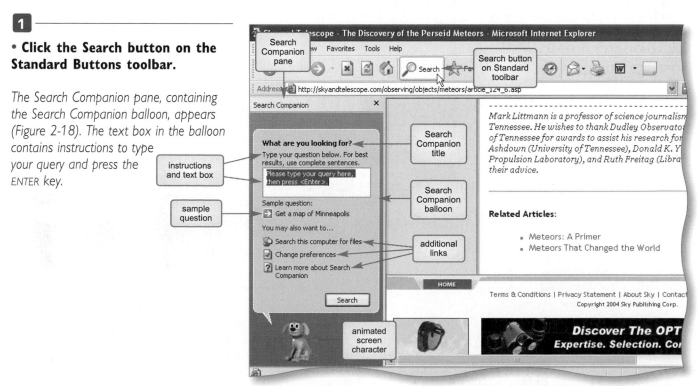

FIGURE 2-18

2

• **Type** In 2003, what were the dates of the perseid meteor shower? **in the text box in the Search Companion balloon.**

Internet Explorer displays the question in the text box (Figure 2-19).

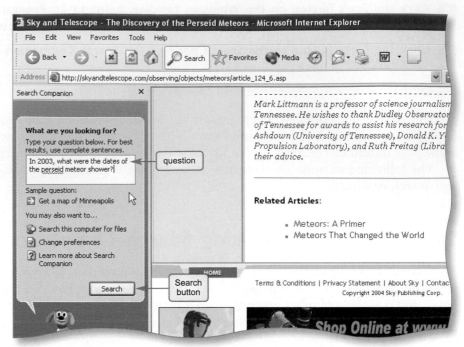

FIGURE 2-19

3

• **Click the Search button in the Search Companion balloon.**

MSN Search searches for and finds 231 Web pages (Figure 2-20). Three links are visible in the display area. Clicking the NEXT link in the display area displays the next fifteen Web pages. The default search engine on your computer may be different.

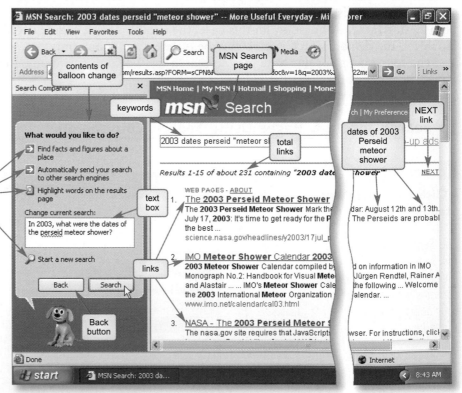

FIGURE 2-20

In Figure 2-18 on the previous page, the Search Companion balloon contains a title (What are you looking for?), instructions and a text box, a sample question, and three links that allow you to search for files on the computer, change search preferences, and learn more about Search Companion. An animated screen character named, Rover, appears below the balloon.

In Figure 2-20, the MSN Search engine translates the question entered in the text box (In 2003, what were the dates of the perseid meteor shower?) into a series of keywords (2003, dates, perseid, meteor, shower), and displays the keywords (2003 dates perseid "meteor shower") in a more organized "sentence" in the text box at the top of the MSN Search page. The MSN Search engine uses the keywords and "sentence" to search for Web pages and display the corresponding links in the display area.

The first link (The 2003 Perseid Meteor Shower) in the list of links contains the dates (August 12th and August 13th) of the 2003 Perseid meteor shower. In addition, the contents of the Search Companion balloon change to contain the Change current search text box and four links that allow you to find facts and figures about a place, automatically send your search to other search engines, highlight words on the results page, and start a new search. The text box contains the original question. Clicking the Back button in the Search Companion pane displays the previous Search Companion balloon.

Closing the Search Companion Pane

When you are finished using Search Companion, you may want to close the Search Companion pane. The following step shows how to close the Search Companion pane.

To Close the Search Companion Pane

1 **Click the Close button in the Search Companion pane.**

Internet Explorer closes the Search Companion pane.

Searching the Web Using Search Assistant

The second method to search the Web is to use Search Assistant. **Search Assistant** allows you to search for Web pages, mailing or e-mail addresses, business information, maps, definitions, encyclopedia articles, pictures, and more. If you want to use Search Assistant instead of Search Companion, you must first select the search preference for Search Assistant.

Search preferences include using or not using an animated screen character (Rover, Merlin, and so on), selecting a different animated screen character, using or not using the Indexing Service for faster local searches, selecting the Standard or Advanced method to search for files and folders, selecting the Search Companion behavior or Classic Internet Search behavior, show or not show balloon tips, and turn on or turn off the AutoComplete feature (Figure 2-22 on the next page).

Selecting an Internet Search Behavior

The Internet search behavior for Search Companion, which is the default Internet search behavior, is the **Search Companion behavior**. The Internet search behavior for Search Assistant is the **Classic Internet Search behavior**. If you want to use Search Assistant, you must select the Classic Internet Search behavior as the Internet search behavior. The steps on the next page illustrate how to select an Internet search behavior.

Q: What search engines does Search Assistant allow me to use?

A: Search Assistant allows you to use the following 14 search engines: MSN Search, Overture, AltaVista, Lycos, Excite, Yahoo!, Euroseek, InfoSpace, Expedia.com, MapQuest, Encarta, Dictionary.com, Merriam-Webster, and Corbis.

To Select an Internet Search Behavior

1

• **Click the Search button on the Standard Buttons toolbar.**

The Search Companion pane appears (Figure 2-21).

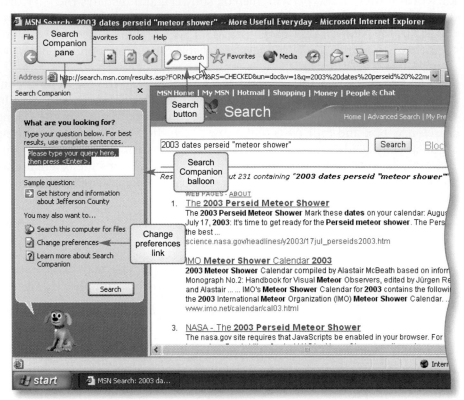

FIGURE 2-21

2

• **Click the Change preferences link in the Search Companion balloon.**

The balloon title and seven preferences appear in the Search Companion balloon (Figure 2-22). The Change Internet search behavior preference is displayed among the preferences.

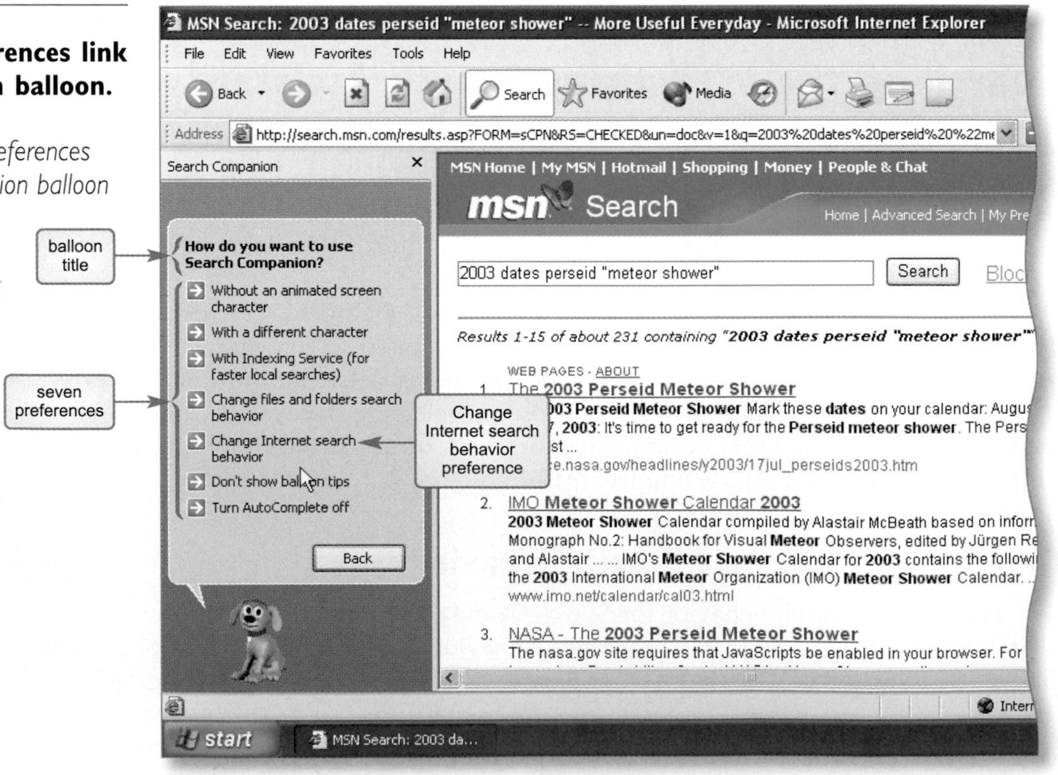

FIGURE 2-22

3

• **Click the Change Internet search behavior button.**

The balloon contains a title, a question, two option buttons associated with links, and a list of search engine names in the Select the default search engine list (Figure 2-23). The With Search Companion option button is selected and the default MSN search engine name is highlighted in the list box. Five of the twelve search engines are displayed in the list.

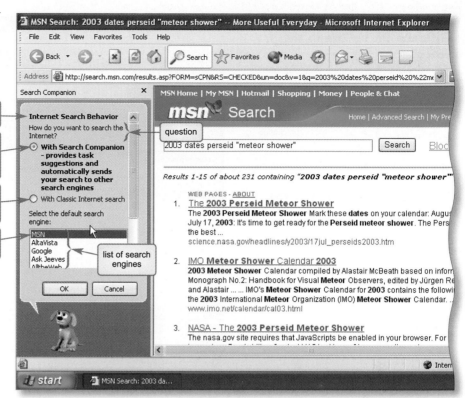

FIGURE 2-23

4

• **Click the With Classic Internet search option button.**

The With Classic Internet search option button is selected (Figure 2-24).

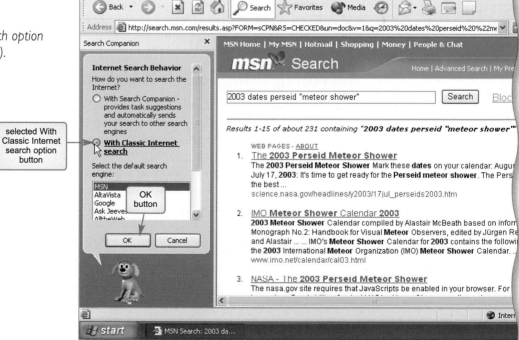

FIGURE 2-24

5

• **Click the OK button in the balloon.**

The contents of the balloon change and the Classic Internet search becomes the default Internet search behavior (Figure 2-25).

6

• **Click the Close button in the Search Companion pane.**

• **Click the Close button in the MSN Search window.**

The Search Companion pane and MSN Search window close.

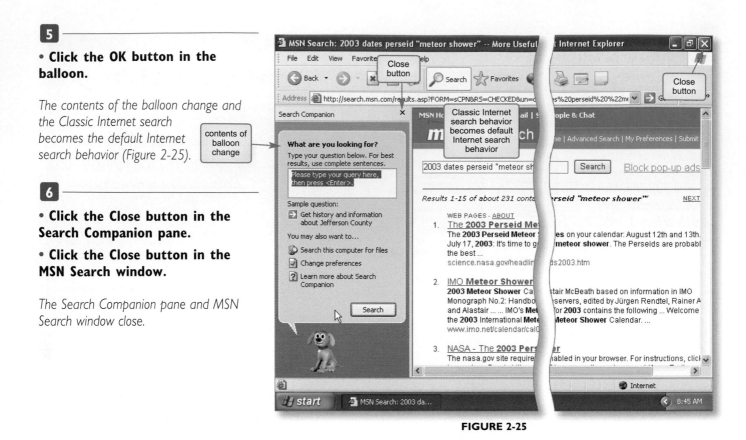

FIGURE 2-25

In Figure 2-23 on the previous page, 12 search engines appear in the Select the default search engine list. The search engines include MSN, AltaVista, Google, Ask Jeeves, AlltheWeb, Teoma, Excite, Overture, Yahoo, AOL Search, Lycos, and Encarta.

Searching Using Search Assistant

After selecting the Classic Internet search as the Internet search behavior and closing the MSN Search window, you can begin searching the Web using Search Assistant. The step on the next page shows how to start Search Assistant and display the Search pane.

The seven search categories that are displayed in the Search pane allow you to search for a Web page (Find a Web page), mailing address or e-mail address (Find a person's address), business name or category (Find a business), address or landmark (Find a map), word in an encyclopedia or dictionary (Look up a word), search for a picture (Find a picture), and perform a previous search (Previous searches).

To Display the Search Pane

1

• **Click the Start button on the Windows taskbar, point to All Programs on the Start menu, and then click Internet Explorer on the All Programs submenu.**

• **Click the Search button on the Standard Buttons toolbar.**

The Search pane appears (Figure 2-26). The Search pane contains a toolbar, seven search categories, a rectangular box, and three links. The Find a Web page option button is selected and the rectangular box contains the Find a Web page containing text box, a message with the default MSN Search name, and Search button. The search engine in the message on your computer may be different.

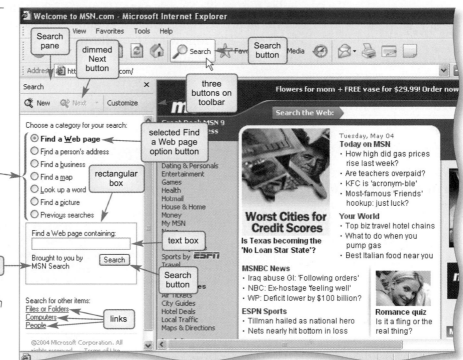

FIGURE 2-26

The Find a Web page option button is selected and the message in the rectangular box (Brought to you by MSN Search) indicates the MSN Search service will be used to search for Web pages. A **search service** allows you to enter a keyword(s) (a word or phrase) about a topic in which you are interested. It then searches for the Web pages that contain the keyword(s) and displays a list of links that you can click to display the associated Web pages. MSN Search is one of the 12 search services (MSN Search, AltaVista, Lycos, InfoSpace, Bigfoot, Expedia.com, MapQuest, Encarta, Dictionary.com, Merriam-Webster, Thesaurus.com, and Corbis) available to search for Web pages based on a keyword.

The toolbar contains three buttons. The New button allows you to start a new search and the Customize button allows you to customize settings. The Next button is dimmed and cannot be used. When the Next button is not dimmed, however, the Next button allows you to select another search engine and search using the same keywords. Three links at the bottom of the Search pane (Files or Folders, Computers, and People) allow you to search for other items.

Typing a keyword in the text box in the Search pane and clicking the Search button will cause MSN Search, or the default search engine on the computer, to search for the keyword and display a list of links to Web pages that contain the keyword. In this case, the **default search engine** is MSN Search. The default search engine may be different on your computer.

Other Ways

1. On View menu point to Explorer Bar, click Search on Explorer Bar submenu
2. Press ALT+V, press E, press S
3. Press CTRL+E

More About

Search Assistant Search Engines

When using Search Assistant, the dimmed Next button indicates you only can use the MSN Search engine. To add additional search engines, click the Customize button in the Search pane and then place a check mark in any of the seven check boxes in the Find a Web page area.

Searching the Web Using Keywords

The search engine name (MSN Search) appears below the text box in the rectangular box in the Search pane (Figure 2-26 on the previous page). MSN Search is one of the many search engines that allow you to search for Web pages based upon a keyword. The following steps illustrate how to use the MSN search engine to search for Web pages that contain the keywords, meteor shower.

To Search Using MSN Search and Keywords

1

• **Type** meteor shower **in the text box in the Search pane.**

The keywords, meteor shower, are entered in the text box (Figure 2-27).

FIGURE 2-27

2

• **Click the Search button.**

*Internet Explorer displays the MSN Search
form in the Search pane and MSN Search
performs the search (Figure 2-28). The
Search pane contains two categories
(Sponsored Sites and Web Pages)
containing several links. The display area
contains the MSN Search Preview of Web
sites. The categories and links on your
computer may be different.*

3

• **Click the Close button
in the Search pane.**

The Search pane closes.

FIGURE 2-28

Other Ways

1. Type keyword, press
ENTER

Although the number of Web pages found does not appear in Figure 2-28, the
search using the keywords, meteor shower, results in more than 60,000 links (Web
pages). To view additional links in the Search pane, scroll the Search pane. To view
links not visible in the Search pane, scroll to the bottom of the Search pane and then
click the NEXT link. Continue clicking the NEXT link to display additional groups
of links.

As you can see, it easy to find many Web pages using a keyword-based search
engine. You can obtain a more reasonable amount of links by refining the search.
Techniques to refine a search will be shown later in this project.

Selecting Another Search Engine While Using Search Assistant

In the previous section, Search Assistant used the MSN Search default search
engine to search for Web pages. Other search engines may be available. If the Next
button on the Search pane toolbar is dimmed, Search Assistant uses the default MSN
Search engine. If the Next button is not dimmed, additional search engines may be
used to search the Web. Clicking the Next button arrow on the Search pane toolbar
allows you to select another search engine and perform another search using the
same keywords.

Simple Search Forms

Google is one of the more widely used search engines. It has an index of more
than 3 billion Web pages. Each day, its robots visit more than 50 million sites, cap-
turing URLs and corresponding text to update its index. Robot programs also check
for **dead links**, which are URLs that no longer work.

More About

Web Search Engines

Fierce competition exists
among search engines. Each
search engine claims to have
the largest index of Web
resources. This competition is
healthy and ensures that
there are large, up-to-date
indexes of Web resources.

As with most search engines, Google has both a simple search form and an advanced search form. The simple search form appears on its home page and consists of a text box and the Google Search button. Typing a keyword in the text box and clicking the Google Search button will cause Google to search for the keyword and display a list of links to Web pages that contain the keyword.

The following steps illustrate how to search for Web pages that contain the keywords, meteor shower.

To Search Using the Google Simple Search

1

• **Click the Address box, type** www.google.com **and then click the Go button.**

The URL for the Google home page (http://www.google.com/) appears in the Address box (Figure 2-29).

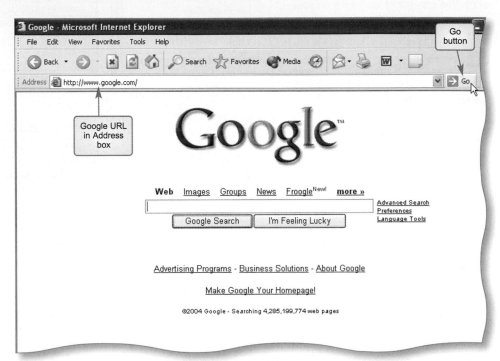

FIGURE 2-29

2

• **Type** meteor shower **in the text box.**

Internet Explorer displays the words, meteor shower, in the text box (Figure 2-30).

FIGURE 2-30

3

• **Click the Google Search button.**

Google performs the search for meteor shower (Figure 2-31). The search results in 209,000 links and four links appear in the display area. The links in the display area on your computer may be different.

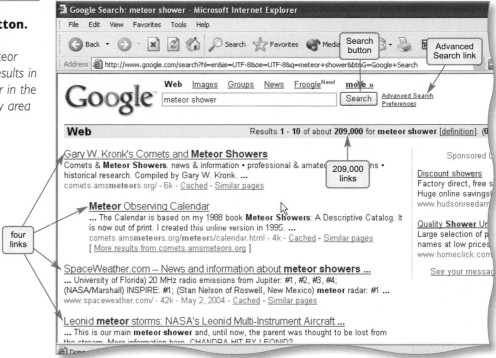

FIGURE 2-31

Other Ways

1. In Address box type URL, press ENTER

The Google search (Figure 2-31) results in 209,000 links. In comparison, the MSN Search (Figure 2-28 on page IE 97) returned approximately 60,000 links. As you can see, different search engines return different numbers of links.

If you spent just one minute looking at each Web page the Google search returned, it would take you almost five months to view all of them. You can obtain more reasonable results by refining the search. The next section illustrates how to refine a search.

Refining a Web Search

You **refine** a search by providing more information the search engine can use to select a smaller, more useful set of results. Most search engines will perform a search for multiple keywords as if each word carries the same weight. This means Web pages containing any one of a set of multiple keywords or any combination of a set of multiple keywords will satisfy the search engine and be returned as a successful match. Web pages that contain the word, meteor, for example, are included in the 209,000 links returned by the search, even though some of those pages have nothing to do with a meteor shower. To eliminate these Web pages, the keywords need to be more selective and better organized.

In addition to entering keywords, Google also allows the use of operators, advanced operators, and some compound search criteria to refine a search. The following paragraphs describe the operators, advanced operators, and compound search criteria.

Operators increase the accuracy of a search by fine-tuning the keywords in the search. Operators include the +, -, and ~ symbols and the OR logical operator. Placing a blank space and the **+ symbol** following a keyword guarantees the keyword will be included in the search. In place of using the + symbol, placing quotation

Q&A

Q: How can I get help while using Google?

A: The Google Help Central Web page contains many helpful topics. To view the topics, enter www.google.com /help/index.html in the Address box and then click the Go button.

marks around two or more keywords also includes the keywords in the search. Placing a blank space and the **– symbol** to the right of a keyword guarantees that the keyword is excluded from the search. Placing the **~ symbol** immediately preceding a keyword causes a search for the keyword and its synonym.

The **OR logical operator**, also referred to as a **Boolean operator**, is a compound search criteria that allows you to control how individual words in a keyword phrase are used. For example, the phrase, peanut OR butter, finds Web pages containing either peanut or butter. The Web pages found also can contain both words, but do not have to.

Although the Google search engine allows only the OR logical operator, other search engines allow the use of other Boolean operators. The logical operators include AND, OR, NOT, and NEAR. The **AND operator** and **OR operator** allow you to create keyword searches containing compound conditions. The **NOT operator** is used to find pages that do not contain certain keywords. The **NEAR operator** is used to find pages in which two keywords are within ten words of each other.

Table 2-3 describes the Boolean operators and gives an example of each one.

<table>
<tr><td colspan="2">**Table 2-3 Boolean Operators and Examples**</td></tr>
<tr><td>**BOOLEAN OPERATOR**</td><td>**EXAMPLE**</td></tr>
<tr><td>AND</td><td>Finds only Web pages containing all of the specified words or phrases. Peanut AND butter finds Web pages with both the word, peanut, and the word, butter.</td></tr>
<tr><td>OR</td><td>Finds Web pages containing at least one of the specified words or phrases. Peanut OR butter finds Web pages containing either peanut or butter. The Web pages found also can contain both words, but do not have to.</td></tr>
<tr><td>NOT</td><td>Excludes Web pages containing the specified word or phrase. Peanut AND NOT butter finds Web pages with peanut but not containing butter. With some search engines, NOT cannot stand alone. You must use it with another operator, such as AND. For example, the AltaVista search engine does not accept peanut NOT butter, but does accept peanut AND NOT butter.</td></tr>
<tr><td>NEAR</td><td>Finds Web pages containing both specified words or phrases within ten words of each other. Peanut NEAR butter would find documents with peanut butter, but probably not any other kind of butter.</td></tr>
<tr><td>( )</td><td>Use parentheses to group complex Boolean phrases. For example, (peanut AND butter) AND (jelly OR jam) finds Web pages with the words 'peanut butter and jelly' or 'peanut butter and jam' or both.</td></tr>
</table>

Advanced operators are query words that have special meaning in Google. The advanced operators modify a search or perform a different type of search. The advanced operators include: cache, link, related, info, define, stocks, site, allintitle, intitle, allinurl, and inurl. For example, the [link:www.google.com] operator finds all Web pages that have links to the www.google.com Web site.

Most search engines have a link on their search pages to access advanced search options. The Google **Advanced search link** appears to the right of the Google Search button on the Google home page (Figure 2-31 on the previous page) and to the right of the Search button on other pages. In addition, clicking the **Advanced Search Tips link** on the Google Advanced Search page (Figure 2-32) displays information about advanced searching.

More About

Refining the Search

You can instruct some search engines to search for two or more words that are physically close to each other by using the NEAR operator. If the keywords are within 10 words of each other, the search engine adds the Web page to the list of Web pages found during the search.

More About

Advanced Searches

If you use Boolean operators in a search query, you can substitute symbols for the operators. The symbol equivalents for the Boolean operators are AND (&), OR (|), AND NOT (!), and NEAR (~).

The following step shows how to refine a search using the Google advanced search capability.

To Display the Google Advanced Search Form

1

• **Click the Advanced Search link to the right of the Search button.**

Google displays the Advanced Search form containing the highlighted Find results area and Language, File Format, Date, Numeric Range, Occurrences, Domain, and SafeSearch entries (Figure 2-32).

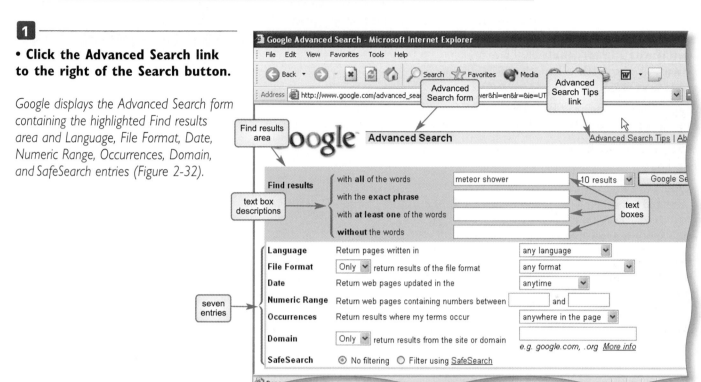

FIGURE 2-32

The **Find results area** contains four descriptions and four text boxes. Table 2-4 describes the text box descriptions and gives an example of each Web page rule.

Table 2-4 Find Results Area	
TEXT BOX DESCRIPTIONS	WEB PAGE RULES
with all of the words	Web pages must contain all the words you typed in the text box.
with the exact phrase	Web pages must contain the exact words in the order they were typed in the text box.
with at least one of the words	Web pages must contain at least one of the words in the text box.
without the words	Web pages must not contain the word or words in the text box.

The following steps show how to use the Google Advanced Search form to refine the search.

To Search Using Google Advanced Search

1

• **Delete the phrase, meteor shower, in the with all of the words text box.**

• **Type** Edward Herrick **in the with all of the words text box.**

• **Click the with the exact phrase text box.**

• **Type** perseid meteor shower **in the text box.**

The Google Advanced Search form contains the words, Edward Herrick, in the with all of the words text box and the phrase, perseid meteor shower, in the with the exact phrase text box (Figure 2-33).

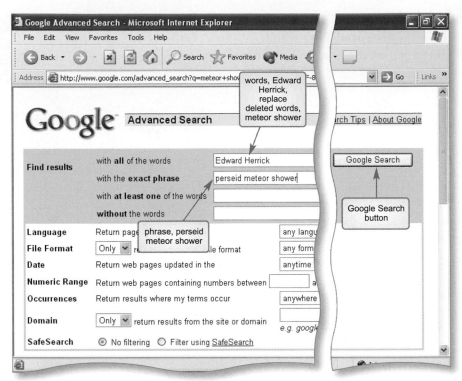

FIGURE 2-33

2

• **Click the Google Search button.**

• **If necessary, scroll down to display the Yahoo! Directory Perseid Meteor Shower link.**

Google performs the search and finds 38 links (Figure 2-34). The Yahoo! Directory Perseid Meteor Shower link appears in the display area.

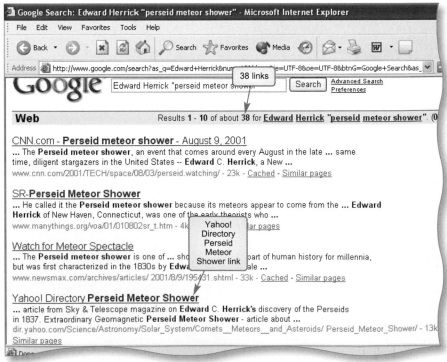

FIGURE 2-34

3

• **Click the Yahoo! Directory Perseid Meteor Shower link in the display area.**

Related links, including the Discovery of the Perseid Meteors link, appear (Figure 2-35).

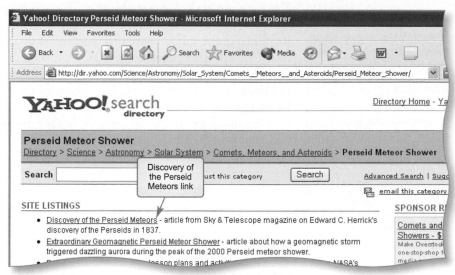

FIGURE 2-35

4

• **Click the Discovery of the Perseid Meteors link in the Yahoo! Search directory.**

The Sky and Telescope - The Discovery of the Perseid Meteors Web page containing The Discovery of the Perseid Meteors article appears (Figure 2-36). This is the same Web page found by searching the Yahoo! directory (Figure 2-14 on page IE 86).

FIGURE 2-36

In Figure 2-33, the first name, Edward, and last name, Herrick, appear in the with all of the words text box. Searching using the names in the text box causes a search for both names (first name and last name) and displays Web pages that contain both names. The phrase, perseid meteor shower, in the with the exact phrase text box causes a search for the exact phrase, perseid meteor shower, and displays Web pages that contain the exact phrase.

Using keywords and advanced searching techniques, you have refined a search to locate many useful Web resources successfully.

Successful Searching Techniques

Recall that the initial search for meteor showers using the Google simple search form returned 209,000 links (Figure 2-31 on page IE 99). The second attempt using the Google Advanced Search form returned 38 links (Figure 2-34 on page IE 102) and the pages were more useful. This illustrates the first successful searching technique: **be as specific as possible with keywords**. Put some thought into what small group of words most represents the topic or is used frequently with it. Choose the best from this group of words to use with the search engine.

If you receive only a few or no useful links, make the keywords slightly more general and try again. For example, assume you want to find information about tax-exempt municipal bonds. A specific-to-very-general list of keywords might be: *tax-exempt bonds*, *municipal bonds*, *tax-free bonds*, *tax-free investments*, *bonds*, or *investments*.

Try to match as many relevant words as possible. This returns more links with better odds that something useful will be among them, although you may have to spend some time looking through all of them. Most search engines support the use of Boolean operators, such as AND, OR, NOT, and NEAR, and parenthesis for grouping. Use the operators to specify complex phrases and conditions. For example, you might use the keywords, (rocket OR shuttle) AND experiment, to search for experiments that were performed in outer space. Use the search engine's Help feature to learn which Boolean operators are available and how to use them.

Another useful technique offered by most search engines is to indicate that certain keywords must appear on the Web page, or that certain keywords cannot appear on the Web page. A plus sign (+) indicates inclusion and a minus sign (–) indicates exclusion. You place the + or – sign immediately before a particular keyword. You can use the **inclusion or exclusion capability** to help narrow the search. For example, searching for the keywords, gold –motorcycle, will return links containing the keyword gold, but not those containing the keyword motorcycle, thus eliminating any Goldwing motorcycle links.

Another useful feature is the **wildcard character**. Several search engines allow you to use the asterisk (*) to indicate zero, one, or more characters in a word. For example, searching for immun* will return hits for immune, immunology, immunologist, and any other word beginning with the letters, i-m-m-u-n. Use wildcards if the spelling of a keyword is unknown or may be incorrectly specified on the Web page. Table 2-5 provides a guide for useful search tips, including the use of wildcard characters.

Creating a Working Bibliography

Once you find a good Web source, how do you record it? A **working bibliography** will help you organize and compile the resources you find, so that you can cite them as sources in the list of works cited. For Web resources, you should note the author or authors, title of the page, URL, date of publication, date of the last revision, date you accessed the resource, heading of any part or section where the relevant information is located, navigation instructions necessary to find the resource, and other pertinent information.

Table 2-5 Successful Search Techniques	
TIP OR WILDCARD	**EXAMPLE**
Use parentheses to group items	Use parentheses ( ) to specify precedence in a search. For example, to search for Web pages that contain information about both President Clinton and President Bush try this advanced query: president AND ((George NEAR Bush) AND ((Bill OR William) NEAR Clinton)).
Use wildcard character	Use an asterisk (*) to broaden a search. To find any words that start with gold, use gold* to find matches for gold, goldfinch, goldfinger, golden, and so on. Use this character if the word you are searching for could have different endings (for example, do not search for dog, search for dog* if it may be plural).
Use quotes to surround a phrase	If you know a certain phrase will appear on the page you are looking for, put the phrase in quotes (for example, try entering song lyrics such as "you ain't nothin' but a hound dog").
Use either specific or general keywords	Carry out searches using specific keywords to obtain fewer, more precise links, or general keywords to obtain numerous, less precise links.

When you are compiling the information, you often will need to look for an e-mail address on the Web page to find the author. You may have to write to the person responsible for the Web site, or **Webmaster**, and ask for the author's name. First, display the home page of the Web site to see if a directory or contact section is listed. If you do not find a directory or contact section, display the bottom of the Web page or other pages in the Web page. Many Web pages include the e-mail address of the Webmaster at the bottom of the page.

Traditionally, index cards have been used to record relevant information about a work, and you still can use index cards to record Web research. Several electronic means, however, are now available for keeping track of the Web sites you visit and the information you find.

- You can e-mail pertinent information to yourself and store the messages in separate folders. Use one folder for each point or category you are researching.
- You can store the pertinent information in separate document files using copy and paste techniques. Use a separate file for each point or category you research.
- You can create a folder in the Favorites list and then place related favorites you find on the Web in that folder.
- You can print the promising Web page.

To demonstrate how to record relevant information about a Web resource, the following steps illustrate how to copy information from the Sky and Telescope - The Discovery of the Perseid Meteors Web page and paste it into a WordPad document. The copy and paste technique you will use was illustrated in Project 1 on pages IE 35-37.

To Record Relevant Information About a Web Research Source

1

• **Click the Start button on the Windows taskbar, point to All Programs on the Start menu, point to Accessories on the All Programs submenu, and then click WordPad on the Accessories submenu.**

Windows starts the WordPad application and the Document - WordPad window appears (Figure 2-37). The Document - WordPad button is displayed on the taskbar.

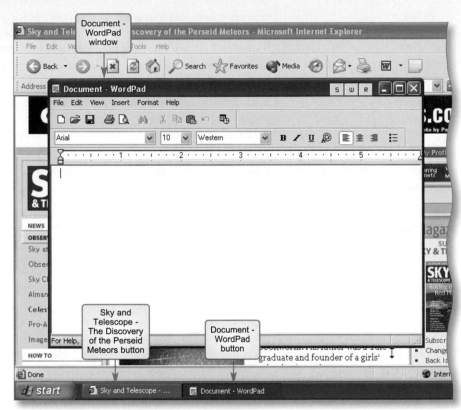

FIGURE 2-37

2

• **Click the Sky and Telescope button on the taskbar to display the Sky and Telescope - The Discovery of the Perseid Meteors window.**

• **Scroll to display the beginning of the article.**

The Sky and Telescope - The Discovery of the Perseid Meteors window, containing the Sky and Telescope Web page, appears (Figure 2-38).

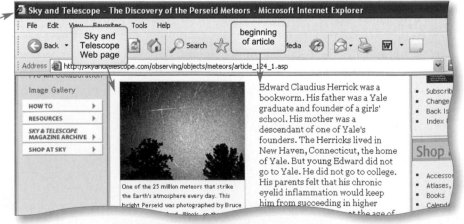

FIGURE 2-38

3

* **Point to the left of the first line of the article.**
* **Drag to select the first paragraph in the article.**
* **Right-click the selected text.**

The text is selected and a shortcut menu appears (Figure 2-39).

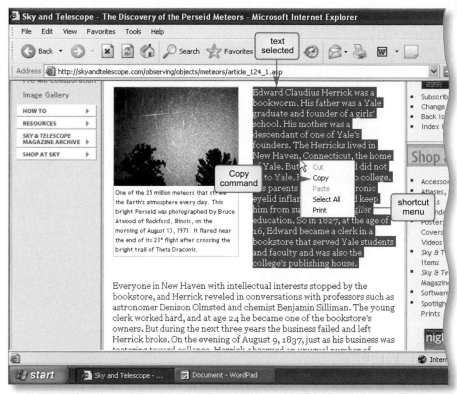

FIGURE 2-39

4

* **Click Copy on the shortcut menu.**
* **Click the Document - WordPad button on the taskbar.**

Windows copies the highlighted text to the Clipboard and the Document - WordPad window appears (Figure 2-40).

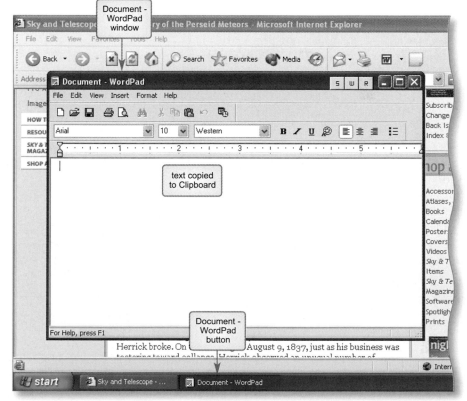

FIGURE 2-40

5

• **Type**
http://skyandtelescope.com
/observing/objects/meteors
/article_124_1.asp **in the**
WordPad document.

• **Press the ENTER key and then**
type Sky & Telescope Magazine
in the WordPad document.

• **Press the ENTER key and then**
type today's date in the WordPad
document.

• **Press the ENTER key twice.**

The URL, organization name, and today's date
appear in the WordPad window (Figure 2-41).
These are some of the pieces of information
needed when citing the work in a research paper.

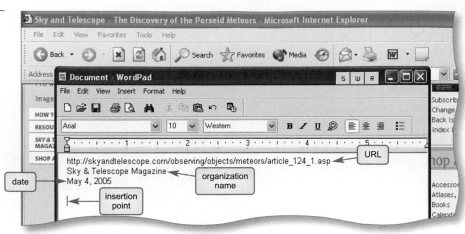

FIGURE 2-41

6

• **Right-click a blank area of the**
document and then click Paste on
the shortcut menu.

Windows pastes the contents of the
Clipboard in the WordPad window at the
location of the insertion point
(Figure 2-42).

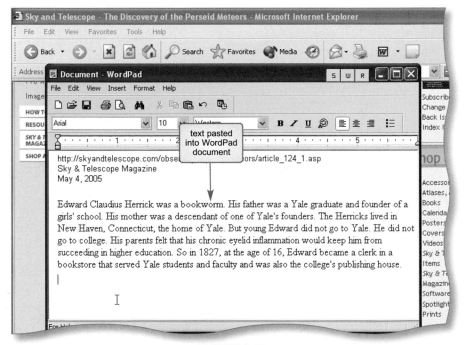

FIGURE 2-42

Saving a WordPad Document

To prevent the accidental loss of the WordPad document, you should formulate an
appropriate file name, such as Discovery of Perseid Meteors, for the document and save
the document on a 3½-inch floppy disk in drive A. After saving the file, quit WordPad.

The next steps show how to save the WordPad document on the floppy disk in
drive A using the file name, Discovery of Perseid Meteors, and quit WordPad.

To Save a WordPad Document

1 **Insert a formatted floppy disk in drive A.**

2 **Click the Save button on the toolbar.**

3 **Type** `Discovery of Perseid Meteors` **in the File name box.**

4 **Click the Save in box arrow.**

5 **Click 3½ Floppy (A:) in the Save in list.**

6 **Click the Save button in the Save As dialog box.**

7 **Remove the floppy disk from drive A.**

8 **Click the Close button on the WordPad title bar to quit WordPad.**

WordPad saves the WordPad document on the floppy disk in drive A using the Discovery of Perseid Meteors file name, closes the WordPad window, and quits WordPad.

If you are using the electronic technique for evaluating a Web source, you can save the research information at the bottom of the worksheet document. Then, both the evaluation criteria and the research information for a particular Web page are stored in the same document.

Citing Web Sources

Most of the preferred style authorities, such as **Modern Language Association** (**MLA**) and **American Psychological Association (APA)**, publish standards for citing Web resources. You can find these guides at a library or on the Web. Online information about these style guides can be found at www.mla.org and www.apa.org.

Figure 2-43 contains an example of using and citing a Web resource using the MLA style. The example documents the source of the criteria for the activity of the Perseid meteor shower.

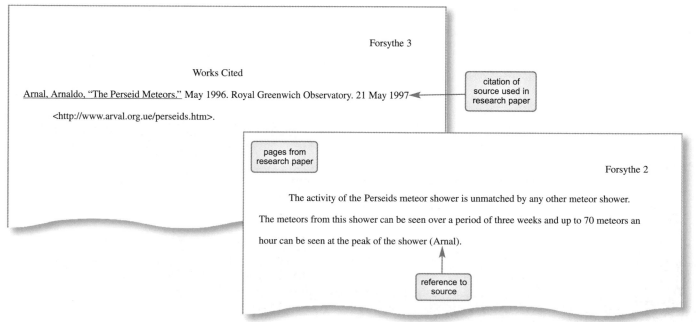

Forsythe 3

Works Cited

Arnal, Arnaldo, "The Perseid Meteors." May 1996. Royal Greenwich Observatory. 21 May 1997 ← citation of source used in research paper

<http://www.arval.org.ue/perseids.htm>.

pages from research paper

Forsythe 2

The activity of the Perseids meteor shower is unmatched by any other meteor shower. The meteors from this shower can be seen over a period of three weeks and up to 70 meteors an hour can be seen at the peak of the shower (Arnal). ← reference to source

FIGURE 2-43

As you have learned in this project, the World Wide Web can be an informative and valuable source of information. By using proper searching and note-taking techniques, and asking the right questions about the usefulness of a Web resource, you can add to the information base you use to write a paper or speech. Always remember, however, that Web sources should complement, not replace, printed sources for locating information.

Other Ways to Use Search Assistant

In this project, you first searched for Web pages using the Yahoo! directory and then searched for Web pages using Search Assistant and the keyword-based MSN Search engine. You also can use Search Assistant to search for mailing addresses and e-mail addresses, business names and business categories, maps, words, and encyclopedia articles, and pictures. The following sections illustrate how to search for a mailing address, a landmark, a word in a dictionary, and a picture.

Searching the Web for a Mailing Address

When you click the Find a person's address button in the Search pane, Search Assistant prompts you to search for a mailing address or an e-mail address by entering the first and last name, city, and state/province. The InfoSpace or BigFoot Web sites are used to perform a search for mailing address and e-mail address.

The following steps illustrate how to search for the mailing address of one of the authors of this book when you know only the author's first and last name.

To Search for a Mailing Address Using Search Assistant

1

• **Click the Search button on the Standard Buttons toolbar.**

• **Click the New button on the Search pane toolbar.**

The Search pane appears in the MSN Search window and the Find a Web page option button is selected (Figure 2-44).

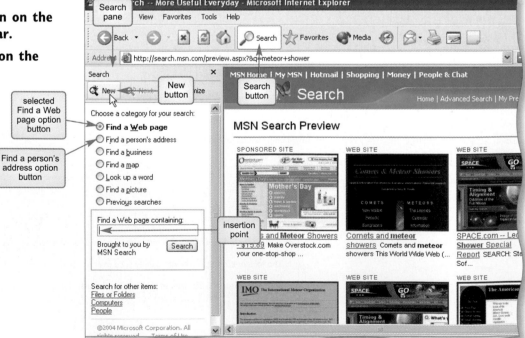

FIGURE 2-44

2

• **Click Find a person's address in the Search pane.**

The Find a person's address option button is selected and the rectangular box contains the Search For box, First Name text box, Last Name text box, City text box, and State/Province text box (Figure 2-45). The mailing address entry appears in the Search For box and the InfoSpace entry replaces the MSN Search entry in the Search pane. The search engine name may be different on your computer.

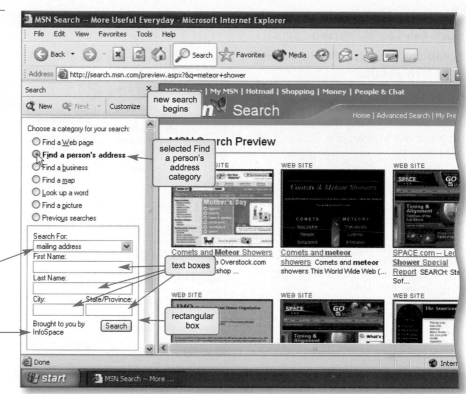

FIGURE 2-45

3

• **Type** Steven **in the First Name text box.**

• **Type** Forsythe **in the Last Name text box.**

The author's first name (Steven) appears in the First Name text box and the author's last name (Forsythe) is displayed in the Last Name text box (Figure 2-46). The City and State/Province entries are not required.

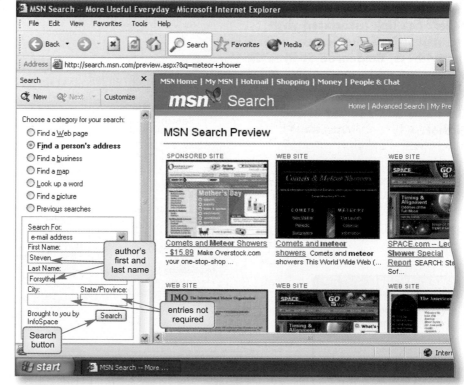

FIGURE 2-46

4

• **Click the Search button.**

• **Scroll the Search pane to display the search results.**

Internet Explorer searches the InfoSpace database for the mailing address of the author and the Search pane displays 5 of the 21 links found during the search (Figure 2-47). The links on your computer may be different.

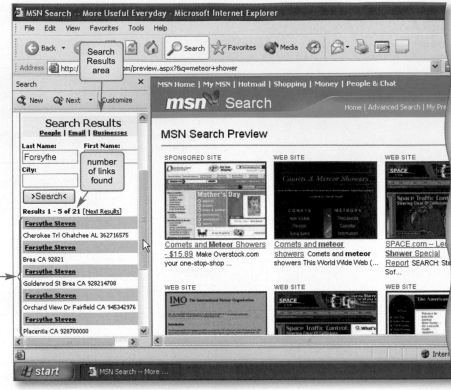

FIGURE 2-47

5

• **Click the link associated with the name, Forsythe Steven, and the address, Goldenrod St Brea CA 928214708 address.**

• **Scroll the display area to display the name and address of the author.**

The name and address of the author appears in the display area (Figure 2-48).

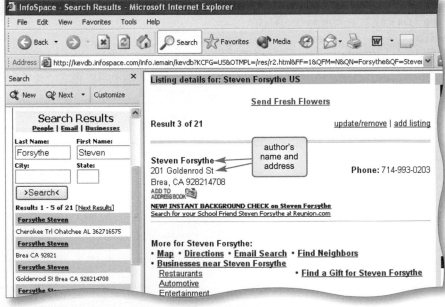

FIGURE 2-48

Other Ways

1. In Address box type
   www.infospace.com,
   click Go button, click Find
   a Person option button,
   type last name, type first
   name, type city or zip
   code, select state, click
   Search button

2. In address box type
   www.bigfoot.com, click
   Go button, type first and
   last name, select a state,
   click Go button

Searching the Web for a Map

When you click the Find a map button in the Search pane, Search Assistant prompts you to search for an address and place or landmark, and then enter the appropriate information to perform the search. When you enter a place or landmark and then click the Search button, the Expedia.com Web site is searched for the appropriate map. The next steps show how to search for the Staples Center landmark in Los Angeles, California.

To Search for a Place or Landmark Using Search Assistant

1

• **Click the New button on the Search pane toolbar and then click the Find a map option button.**

The selected Find a map category appears in the Search pane, the word Address appears in the Search For box, and the Expedia.com search engine name is displayed (Figure 2-49). Unless you decide to use another search engine, Expedia.com will search for an address.

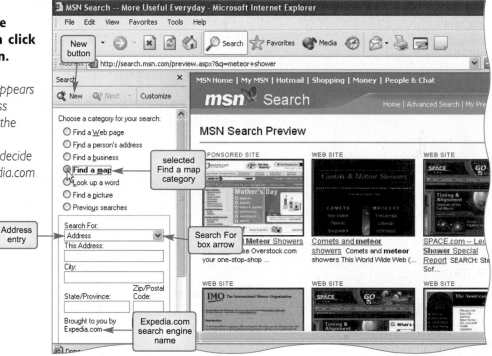

FIGURE 2-49

2

• **Click the Search For box arrow and then click Place or landmark.**

• **Type** Staples Center **in the This place or landmark text box.**

The words, Place or landmark, appear in the Search For box and the landmark name, Staples Center, is displayed in the This place or landmark text box (Figure 2-50).

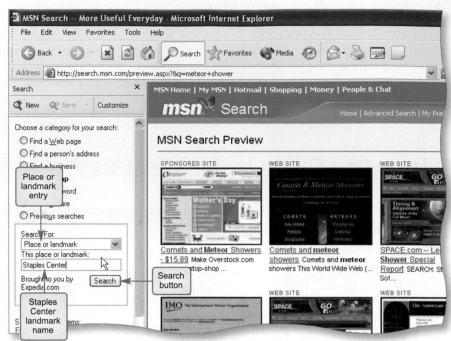

FIGURE 2-50

3

• **Click the Search button in the Search pane.**

Internet Explorer searches the Microsoft Expedia Maps database and displays the Expedia.com home page in the display area (Figure 2-51). The home page contains 10 tabs, several links, and the Los Angeles area map, including the location of the Staples Center.

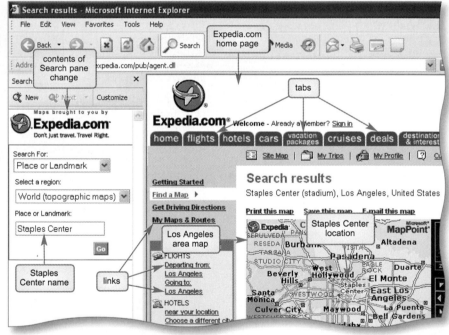

FIGURE 2-51

Other Ways

1. In Address box type www.mapquest.com, click Go button, type address or intersection, type city, type state, type zip code, click Search button

Searching the Web for the Definition of a Word

When you click the Look up a word option button in the Search pane, Search Assistant prompts you to search for an encyclopedia article, word, or synonym and antonym, and then enter the appropriate information to perform the search. When you enter a word and then click the Search button, the Dictionary.com Web site is searched for the appropriate word and a definition is displayed. The next steps show how to find the definition of the abbreviation, DVD.

To Search for a Definition Using Search Assistant

1

• **Click the New button on the Search pane toolbar.**

• **Click the Look up a word option button.**

• **Click the Look in box arrow and then click Dictionary.**

• **Type** DVD **in the Find information on text box.**

A new search begins, the Look up a word option button is selected in the Search pane, the word, Dictionary, appears in the Look in box, and the abbreviation, DVD, is displayed in the Find information on text box (Figure 2-52). The Dictionary.com name appears to the left of the Search button.

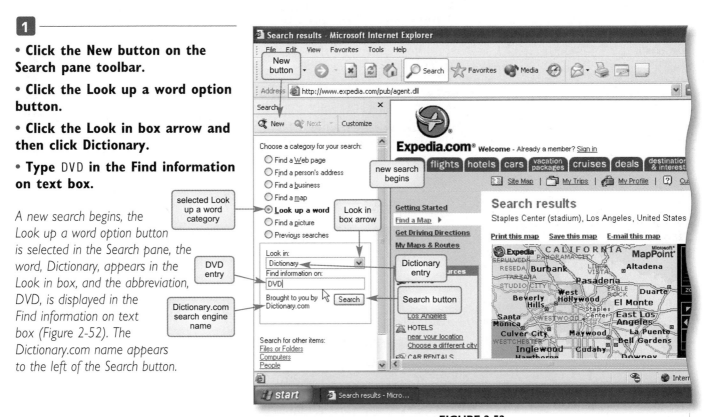

FIGURE 2-52

2

• **Click the Search button in the Search pane.**

Dictionary.com searches for and displays a partial list of links (3 entries and 134 matches) to Web pages that contain the definition of the abbreviation, DVD, in the Search pane (Figure 2-53). The first entry in the list is DVD American Heritage Dictionary. The search results on your computer may be different.

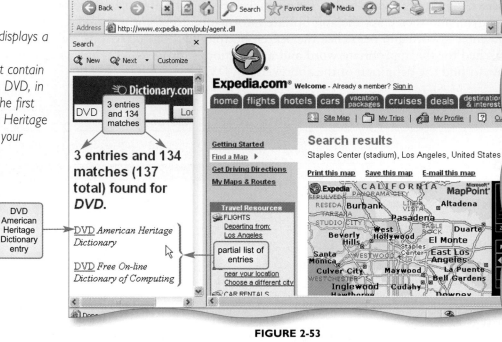

FIGURE 2-53

3

• **Click the DVD American Heritage Dictionary link in the Search pane.**
• **Scroll the display area to read the first definition.**

Internet Explorer displays the Dictionary.com home page and the definition for DVD (Figure 2-54).

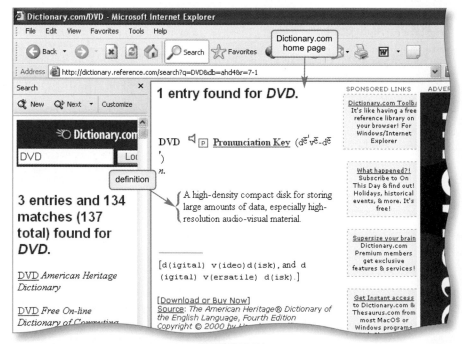

FIGURE 2-54

Searching the Web for a Picture

When you click the Find a picture option button in the Search pane, Search Assistant prompts you to enter the type of picture you want to find. When you enter the type of picture and then click the Search button, the Corbis Web site is searched and a list of pictures appear in the Search pane. The following steps illustrate how to search for surfing pictures.

To Search for a Picture Using Search Assistant

1

• **Click the New button on the Search pane toolbar.**

• **Click the Find a picture option button.**

• **Type** surfing **in the Find a picture relating to text box.**

A new search begins and the contents of the Search pane change (Figure 2-55). The Find a picture option button is selected, and the word, surfing, appears in the Find a picture relating to text box. The Corbis search engine name is displayed to the left of the Search button.

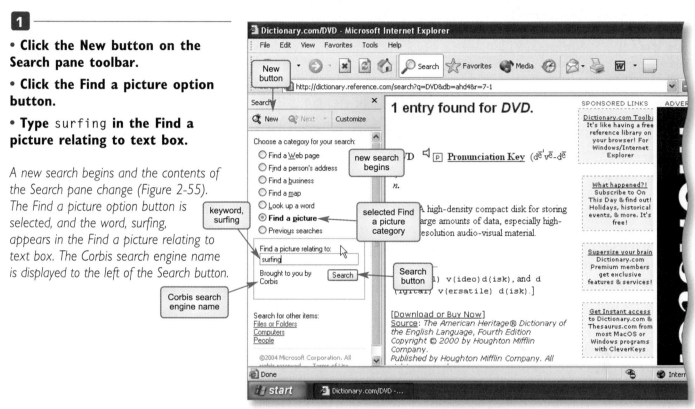

FIGURE 2-55

2

• **Click the Search button.**

Searching the Corbis Web site results in finding 38 pictures (Figure 2-56). Nine pictures and their titles appear per page and the first picture (Surfer Cutting Across Blue Waves) is displayed in the Search pane. Clicking the Next button displays the next set of nine pictures. The list of pictures on your computer may be different.

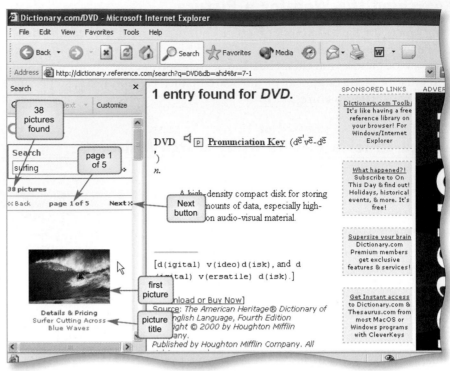

FIGURE 2-56

3

• **Click the first picture in the Search pane.**

Internet Explorer displays a Web page from the Corbis Web site containing the enlarged (Surfer Cutting Across Blue Waves) picture in the display area (Figure 2-57). You can search for images using option buttons or a text box, and display the editor's pick of images.

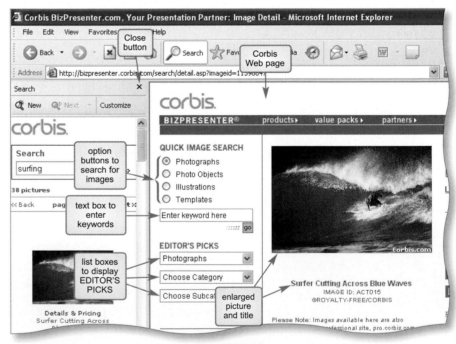

FIGURE 2-57

Other Ways

1. In Address box type
   www.corbis.com, click
   Go button, type surfing
   in text box, click Search
   button, click picture

Closing the Search pane

Upon completion of searching, the Search pane should be closed. The following step closes the Search pane.

To Close the Search Pane

1 **Click the Close button on the Search pane.**

Other Ways to Search the Web

Previously, this project used Search Assistant to search for information (Web page, mailing address, place or landmark, definitions, pictures, and so on). Using the Address bar also allows you to search for information on the Web. As mentioned previously, this type of search tool is called a Keyword system. A **Keyword system** allows you to enter a name or word on the Address bar to display a list of corresponding Web pages.

You can use the Address bar to type an address (URL) and display the associated Web page or type a keyword or phrase (search inquiry) to display a list of Web pages relating to the keyword or phrase. In addition, you can type a folder location (path) to display the contents of the folder, type an application program name to start a program, and type a document name to start an application and display the document in the application window. Three of these operations are illustrated in the following sections.

Using the Address Bar and a URL to Display a Web Page

One method to search for and display a Web page using the Address bar is to type an address (URL) and then click the Go button. For example, the URL for the Kelley Blue Book Web page is www.kelleybluebook.com. The next steps illustrate how to type the URL for the Kelley Blue Book Web page in the Address box and display the Kelley Blue Book Web page.

To Search for a Web Page Using the Address Bar

1

• **Click the Address box and then type** www.kelleybluebook.com **in the Address box.**

The URL for the Kelley Blue Book Web page appears in the Address box (Figure 2-58).

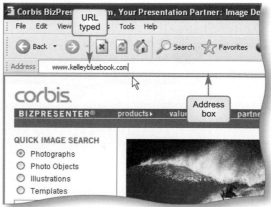

FIGURE 2-58

2

• **Click the Go button.**

The Kelley Blue Book Web page appears in the Kelley Blue Book - New Car Pricing, Used Car Values window (Figure 2-59).

FIGURE 2-59

Using the Address Bar and a Keyword to Display a Home Page

If you type a specific product, trademark, company name, or institution name in the Address box and then click the Go button, MSN Search will search for and display a list of Web pages relating to the entry in the Address box. Any Address box entry that does not end with a .com, .net, .org, .de, or .jp is passed to the Keyword system.

Assume you want information on the University of Michigan, but do not know the university's URL. After entering the phrase, university of michigan, MSN Search searches for and displays a list of Web pages. In most cases, the MSN butterfly and the phrase, Top Pick, identify the Web page as the home page.

The following steps show how to display the home page of the University of Michigan using the Keyword system.

To Search for a Home Page Using the Keyword System

1

• **Click the Address box and then type** university of michigan **in the Address box.**

The Address box contains the entry, university of michigan, and a text box below the Address box contains the entry, Search for "university of michigan" (Figure 2-60).

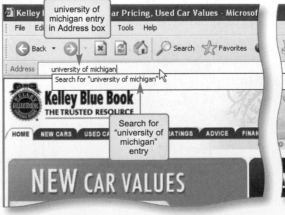

FIGURE 2-60

Internet Explorer Project 2

2

• **Click the Go button.**

Because the university of michigan entry does not have a www. or .com or .org, Internet Explorer sends the keywords (university of michigan) to the Keyword system. The Keyword system matches the keywords to its database of keywords and displays a list of links containing the keywords (Figure 2-61). The MSN butterfly and the words, Top Pick, identify the Web page as the home page.

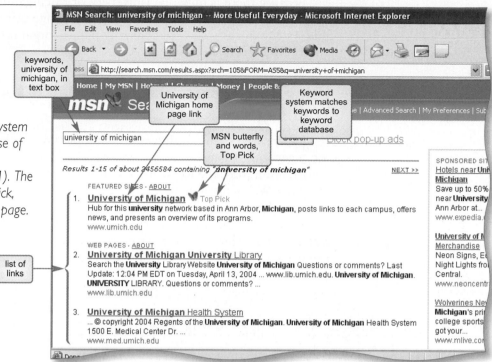

FIGURE 2-61

3

• **Click the University of Michigan link identified by the MSN butterfly and the words, Top Pick.**

The University of Michigan home page appears (Figure 2-62).

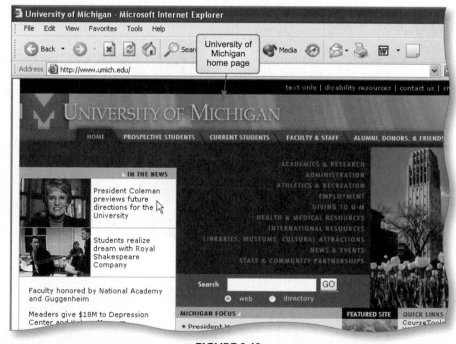

FIGURE 2-62

Other Ways

1. In Address box press TAB key to select entry, type keyword, press ENTER key

Because there is only one University of Michigan home page, the Keyword system identifies one Web page as the home page using the entry, Top Pick. Thus, this system works well with company names, organization names, association names, and specific products and services.

Using the Address Bar to Display a List of Related Web Pages

More often than not, however, the topic on which you want information is much more general. If you enter a general keyword, such as concerts, home gardening, or construction jobs, the Keyword system passes the keyword to MSN Search, which returns a Web page with several related links from which you can choose. MSN Search is Internet Explorer's default search engine.

As an example, assume you need information on the topic, stem cell research, for a term paper. The following steps show how the Keyword system passes the general topic, stem cell research, to MSN Search, which displays a page of links from which you can choose.

To Search for Related Web Pages Using the Keyword System

1

• **Click the Address box and then type** stem cell research **in the Address box.**

The keywords, stem cell research, appear in the Address box and a text box below the Address box contains the entry, Search for "stem cell research" (Figure 2-63).

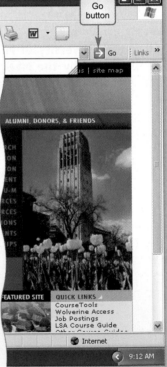

FIGURE 2-63

2

• **Click the Go button.**

Because the keywords, stem cell research, have no specific Web page, the Keyword system passes the entry to MSN Search, which displays a list of related links, rather than a specific Web page (Figure 2-64). The window contains several links to other Web pages containing information about stem cell research.

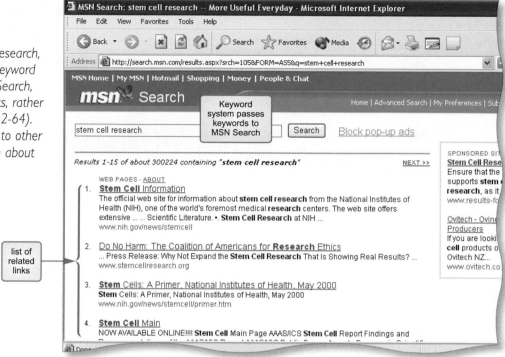

list of related links

FIGURE 2-64

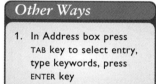

Other Ways

1. In Address box press TAB key to select entry, type keywords, press ENTER key

Using the Address Bar to Search for a Folder on the Computer

To display the contents of a folder using the Address bar, you must type the path of the folder and then click the Go button. A **path** is the means of navigating to a specific location on a computer or network. To specify a path, you must type the drive letter, followed by a colon (:), a backslash (\), and the folder name. For example, the path for the WINDOWS folder on drive C is C:\WINDOWS. The steps on the next page show how to type the path of the WINDOWS folder and display the contents of the WINDOWS folder.

To Search for a Folder and Its Contents

1

• **Click the Address box and then type** c:\windows **in the Address box.**

The path of the WINDOWS folder appears in the Address box (Figure 2-65).

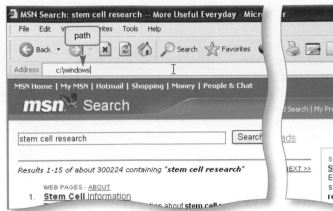

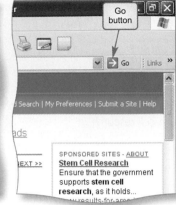

FIGURE 2-65

2

• **Click the Go button.**

• **If the message, These files are hidden, displays in the WINDOWS - Microsoft Internet Explorer window, click the Show the contents of this folder link.**

A folder icon and the path of the WINDOWS folder appear in the Address box and the WINDOWS - Microsoft Internet Explorer window containing the files and folders in the WINDOWS folder is displayed (Figure 2-66).

3

• **Click the Close button on the WINDOWS window.**

The WINDOWS window closes.

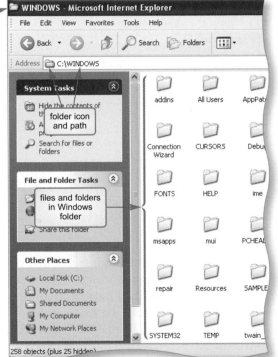

FIGURE 2-66

Other Ways

1. In Address box press TAB key to select entry, type path, click GO button.

In addition to using the Address bar to display a Web page, search for information on the Web, and display the contents of a folder, you also can use the Address bar to start a program and open a document. To start an application, such as the WordPad application, you type the application name (WordPad) in the Address box and then click the Go button. The Document - WordPad window will appear on the desktop. To display a document, you type the document name in the Address box and then click the Go button. The document will appear in a separate window.

Displaying the Search Companion Pane

As mentioned earlier in this project, Internet Explorer allows you to search the Web using either Search Companion or Search Assistant. When you are finished using Search Assistant, you should display the Search Companion pane.

The following steps illustrate how to display the Search Companion pane.

To Display the Search Companion Pane

1 Click the Search button on the Standard Buttons toolbar.

2 Click the Customize button on the Search pane.

3 Click the Use Search Companion option button in the Customize Search Settings dialog box and then click the OK button.

4 Click the Close button in the Search pane.

5 Click the Close button in the Microsoft Internet Explorer window to close Internet Explorer.

The Search Companion pane is displayed in the Microsoft Internet Explorer window. Then, the Search Companion pane and the Microsoft Explorer window are closed.

Project Summary

In this project, the nine general types of Web pages and the three general types of search tools were described. You learned how to evaluate a Web page as a potential source for research. You learned how to search the Internet using the Yahoo! directory. You learned the techniques for using the MSN Search and Google search engines to enter keywords and use advanced search techniques. You learned how to record relevant information about a potential source for future reference and learned how to write a citation for a Web resource. You saw how Search Assistant was used to search the Internet for an e-mail address, a map, a definition, and a picture. In addition, you learned how to search the Web using the Address bar and the Keyword system.

What You Should Know

Having completed the project, you now should be able to perform the tasks below. The tasks are listed in the same order they were presented in this project.

1. Start Internet Explorer (IE 81)
2. Display the Yahoo! Home Page (IE 82)
3. Search Using the Yahoo! Directory (IE 83)
4. Evaluate a Web Resource (IE 86)
5. Display the Search Companion Pane (IE 88)
6. Search for Web Pages Using Search Companion (IE 89)
7. Close the Search Companion Pane (IE 91)
8. Select an Internet Search Behavior (IE 92)
9. Display the Search Pane (IE 95)
10. Search Using MSN Search and Keywords (IE 96)
11. Search Using the Google Simple Search (IE 98)
12. Display the Google Advanced Search Form (IE 101)
13. Search Using the Google Advanced Search (IE 102)
14. Record Relevant Information about a Research Source (IE 106)
15. Save a WordPad Document (IE 109)
16. Search for a Mailing Address Using Search Assistant (IE 110)
17. Search for a Place or Landmark Using Search Assistant (IE 113)
18. Search for a Definition Using Search Assistant (IE 115)
19. Search for a Picture Using Search Assistant (IE 117)
20. Close the Search Pane (IE 119)
21. Search for a Web Page Using the Address Bar (IE 119)
22. Search for a Home Page Using the Keyword System (IE 120)
23. Search for Related Web Pages Using the Keyword System (IE 122)
24. Search for a Folder and Its Contents (IE 124)
25. Display the Search Companion Pane (IE 125)

Learn It Online

Instructions: To complete the Learn It Online exercises, start your browser, click the Address box, enter scsite.com/ie6winxp/learn, and then click the Go button. When the Internet Explorer Learn It Online page is displayed, follow the instructions in the exercises below. Each exercise has instructions for printing your results, either for your own records or for submission to your instructor.

1 Project Reinforcement TF, MC, and SA

Below Internet Explorer Project 2, click the Project Reinforcement link. Print the quiz by clicking Print on the File menu for each page. Answer each question.

2 Flash Cards

Below Internet Explorer Project 2, click the Flash Cards link and read the instructions. Type 20 (or a number specified by your instructor) in the Number of playing cards text box, type your name in the Enter your name text box, and then click the Flip Card button. When the flash card is displayed, read the question and then click the ANSWER box arrow to select an answer. Flip through Flash Cards. If your score is 15 (75%) correct or greater, click Print on the File menu to print your results. If your score is less than 15 (75%) correct, then redo this exercise by clicking the Replay button.

3 Practice Test

Below Internet Explorer Project 2, click the Practice Test link. Answer each question, enter your first and last name at the bottom of the page, and then click the Grade Test button. When the graded practice test is displayed on your screen, click Print on the File menu to print a hard copy. Continue to take practice tests until you score 80% or better.

4 Who Wants To Be a Computer Genius?

Below Internet Explorer Project 2, click the Computer Genius link. Read the instructions, enter your first and last name at the bottom of the page, and then click the PLAY button. When your score is displayed, click the PRINT RESULTS link to print a hard copy.

5 Wheel of Terms

Below Internet Explorer Project 2, click the Wheel of Terms link. Read the instructions, and then enter your first and last name and your school name. Click the PLAY button. When your score is displayed, right-click the scores and then click Print on the shortcut menu to print a hard copy.

6 Crossword Puzzle Challenge

Below Internet Explorer Project 2, click the Crossword Puzzle Challenge link. Read the instructions, and then enter your first and last name. Click the SUBMIT button. Work the crossword puzzle. When you are finished, click the Submit button. When the crossword puzzle is displayed, click the Print Puzzle button to print a hard copy.

7 Tips and Tricks

Below Internet Explorer Project 2, click the Tips and Tricks link. Click a topic that pertains to Project 2. Right-click the information and then click Print on the shortcut menu. Construct a brief example of what the information relates to in Internet Explorer to confirm you understand how to use the tip or trick.

8 Newsgroups

Below Internet Explorer Project 2, click the Newsgroups link. Click a topic that pertains to Project 2. Print three comments.

9 Expanding Your Horizons

Below Internet Explorer Project 2, click the Articles for Microsoft Windows XP link. Click a topic that pertains to Project 2. Print the information. Construct a brief example of what the information relates to in Internet Explorer to confirm you understand the contents of the article.

10 Search Sleuth

Below Internet Explorer Project 2, click the Search Sleuth link. To search for a term that pertains to this project, select a term below the Project 2 title and then use the Google search engine at google.com (or any major search engine) to display and print two Web pages that present information on the term.

11 Internet Explorer How-To Article

Below Internet Explorer Project 2, click the Internet Explorer How-To Articles link. When your browser displays the Internet Explorer How-to Articles Web page, scroll down and click one of the links that covers one or more of the objectives listed at the beginning of the project on page IE 74. Print the first page of the how-to article before stepping through it.

12 Getting More From the Web

Below Internet Explorer Project 2, click the Getting More from the Web link. When your browser displays the Getting More from the Web with Internet Explorer 6 Web page, click one of the Top Stories or Featured Contents links. Print the first page.

In the Lab

1 Searching the Web Using the Yahoo! Directory

Problem: You work full-time for the San Antonio Community Center. Your boss has asked you to search for information on several unrelated topics and print the first page of each Web site.

Instructions: Use Internet Explorer and a computer to perform the following tasks.

Part 1: *Displaying the Yahoo! Directory*

1. If necessary, connect to the Internet and start Internet Explorer.
2. Click the Address box, type www.yahoo.com and then click the Go button to display the Yahoo! directory.

Part 2: *Finding Information about Alternative Medicine Using the Yahoo! Directory*

1. Using the Yahoo! directory and the Health category locate information on an alternative form of medicine called rolfing. Rolfing involves working the body to improve structural integrity and also is referred to as Body Working. Answer the following questions.
   a. What is rolfing? _____
   b. Who founded and taught rolfing? _____
   c. What is the benefit of rolfing? _____
2. Print the home page for the Guild for Structural Integration and write your name on the printout (Figure 2-67).

FIGURE 2-67

In the Lab

Part 3: *Finding a College Using the Yahoo! Directory*

1. Using the Yahoo! directory and the Education category, locate the home page of the only private college in Cherokee county, South Carolina. Answer the following questions.
   a. What is the college name? _____
   b. In what city is the college located? _____
   c. What team name does the Athletic department use? _____
2. Print the home page of the college and write your name on the printout.

Part 4: *Finding Information about Roller Coasters Using the Yahoo! Directory*

1. Using the Yahoo! directory and the Recreation & Sports category, locate information about amusement parks that have roller coasters and then use the roller coaster database to answer the following questions.
   a. In which city is the Michigan's Adventure park located? _____
   b. How many steel roller coasters does the park have? _____
   c. In what amusement park is the oldest indoor roller coaster located? _____
2. Print the Roller Coaster DataBase Web page and write your name on the printout.

Part 5: *Finding Information about Chemistry Using the Yahoo! Directory*

1. Using the Yahoo! directory and the Science category, locate information about the periodic table of elements. Answer the following questions.
   a. What is the symbol for Gold? _____
   b. Which element is associated with the symbol Ca? _____
   c. What is the atomic weight of Californium? _____
2. Print the Web page containing the periodic table and write your name on the printout.
3. Hand in all printouts to your instructor.
4. Quit Internet Explorer.

2 Searching the Web Using the Yahoo! Directory

Problem: Your instructor would like you to practice using the Yahoo! directory. She recommends searching for graphic images of different types of artwork. As proof of completing this assignment, you should print the Web page containing the graphic image.

Instructions: Use Internet Explorer and a computer to perform the following tasks.

Part 1: *Displaying the Yahoo! Directory*

1. If necessary, connect to the Internet and start Internet Explorer.
2. Click the Address box, type www.yahoo.com, and then click the Go button to display the Yahoo! directory.

(continued)

In the Lab

Searching the Web Using the Yahoo! Directory *(continued)*

Part 2: *Finding Art Work Using the Yahoo! Directory*

1. Using the Yahoo! directory and the Arts & Humanities category, search for and print the Web page containing a graphic image that is representative of each of the following types of artwork: animation, body art, computer generated, public art, graffiti, and stone sculpture. Figure 2-68 shows a collection of Alabaster bowls created by Ron Christie.
2. On each printout, write your name and the type of artwork the Web page represents. Hand in the pages to your instructor.
3. Quit Internet Explorer.

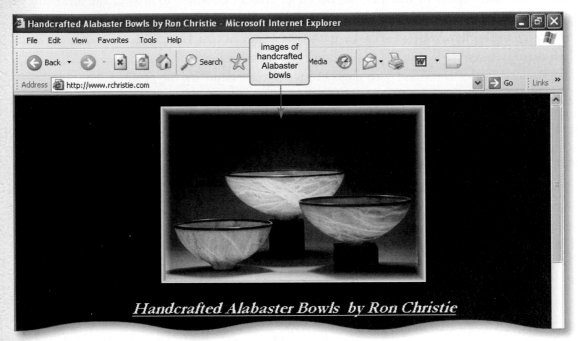

FIGURE 2-68

3 Searching the Web Using the Google Directory

Problem: Your instructor would like you to practice searching Web sites using the Google directory. He would like you to focus on finding Web pages that contain antiques, rules of card games, and images of birds. As proof of completing this assignment, print out the first page of each Web site you visit.

Instructions: Use Internet Explorer and a computer to perform the following tasks.

Part 1: *Displaying the Google Directory*

1. If necessary, connect to the Internet and start Internet Explorer.
2. Click the Address box, type www.google.com, and then click the Go button to display the Google home page.
3. Click the more link and then click Directory on the resulting page (Figure 2-69).

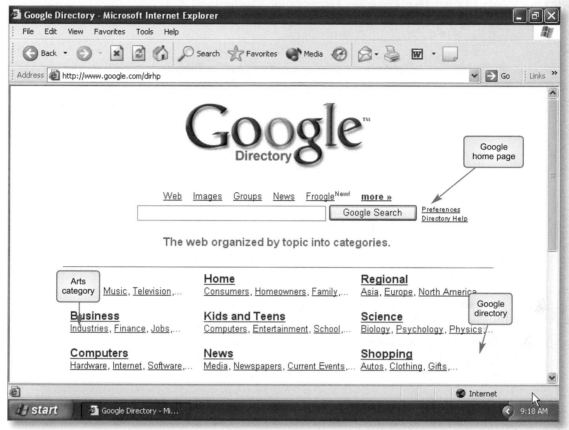

FIGURE 2-69

Part 2: *Finding Antiques Using the Google Directory*

1. Using the Google directory and the Arts category, locate a Web page that contains information on antique Nikon cameras. Print the Web page and write your name on the printout.
2. Locate a Web page that contains information about antique salt and pepper shakers. Print the Web page and write your name on the printout.
3. Locate a Web page that contains information about antique stamps. Print the Web page and write your name on the printout.

Part 3: *Finding Games Using the Google Directory*

1. Using the Google directory and the Games category, locate a Web page that contains the rules for the Hearts card game. Print the Web page and write your name on the printout.
2. Locate a Web page that contains the rules for the Canasta card game. Print the Web page and write your name on the printout.
3. Locate a Web page that contains rules for the Euchre card game. Print the Web page and write your name on the printout.

(continued)

In the Lab

Searching the Web Using the Google Directory *(continued)*

Part 4: *Finding Recreational Activities Using the Google Directory*

1. Using the Google directory and the Recreation category, locate a Web page that contains images of Hot Air Ballooning. Print the Web page and write your name on the printout.
2. Locate a Web page that contains images of birds. Print the Web page and write your name on the printout.
3. Locate a Web page that contains images of miniature trains. Print the Web page and write your name on the printout.
4. Hand in all printouts to your instructor. Quit Internet Explorer.

4 Searching the Web Using AltaVista and Keywords

Problem: Your instructor would like you to practice using the AltaVista search engine. He wants you to search for two interesting articles and then record the URL for each article and develop a short report on each article using WordPad.

Instructions: Use Internet Explorer and a computer to perform the following tasks.

Part 1: *Displaying the AltaVista Home Page*

1. If necessary, connect to the Internet and start Internet Explorer.
2. Click the Address box, type www.altavista.com, and then click the Go button to display the AltaVista home page. The home page contains the AltaVista simple search form.

Part 2: *Performing an AltaVista Simple Search*

1. Use the text box and the Find button in the AltaVista simple search form to search for two of the following topics: virtual reality, computer generated graphics, Java applets, MLA style, APA style, or any extreme sport. Figure 2-70 shows a Web page about bungee jumping from the Bridge To Nowhere in Southern California.
2. Find one or more informative Web pages about each topic you select.
3. Using WordPad, copy information about each topic from the Web pages into a WordPad document and develop a short report about each topic. Add the URLs of the Web sites you used and your name to the end of the report.
4. Print the WordPad document.

Part 3: *Performing an AltaVista Advanced Search*

1. Click the Advanced Search link in the AltaVista simple search form.
2. Use the Advanced Search form to find three Web pages that contain information about three different universities that are not public universities. Sort the resulting Web pages using the word, university.
3. Print the three Web pages and write your name on each printout.
4. Hand in all printouts to your instructor. Quit Internet Explorer.

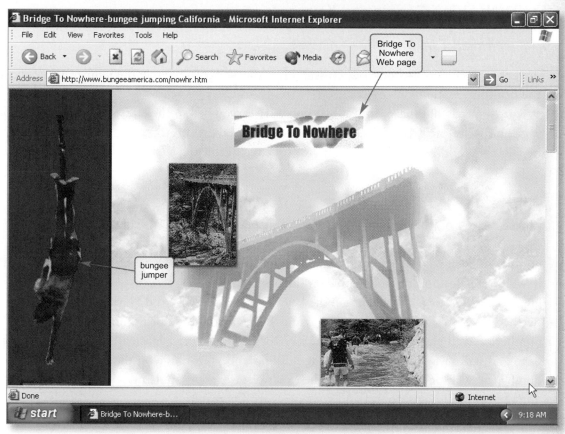

FIGURE 2-70

5 Searching the Web Using Google and Keywords

Problem: You want to use both the Google simple search and advanced search to find Web pages relating to several of your hobbies. You decide to print out the first page of each Web page you visit.

Instructions: Use Internet Explorer and a computer to perform the following tasks.

Part 1: *Starting the Google Search Engine*

1. If necessary, connect to the Internet and start Internet Explorer.
2. Click the Address box, type www.google.com, and then click the Go button to display the Google home page.

Part 2: *Searching for a Web Page*

1. Find a Web page containing inspirational quotations about children. Print the Web page and write your name on the printout.
2. Find the Web page containing the address, phone number, and e-mail address of your representative in the U.S. House of Representatives. Print the Web page and write your name on the printout.
3. Find the Official Web site of Tiger Woods. Print the Web page and write your name on the printout.

(continued)

In the Lab

Searching the Web Using Google and Keywords *(continued)*

Part 3: *Searching for Information*

1. Find the current temperature in Moscow, Russia. Print the Web page, circle the temperature, and write your name on the printout.
2. Use the keywords, movie database, to find who played Harvey Pell in the classic movie *High Noon*. Print the Web page and write the actor name and your name on the printout.
3. What is the URL and address of the University of Chicago? Print the Web page and write your name on the printout.

Part 4: *Using the Google Advanced Search*

1. Click Advanced Search on the Google home page to display the Google Advanced Search form (Figure 2-71).
2. Find the number of Web pages that contain the keyword, motorcycle. Print the Web page and write the number of Web pages found and your name on the printout.
3. Find the number of Web pages that contain the keywords, motorcycle and Harley-Davidson. Print the Web page and write the number of Web pages found and your name on the printout.
4. Find the number of Web pages that contain the keywords, motorcycle, Harley-Davidson, and parts. Print the Web page and write the number of Web pages found and your name on the printout.
5. Find the number of Web pages that contains the exact phrase, geographic map. Print the Web page and write the number of Web pages found and your name on the printout.

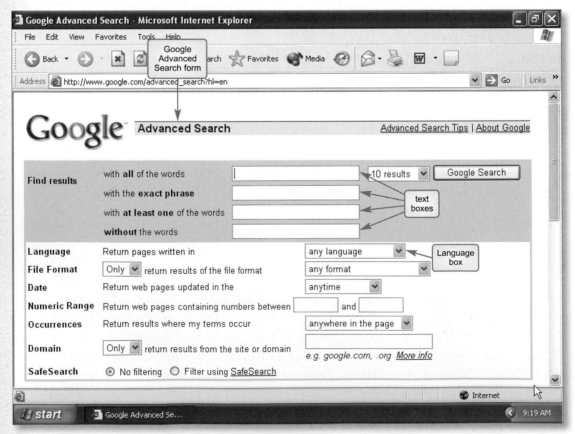

FIGURE 2-71

In the Lab

6. Find the number of Web pages that contain the exact phrase, geographic map, and the keyword, France. Print the Web page and write the number of Web pages found and your name on the printout.
7. Find the number of Web pages that contain an exact phrase (geographic map), keyword (France), and are written in the French language. Print the Web page and write the number of Web pages found and your name on the printout.
8. Hand in all printouts to your instructor.

6 Searching the Web Using Excite and Keywords

Problem: Your instructor would like you to practice using the Excite search engine and keywords. He wants you to find one or more interesting topics, copy information about the topic(s) into a WordPad document, and develop a short report. Add the URLs of each Web site you used and your name to the end of the report.

Instructions: Use Internet Explorer and a computer to perform the following tasks.

Part 1: Displaying the Excite Home Page

1. If necessary, connect to the Internet and start Internet Explorer.
2. Click the Address box, type www.excite.com, and then click the Go button to display the Excite home page. The home page contains the Excite simple search form.
3. Perform a search using Excite and any one of the following topics: government spending, a historical event, the life of a current political figure, an extreme weather event, asteroid collisions with the earth, an extraterrestrial sighting, or genetic engineering. Figure 2-72 shows the Web page of an organization that explores, understands, and explains the origin, nature and prevalence of life in the universe.
4. Find one or more informative Web pages about the topic you select. Using WordPad copy information about the topic from the Web pages into a WordPad document and develop a short report about the topic.
5. Add the URLs of the Web sites you used and your name to the end of the report.
6. Print out the WordPad document and hand in the report to your instructor.
7. Quit Internet Explorer.

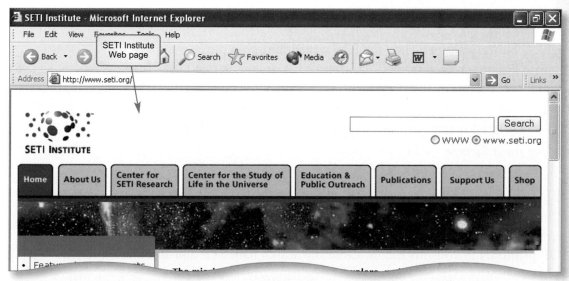

FIGURE 2-72

7 Searching the Web Using Search Assistant

Problem: You would like to become more familiar with Search Assistant and be able to search for pictures, business addresses, and maps. You decide to print out the first page of each Web page you visit.

Instructions: Use Internet Explorer and a computer to perform the following tasks.

Part 1: *Using Search Assistant*

1. If necessary, connect to the Internet and start Internet Explorer.
2. Click the Search button on the Standard Buttons toolbar.
3. If the Search Assistant pane does not appear, perform the steps in Figure 2-21 through Figure 2-25 on pages IE 92-94.
4. Click the Find a Web page button in the Search pane.

Part 2: *Searching for Web Pages Using Search Assistant*

1. Locate a Web page for each of the topics listed in steps 2, 3, 4, and 5 below.
2. Search for a Web page containing a picture of the northern lights (aurora borealis). Print the Web page and write your name on the printout.
3. Search for a Web page containing a picture of a porcupine puffer fish (diodon nicthemerus). Print the Web page and write your name on the printout.
4. Search for a Web page containing a picture of Brad Pitt or Elle MacPherson. Print the Web page and write your name on the printout.

Part 3: *Searching for a Business Address*

1. Click the New button in the Search pane and then click the Find a business button in the Search pane.
2. Use WordPad to create a list of business names, addresses, and telephone numbers for each of the following businesses: Course Technology (Massachusetts), Microsoft Corporation (Washington), Flagler Museum (Florida), and Recreational Equipment (Seattle, Washington). Click the New button after completing each search.
3. Print out the WordPad document and write your name on the printout.

Part 4: *Searching for a Map*

1. Click the New button and then click the Find a map button in the Search pane.
2. Find and print a map for each of the following places or landmarks: Eiffel Tower (France), Key West (Florida), and White House (District of Columbia). Click the New button after completing each search.
3. Circle the place or landmark on the map and write your name on each map.
4. Print out the WordPad documents and write your name on each report.

Part 5: *Searching for a Picture*

1. Click the New button and then click the Find a picture button.
2. Find and print a picture of the Golden Gate Bridge. Write your name on the printout.
3. Find and print a picture of the Seattle Space Needle. Write your name on the printout.
4. Find and print a picture of the Statue of Liberty. Write your name on the printout.
5. Hand in all printouts to your instructor. Close the Search pane and quit Internet Explorer.

In the Lab

8 Searching the Web Using Multiple Search Engines

Problem: You are currently using MSN Search but would like to try using AltaVista. You decide to find five Web pages using MSN Search and five Web pages using AltaVista. You want to record the names of the top five Web pages for both search engines and record them using WordPad.

Instructions: Use Internet Explorer and a computer to perform the following tasks.

Part 1: *Starting Search Assistant*

1. If necessary, connect to the Internet and start Internet Explorer.
2. Click the Search button on the Standard Buttons toolbar.
3. If the Search Assistant pane does not appear, perform the steps in Figure 2-21 through Figure 2-25 on pages IE 92-94.

Part 2: *Customizing Search Settings*

1. Click the Customize button in the Search pane.
2. In the Find a Web page area, click the AltaVista check box to place a check mark in the check box.
3. In the Find a Web page area, click the Lycos check box to place a check mark in the check box.
4. Click the OK button in the Customize Search Settings dialog box.

Part 3: *Searching the Web Using the MSN Search Engine*

1. Click the Find a Web page button in the Search pane.
2. Type niagara falls in the Find a Web page containing box.
3. Click the Search button.
4. Use WordPad to record the names of the top five Web pages found during the MSN Search.

Part 4: *Searching the Web Using the AltaVista Search Engine*

1. Click the down arrow on the Next button in the Search pane.
2. Click AltaVista on the Next button list.
3. Type niagara falls in the AltaVista text box.
4. Click the Find button.
5. Record the names of the top five Web pages found during the AltaVista search.

Part 5: *Searching the Web Using the Lycos Search Engine*

1. Click the down arrow on the Next button in the Search pane.
2. Click Lycos on the Next button list.
3. Record the names of the top five Web pages found during the Lycos search.

(continued)

In the Lab

Searching the Web Using Multiple Search Engines *(continued)*

Part 6: *Comparing the Web Sites Found*

1. Compare the results of each search. Answer the following questions by typing your answers in the WordPad document.
   a. Which search engine returned the most duplicated Web pages?

   _____

   b. Were there any Web pages that displayed in all four searches?

   _____

   c. Which search engine do you think returned the best selection of Web pages? Explain.
   d. What are your general comments about the four search engines?

   _____

2. Print the WordPad document and write your name on the document.
3. Hand in the WordPad document to your instructor.

Part 7: *Resetting the Search Settings*

1. Click the Customize button in the Search pane.
2. In the Find a Web page area, click the AltaVista check box to remove the check mark from the check box.
3. In the Find a Web page area, click the Lycos check box to remove the check mark from the check box.
4. Click the OK button in the Customize Search Settings dialog box.
5. Close the Search pane and quit Internet Explorer.

Cases and Places

The difficulty of these case studies varies:
■ are the least difficult and ■■ are more difficult. The last exercise is a group exercise.

1 ■ Many new bands have their own home pages on the Web. Using the search engine of your choice, find out when and where the Red Elvises will be playing next. Find and print their home page. Next, find out when and where your favorite performer, band, or musical group will be playing next. Find and print their home page. Do these pages qualify as informational Web pages? Write your answer and the reasons supporting your position on one of the printouts and hand it in to your instructor.

2 ■ You have been hired by a local bicycle shop to compare their store prices with the prices available on the Internet. Search the Internet for Web pages that sell bicycles and bicycle parts. Find at least 10 items being sold by three different online bicycle stores. Develop a price list to compare the prices of the 10 items and hand in the price list to your instructor.

3 ■ You recently graduated from college and took a job at a small investment firm. Your first job is to search for and compare the services of the major online brokers. Find five online brokers and compare their services, costs to buy and sell stocks, Web sites, and any other pertinent information. Summarize your findings in a report.

4 ■■ Web search engines use different techniques for searching Web resources. If you were designing a search engine, what would you have the engine look for when determining whether a Web page successfully matches the keywords? Visit the Help page of a few search engines to get an idea of what criteria they use, and then write a list containing the criteria you would have your search engine use to determine whether a Web page is a successful match for keywords. Include an explanation for each item, such as the relative importance assigned, and then hand in the list and explanations.

5 ■■ A gopher is a computer system that allows computer users to find files on the Internet. Some federal, state, and local government agencies continue to use a gopher site to provide information and distribute documents and forms. Find one government agency that provides gopher services, learn to use its gopher, and write a brief report about the gopher. Include instructions to use the gopher, documents you found using the gopher, and whether you liked or disliked this method of finding information on the Internet.

Cases and Places

6 ■■ **Working Together** Computer security is a major concern for systems administrators. A very important first line of defense is an account name or user name and password. Choosing good passwords is important for security issues. Have each member of your group select a different search engine and then find three different Web sources (Web sites) that describe criteria for creating a good password. Each member should record the relevant information necessary for citing the sources using the MLA or APA style. Print the three Web pages and write the citation on each page using either the MLA or APA style. As a group, each member should present their findings to the class.

Communicating Over the Internet

PROJECT

3

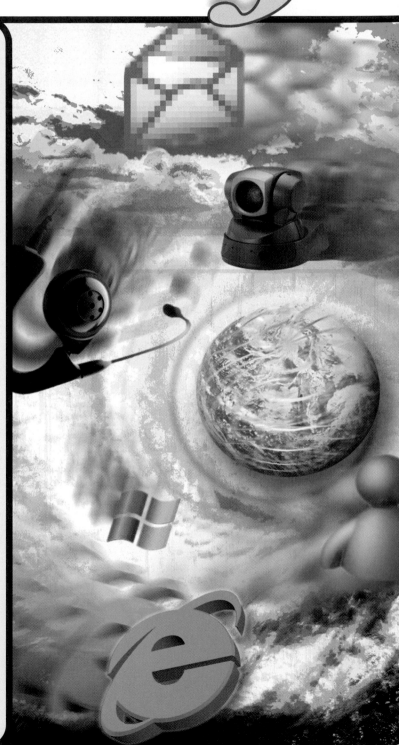

CASE PERSPECTIVE

Taking an Internet class at the local community college allowed you to learn more about the Internet. Now you think it would be a good idea to have some real-world experience. A fellow student tells you that you can find information about free Microsoft seminars on the Microsoft Web site. You take her recommendation and search the Microsoft Web site for free seminars. You find a seminar entitled, Communicating Over the Internet. You enroll in the free seminar.

You attend the Microsoft seminar. Before attending the seminar, you were unsure how to use the Internet to communicate. At the seminar, you watched an impressive presentation that included using Microsoft Outlook Express to send and receive e-mail messages and read and post messages to a newsgroup, using MSN Messenger to send instant messages, using a Web camera to conduct online meetings, and using Internet Explorer to listen to music from radio stations.

You were careful to make a list of the various ways to communicate over the Internet and the software programs that allow you to communicate. The list also included a reminder to buy a video camera and headset for your computer.

After purchasing and installing your newly acquired video camera and headset, you are ready to start communicating via online meetings. This idea seems to be a possible solution to the high cost of using the telephone to communicate with out-of-town friends, family, and business associates. Indeed! After only four months, you saved enough money to recover the original cost of the video camera.

As you read through this project, you will learn how to send and receive e-mail messages, read and post messages to a newsgroup, send instant messages, have an online meeting, and listen to music from radio stations around the world.

Communicating
Over the Internet

PROJECT

3

Objectives

You will have mastered the material in this project when you can:

- Open, read, print, reply to, and delete electronic mail messages
- View a file attachment
- Compose, format, and send electronic mail messages
- Add and delete an Address Book contact
- Search for and display newsgroups

- Read, post, and print newsgroup articles
- Subscribe and unsubscribe to a newsgroup
- Start and sign in to MSN Messenger
- Add and remove an MSN Messenger contact
- Send an instant message
- Have an online meeting
- Listen to an Internet radio station

Introduction

In Projects 1 and 2, you used Internet Explorer to search for information on the World Wide Web. In addition to searching for information, you also may use the Internet to communicate with other individuals. Web services designed for communicating over the Internet include Microsoft Outlook Express, which allows you to send and receive electronic mail and read and post messages to a newsgroup; MSN Messenger, which allows you to communicate with other MSN Messenger members by sending and receiving instant messages, and permitting you to engage in an online meeting; and the Media bar, which allows you to play music, video, or multimedia files, and listen to Internet radio stations. Project 3 illustrates the different types of communications available while using Internet Explorer.

Starting Internet Explorer

Before you can send and receive e-mail messages, read and post messages to a newsgroup, send and receive instant messages, engage in an online meeting, and work with multimedia, you must start Internet Explorer following the procedure you used in Project 1. The following step shows how to start Internet Explorer.

To Start Internet Explorer

1 **Click the Start button on the Windows taskbar, point to All Programs on the Start menu, and then click Internet Explorer on the All Programs submenu.**

The Microsoft Internet Explorer window with the MSN.com home page appears (Figure 3-1). The home page may be different on your computer.

FIGURE 3-1

Electronic (E-Mail) Messages

Electronic mail (**e-mail**) has become an important means of exchanging messages and files between business associates and friends. Businesses find that using e-mail to send documents electronically saves both time and money. Parents with students away at college or relatives who are scattered across the country find that exchanging e-mail messages is an inexpensive and easy way to stay in touch with their family members. In fact, exchanging e-mail messages is one of the more widely used features of the Internet.

Besides exchanging e-mail messages, another popular method of sharing information among individuals is to use Internet newsgroups. An **Internet newsgroup** contains articles and messages about many varied and interesting topics.

Microsoft Outlook Express allows you to receive and store incoming e-mail messages, compose and send e-mail messages, maintain a list of frequently used e-mail addresses, and read and post messages to Internet newsgroups.

Starting Microsoft Outlook Express

After starting Internet Explorer, you can start Microsoft Outlook Express using the Mail button on the Standard Buttons toolbar in the Microsoft Internet Explorer window. The following steps illustrate how to start Outlook Express.

To Start Microsoft Outlook Express

1

• **Click the Mail button on the Standard Buttons toolbar.**

The Mail menu containing five commands appears (Figure 3-2). Clicking the Read Mail command starts Outlook Express.

2

• **Click Read Mail on the Mail menu.**

• **If necessary, maximize the Inbox - Outlook Express window.**

The Outlook Express introductory screen appears momentarily while Outlook Express starts and then the maximized Inbox - Outlook Express - Steven Forsythe window is displayed (Figure 3-3). The window contains the Folders list, Contacts list, message list, and preview pane. The e-mail messages in the message list on your computer will be different.

Other Ways

1. Click Start button on Windows taskbar, point to All Programs, click Outlook Express on All Programs submenu
2. Press CTRL+ESC, press P, press O, press ENTER

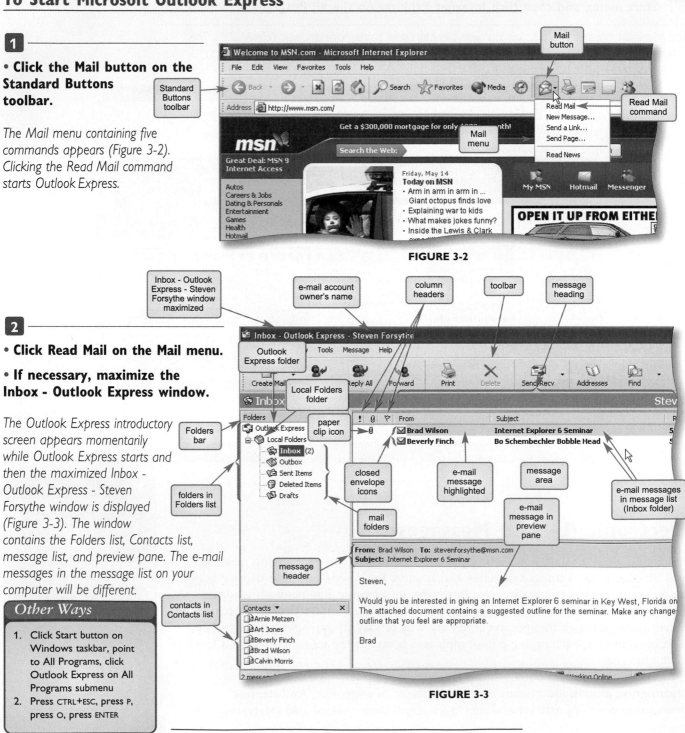

FIGURE 3-2

FIGURE 3-3

The Mail menu shown in Figure 3-2 contains commands to start Outlook Express (Read Mail), compose a new e-mail message (New Message), send an e-mail message containing a link of the currently displayed Web page (Send a Link), send an e-mail message containing the currently displayed Web page (Send Page), and access a newsgroup (Read News).

The Inbox - Outlook Express - Steven Forsythe window shown in Figure 3-3 contains a number of elements. The title bar contains the folder name (Inbox), the application name (Outlook Express), and the e-mail account owner's name (Steven Forsythe). The e-mail account owner's name and the e-mail messages in the message list may be different on your computer. Below the title bar and menu bar is a toolbar containing buttons specific to Outlook Express (Create Mail, Reply, Reply All, Forward, and so on). Table 3-1 contains the toolbar buttons and a brief explanation of their functions.

Table 3-1 Toolbar Buttons and Functions

BUTTON	FUNCTION
Create Mail	Displays the New Message window used to compose a new e-mail message.
Reply	Displays a window used to reply to an e-mail message. The recipient's name, original subject of the e-mail message preceded by the Re: entry, and the original e-mail message appear in the window.
Reply All	Displays a window used to reply to an e-mail message. The names of all recipients, subject of the e-mail message preceded by the Re: entry, and the original e-mail message appear in the window.
Forward	Displays a window used to forward an e-mail message to another recipient. The original subject of the e-mail message preceded by the Fw: entry and the original e-mail message appear in the window.
Print	Prints the highlighted e-mail message in the message list.
Delete	Deletes the highlighted e-mail message in the message list by moving the message to the Deleted Items folder.
Send/Recv	Displays the Outlook Express dialog box, contacts the mail server, sends any e-mail messages in the Outbox folder, and places new e-mail messages in the Inbox folder.
Addresses	Displays the Address Book window containing a list of frequently used contacts.
Find	Displays the Find Message window that allows you to search for an e-mail message in the message list based on sender name, recipient name, e-mail subject, e-mail message, and date.

The Inbox - Outlook Express - Steven Forsythe window is divided into four areas. The **Folders list** contains, in hierarchical structure, the Outlook Express folder, Local Folders folder, and the five mail folders contained in the Local Folders folder. Five standard mail folders (Inbox, Outbox, Sent Items, Deleted Items, and Drafts) are displayed when you first start Outlook Express. Although you cannot rename or delete these folders, you can create additional folders.

The two highest levels in the hierarchy are Outlook Express and Local Folders. Connected by a dotted vertical line below the Local Folders icon are the five standard mail folders icons. On some computers, the Local Folders folder may not be displayed and the mail folders are connected by a dotted vertical line below the Outlook Express folder.

The **Inbox folder** in Figure 3-3 on page IE 144 is the destination for incoming mail. The **Outbox folder** temporarily holds messages you send until Outlook Express delivers the messages. The **Sent Items folder** retains copies of messages that you have sent. The **Deleted Items folder** contains messages that you have deleted. As a safety precaution, you can retrieve deleted messages from the Deleted Items folder if you later decide you want to keep them. Deleting messages from the Deleted Items folder removes the messages permanently. The **Drafts folder** retains copies of messages that you are not yet ready to send.

Folders can contain e-mail messages, faxes, and files created in other Windows applications. Folders in bold type followed by a number in parentheses, **Inbox** (2), indicate the number of messages in the folder that are unopened. Other folders may appear on your computer instead of or in addition to the folders shown in Figure 3-3.

The **Contacts list** contains an alphabetical list of contacts in the Address Book. The **Address Book** is a central location for storing business and personal information (name, address, telephone number, e-mail address, and so on) about those individuals you contact frequently. An entry in the Address book is commonly referred to as a **contact**.

MSN Messenger members also may appear in the Contacts list. **MSN Messenger** allows you to communicate with other MSN Messenger members by sending and receiving instant messages. An MSN Messenger member also is referred to as a contact. No MSN Messenger members are displayed in the Contacts list.

The name of five Address book contacts appear in Figure 3-3. Double-clicking an entry in the Contacts list displays the New Message window that allows you to compose and send an e-mail message to another contact. Other contacts may appear on your computer instead of or in addition to the contacts shown in the Contacts list. If the Contacts list is not displayed, read the More About on this page to learn how to display the Contacts list.

The contents of the Inbox folder automatically appear in the **message list** in Figure 3-3 when Internet Explorer starts Outlook Express. Six column headers appear above the message list. An exclamation point icon (High Priority) identifies the first header, a paper clip icon (Attachment) identifies the second header, and a flag (Flagged) identifies the third header. An exclamation point icon in the column below the first header indicates the e-mail message has been marked high priority by the sender and should be read immediately. A paper clip icon in the column below the second header indicates the e-mail message contains an attachment (file or object). The first e-mail message in the message list (Brad Wilson) contains an attachment, as indicated by the paper clip icon. A flag icon in the column below the third header indicates the e-mail message has been flagged by the sender.

Entries in the columns below the fourth header (From), fifth header (Subject), and sixth header (Received) indicate the e-mail author's name or e-mail address, subject of the e-mail message, and date and time the message was received. Collectively, these last three entries are referred to as the **message heading**.

A closed envelope icon in the From column and a message heading that appears in bold type identifies an unread e-mail message. In Figure 3-3, the first e-mail message from Brad Wilson contains a paper clip icon, a closed envelope icon, and a message heading that appears in bold type. The closed envelope icon and bold message heading indicate the e-mail message has not been read (opened) and the paper clip indicates the e-mail message has an attachment. In addition, the e-mail message is highlighted because it is the first message in the message list.

The second e-mail message from Beverly Finch contains a closed envelope icon and a message heading that appears in bold type. The icon and bold message heading indicate the e-mail message has not been read. Other e-mail messages may display on your computer in place of or in addition to these messages.

More About

The Contacts List

If the Contacts list is not displayed in the Inbox - Outlook Express window, click View on the menu bar, click Layout, click Contacts, and then click the OK button.

More About

Column Headings

You can change the width of column headers in the message list by dragging the vertical line between two column headers.

More About

Message Headings

You can change the column widths of the column headers in the message list by dragging the vertical line between two column headers. To change the size of the two areas, drag the vertical line that separates the Folders list and Contacts list from the message list and preview pane.

The closed envelope icon is one of several icons, called **message list icons**, that display in the From column. Different message list icons may display in the From column to indicate the status of the message. The icon may indicate an action that was performed by the sender or one that was performed by the recipient. The actions may include reading, replying to, forwarding, digitally signing, or encrypting a message. Table 3-2 contains a partial list of message list icons and the action performed on the mail message.

Table 3-2 Message List Icons and Actions

MESSAGE LIST ICON	ACTION
	The message has been read.
	The message has not been read.
	The message has been replied to.
	The message has been forwarded.
	The message is in progress in the Drafts folder.
	The message is digitally signed and unopened.
	The message is encrypted and unopened.
	The message is digitally signed, encrypted and unopened.
	The message is digitally signed and has been opened.
	The message is encrypted and has been opened.
	The message is digitally signed, encrypted, and has been opened.

The **preview pane** in Figure 3-3 on page IE 144 contains the text of the highlighted e-mail message (Brad Wilson) in the message pane. The **message header** is displayed at the top of the preview pane and contains the sender's name (Brad Wilson), recipient's e-mail address (stevenforsythe@msn.com), and the e-mail subject (Internet Explorer 6 Seminar). The text of the highlighted e-mail message in the message list appears below the message header.

Opening and Reading E-Mail Messages

In Figure 3-3, the message headings for Brad Wilson and Beverly Finch are displayed in the message list. Double-clicking the closed envelope icon in either heading opens the e-mail message and displays the text of the message in a separate window. The step on the next page shows how to open the e-mail message from Beverly Finch.

To Open (Read) an E-Mail Message

1

• **Double-click the closed envelope icon to the left of the Beverly Finch name in the message list.**

• **Maximize the Bo Schembechler Bobble Head window.**

• **If the envelope icon for Beverly Finch is not displayed in the message list, double-click another closed envelope icon.**

The maximized Bo Schembechler Bobble Head window appears (Figure 3-4). The window contains a menu bar, toolbar, identifying information about the e-mail message, and message area. The subject of the e-mail message (Bo Schembechler Bobble Head) becomes the window title.

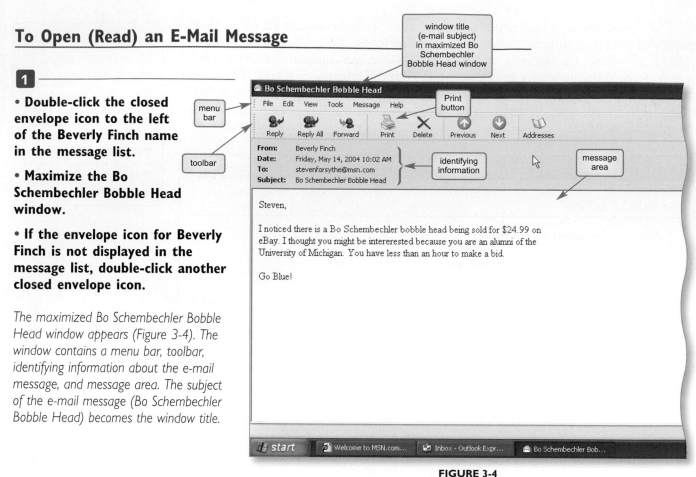

FIGURE 3-4

Other Ways

1. Right-click closed envelope icon, click Open on shortcut menu
2. Click closed envelope icon, on File menu click Open
3. Select message heading, press CTRL+O

When you double-click a closed envelope icon in the message list, Outlook Express displays the message in a separate window, changes the closed envelope icon to an opened envelope icon, and no longer displays the message heading in bold type.

Below the title bar and menu bar shown in Figure 3-4 is a toolbar that contains the buttons needed to work with opened e-mail messages (Reply, Reply All, Forward, and so on). Table 3-3 contains the toolbar buttons and a brief explanation of their functions.

Table 3-3   Toolbar Buttons and Functions

BUTTON	FUNCTION
Reply	Displays a window used to reply to an e-mail message. The e-mail address, original subject of the e-mail message preceded by the Re: entry, and original e-mail message appear in the window.
Reply All	Displays a window used to reply to an e-mail message. The e-mail addresses of all recipients, subject of the e-mail message preceded by the Re: entry, and original e-mail message appear in the window.
Forward	Displays a window used to forward an e-mail message to another recipient. The original subject of the e-mail message preceded by the Fw: entry and the original e-mail message appear in the window.
Print	Prints the e-mail message in the window.
Delete	Deletes the e-mail message in the window by moving the message to the Deleted Items folder and displays the next e-mail message in the message list.
Previous	Displays the previous e-mail message in the message list.
Next	Displays the next e-mail message in the message list.
Addresses	Displays the Address Book window containing a list of frequently used contacts.

Printing an E-Mail Message

You can print the contents of an e-mail message before or after opening the message. The following steps illustrate how to print an opened e-mail message.

To Print an Opened E-Mail Message

1

• **Click the Print button on the toolbar.**

The Print dialog box appears (Figure 3-5).

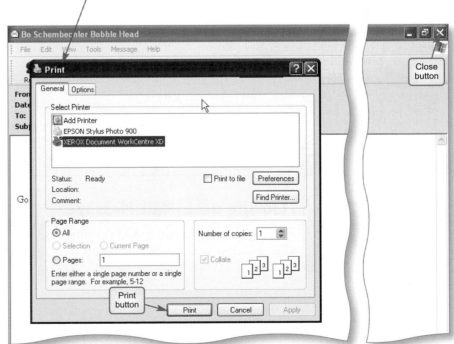

FIGURE 3-5

2

• **Click the Print button in the Print dialog box.**

The printed message consists of a header at the top of the page containing the page number (Page 1 of 1), the recipient's name (Steven Forsythe), and a horizontal line (Figure 3-6). The line is heavier below the recipient's name. Below the recipient's name are the From, To, Sent, and Subject entries, and the e-mail message. A footer at the bottom of the page contains the current date (5/14/2005).

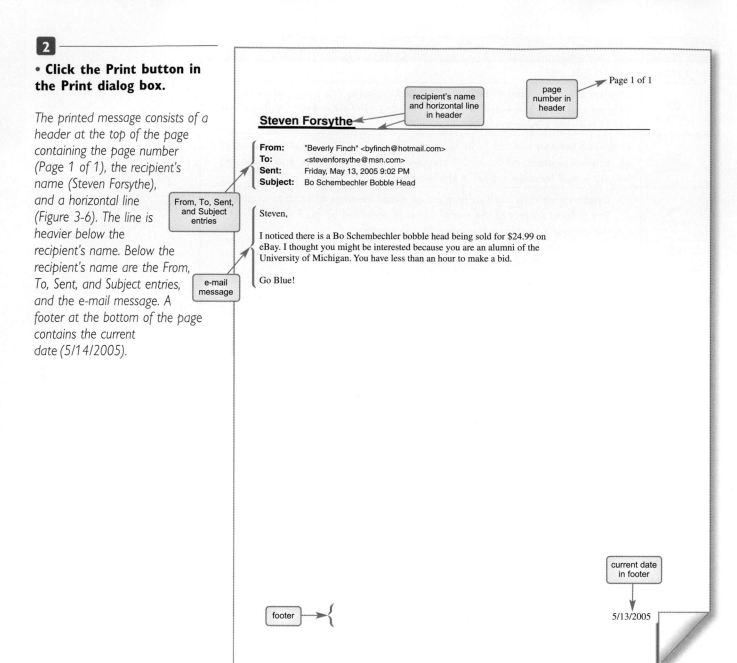

recipient's name and horizontal line in header

page number in header

Page 1 of 1

Steven Forsythe

From:	"Beverly Finch" <byfinch@hotmail.com>
To:	<stevenforsythe@msn.com>
Sent:	Friday, May 13, 2005 9:02 PM
Subject:	Bo Schembechler Bobble Head

From, To, Sent, and Subject entries

Steven,

I noticed there is a Bo Schembechler bobble head being sold for $24.99 on eBay. I thought you might be interested because you are an alumni of the University of Michigan. You have less than an hour to make a bid.

Go Blue!

e-mail message

current date in footer

footer

5/13/2005

FIGURE 3-6

Other Ways

1. On File menu click Print, click Print button in Print dialog box
2. Press ALT+F, press P, press ENTER
3. Press CTRL+P, press ENTER

Closing an E-Mail Message

When you have finished opening and reading an e-mail message, you can close the window containing the e-mail message by following the step on the next page.

To Close an E-Mail Message

1

• **Click the Close button on the title bar (Figure 3-6).**

The Bo Schembechler Bobble Head window closes and the Inbox - Outlook Express - Steven Forsythe window appears (Figure 3-7). An open envelope icon replaces the closed envelope icon preceding the Beverly Finch message heading and the Inbox entry in the Folders list, Inbox (1), indicates one e-mail message (Brad Wilson) remains unopened.

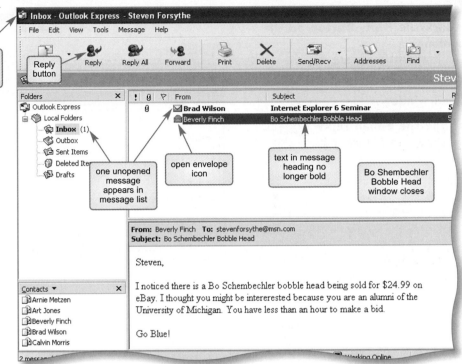

FIGURE 3-7

Other Ways
1. On File menu click Close
2. Press ALT+F4

When you double-click a closed envelope icon in the message list, Outlook Express opens the message and displays its contents in a separate window. When you close the window, the e-mail message heading in the message list in the Inbox - Outlook Express - Steven Forsythe window no longer appears in bold type and the closed envelope icon changes to an open envelope icon to indicate the e-mail message has been opened. In addition, the Inbox entry, Inbox (1), shows only one e-mail message is unopened.

Replying to an E-Mail Message

As mentioned previously, the Address Book is a central location for storing business and personal information about individuals you contact frequently. When you reply to an e-mail message, Outlook Express adds the business and personal information about the sender to the Address Book. Once a contact is added to the Address Book, Outlook Express can use the Address Book to find the e-mail address needed to reply to the e-mail message or to use when composing a new e-mail message.

The next steps illustrate composing and sending an e-mail reply to a sender; in this case, Beverly Finch, using the Reply button. The Reply button on the toolbar allows you to reply quickly to an e-mail message using the sender's e-mail address. The steps on the next page illustrate how to compose and send an e-mail reply to a sender, in this case, Beverly Finch, using the Reply button.

More About

Replying to an E-Mail Message

Some people who receive reply e-mail messages find it awkward that the original e-mail message appears with the reply message. To remove the original message from all e-mail replies, click Tools on the menu bar, click Options, click the Send tab, click the Include message in reply check box, and then click the OK button.

To Reply to an E-Mail Message

1

• **Click the Reply button on the toolbar.**

• **Maximize the Re: Bo Schembechler Bobble Head window.**

• **Type the e-mail reply as shown in Figure 3-8.**

The Re: Bo Schembechler Bobble Head window appears (Figure 3-8). The Re: entry and subject are displayed in the window title and Subject text box. A toolbar and three text boxes are displayed. The e-mail reply and original message appear in the message area.

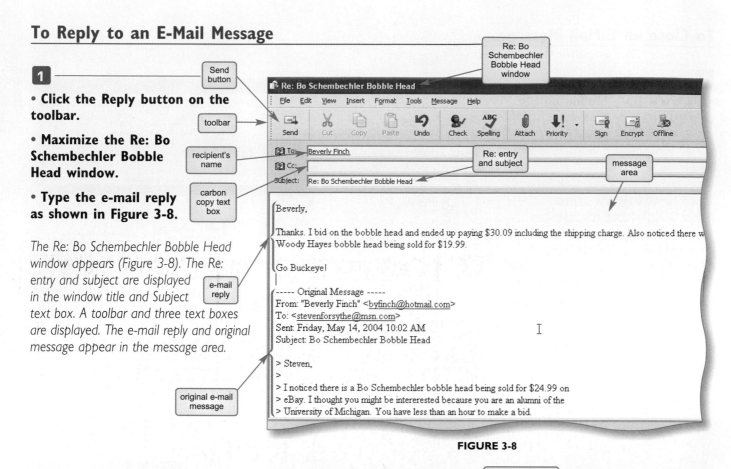

FIGURE 3-8

2

• **Click the Send button on the toolbar.**

The Re: Bo Schembechler Bobble Head window closes, Outlook Express stores the reply e-mail message in the Outbox folder while it sends the message, and then moves the message to the Sent Items folder (Figure 3-9).

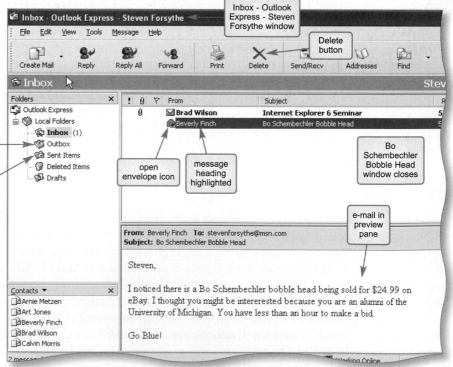

FIGURE 3-9

Other Ways

1. On Message menu click Reply to Sender
2. Press CTRL+R

In Figure 3-9, the highlighted Beverly Finch message heading appears in the message list and the e-mail message is displayed in the preview pane. The open envelope icon to the left of the Beverly Finch entry in the message list contains an arrow to indicate that the message has been replied to.

In Figure 3-8, the underlined Beverly Finch name appears in the To text box and the original e-mail message is identified by the words, Original Message, and the From, To, Sent, and Subject entries in the message list. In addition, the window contains a toolbar below the menu bar. The buttons on the toolbar below the menu bar (Send, Cut, Copy, Paste, and so on) are useful when replying to a message. Table 3-4 shows the buttons on the toolbar below the menu bar and their functions.

Table 3-4 Toolbar Buttons and Functions	
BUTTON	**FUNCTION**
Send	Places the e-mail message in the Outbox folder temporarily while the message is sent and then moves the message to the Sent Items folder.
Cut	Moves a selected item in an e-mail message to the Clipboard.
Copy	Copies a selected item in an e-mail message to the Clipboard.
Paste	Copies an item from the Clipboard to an e-mail message.
Undo	Undoes the previous operation.
Check	Checks the recipient's name against the Address Book.
Spelling	Spell checks the e-mail message.
Attach	Attaches a file to the e-mail message.
Priority	Sets the priority (high, normal, or low) of an e-mail message.
Sign	Digitally signs an e-mail message, allowing the recipient to verify the sender's identity.
Encrypt	Encrypts, or scrambles, an e-mail message, preventing someone other than the recipient from reading the message.
Offline	Allows you to work offline.

As you send and reply to messages, the number of messages in the Sent Items folder increases. To delete an e-mail message from the Sent Items folder, click the Sent Items folder icon in the Folders list, highlight the message in the message list, and then click the Delete button in the Outlook Express dialog box.

More About

Mail Folders

You can reduce the hard disk space required by a mail folder by clicking the folder in the Folders list, clicking File on the menu bar, pointing to Folder, and then clicking Compact on the Folder submenu. To compact all folders, click the Compact All command instead of the Compact command. It may take several minutes to compact all folders.

Deleting an E-Mail Message

After reading and replying to an e-mail message, you may want to delete the original e-mail message from the message list. Deleting a message removes the e-mail message from the Inbox folder. If you do not delete unwanted messages, large numbers of messages in the Inbox folder make it difficult to find and read new messages and wastes disk space. The following step shows how to delete the e-mail message from Beverly Finch.

To Delete an E-Mail Message

1

• **Click the Delete button on the toolbar.**

Outlook Express moves the Beverly Finch e-mail message from the Inbox folder to the Deleted Items folder and removes the e-mail entry from the message list (Figure 3-10).

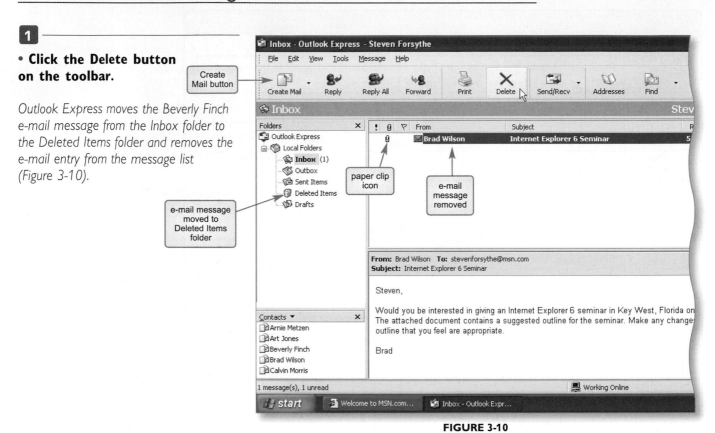

FIGURE 3-10

Other Ways

1. Drag e-mail message to Deleted Items folder in Folders list
2. On Edit menu click Delete
3. Right-click e-mail message, click Delete on shortcut menu
4. Press CTRL+D

As you delete messages from the Inbox, the number of messages in the Deleted Items folder increases. To delete an e-mail message from the Deleted Items folder, click the Deleted Items folder icon in the Folders list, highlight the message in the message list, click the Delete button, and then click the Yes button in the Outlook Express dialog box.

Viewing a File Attachment

The remaining message in the message list, Brad Wilson, contains a file attachment. A paper clip icon in the column below the second header in Figure 3-10 indicates the e-mail message contains a file attachment (file or object). The following steps illustrate how to view the file attachment.

To View a File Attachment

1

• **Double-click the paper clip icon to the left of the Brad Wilson name in the message list.**

• **Maximize the Internet Explorer 6 Seminar window.**

The maximized Internet Explorer 6 Seminar window appears (Figure 3-11). The Attach box, containing a text document icon, Internet Explorer 6 Outline.txt document name, and file size (306 bytes) are displayed above the message list.

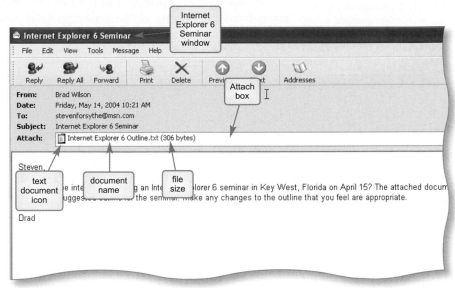

FIGURE 3-11

2

• **Double-click the Internet Explorer 6 Outline.txt icon in the Attach box.**

The Internet Explorer 6 Outline - Notepad window, containing the outline, appears (Figure 3-12).

3

• **Click the Close button in the Internet Explorer 6 Outline - Notepad window.**

• **Click the Close button in the Internet Explorer 6 Seminar window.**

The Internet Explorer 6 Outline - Notepad window and Internet Explorer 6 Seminar window close.

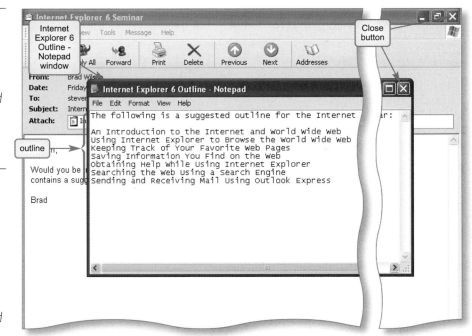

FIGURE 3-12

   File attachments can be anything from spreadsheets to pictures. Outlook Express gives you the option of viewing the attachment as you read the e-mail, or you can save it to a file to view at another time.

Q & A

Q: Can I use stationery for all my outgoing messages?

A: Yes. To uses stationery for all your outgoing messages, click Tools on the menu bar, click Options, click the Compose tab, select the Mail and/or News check box in the Stationery area, and then click the Select button.

Composing a New Mail Message

In addition to opening and reading, replying to, and deleting e-mail messages, users frequently want to compose and send new e-mail messages. When composing an e-mail message, you must know the e-mail address of the recipient of the message, enter a brief one-line subject that identifies the purpose or contents of the message, and type the message itself.

You also can format an e-mail message to enhance the appearance of the message. **Formatting** is the process of enhancing the appearance of a document by changing the background of the document, and the style, size, and color of the text in the document. One method of formatting an e-mail message is to select a stationery. **Stationery** allows you to add a colorful background image, unique text sizes and colors, and custom margins to an e-mail message. In the following steps, selecting the Leaves stationery causes a decorative banner to appear on a light brown background and the text of the e-mail message to appear using the Arial 10-point font and brown text. The **Arial font** is one of many fonts, or typefaces, available to format an e-mail message. In addition, any links within the e-mail message will be underlined and displayed in blue text.

The next steps show how to select the Leaves stationery and compose an e-mail message to one of the authors (Steven Forsythe) of this book.

To Compose an E-Mail Message Using Stationery

1

• **Click the Create Mail button arrow on the toolbar.**

The Create Mail menu, containing a list of ten stationeries, appears (Figure 3-13). The number and types of stationeries in the list may be different on your computer.

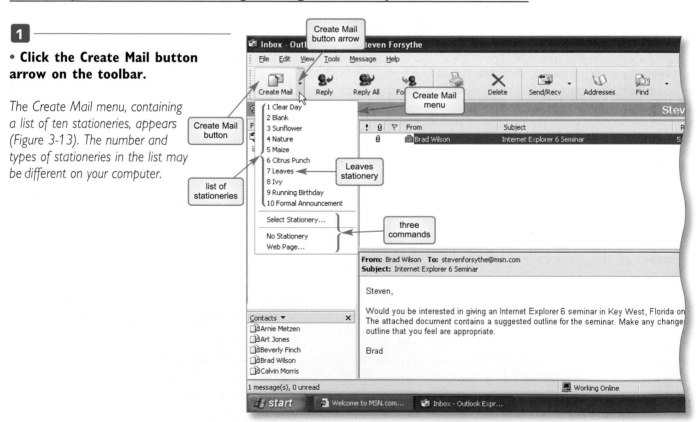

FIGURE 3-13

2

• **Click Leaves on the Create Mail menu.**

• **Maximize the New Message window.**

The New Message window appears (Figure 3-14). The window contains a menu bar, toolbar, three text boxes, dimmed Formatting toolbar, and message area. The insertion point is located in the To text box and the Leaves stationery, containing a decorative banner, is displayed in the message area.

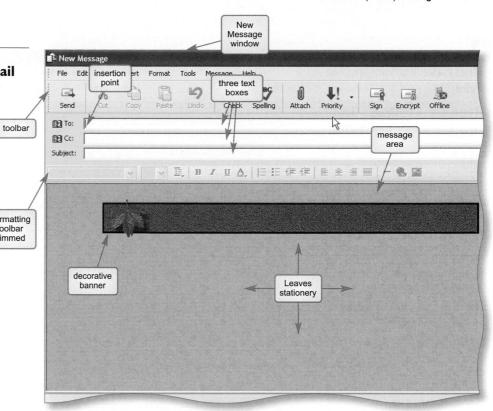

FIGURE 3-14

3

• **Type** stevenforsythe@msn.com **in the To text box.**

• **Click the Subject text box.**

• **Type** Internet Bookstore **in the Subject text box.**

The destination e-mail address appears in the To text box and the subject of the message is displayed in the Subject text box (Figure 3-15). The title of the New Message window changes to the subject of the e-mail message (Internet Bookstore).

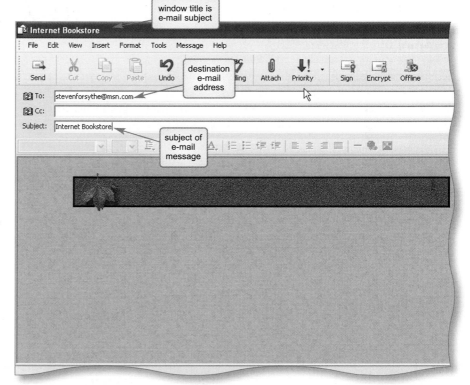

FIGURE 3-15

4

• **Press the TAB key on the keyboard.**

• **Type** Great News! **and then press the ENTER key twice.**

• **Type** Your books are being sold on the Internet. Click this URL to look for your books: www.amazon.com. **in the message area and then press the ENTER key twice.**

• **Type your name and then press the ENTER key.**

The Formatting toolbar is no longer dimmed and the formatted e-mail message appears in the message area (Figure 3-16). The message appears using the Arial 10-point font in brown color and the link is underlined and displayed in blue text. In this case, the sender's name is Pam Wilson.

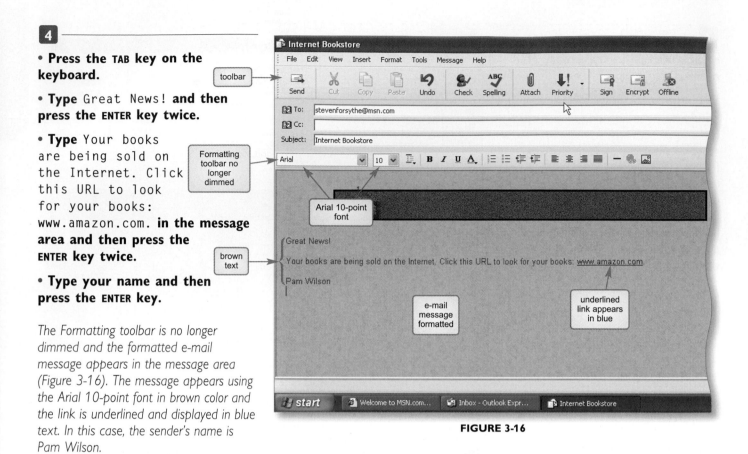

FIGURE 3-16

In Figure 3-13 on page IE 156, the three commands at the bottom of the menu allow you to select from a larger list of stationeries, select to use no stationery, or to send a Web page as an e-mail message.

The **Formatting toolbar** shown in Figure 3-16 allows you to change the appearance, size, and color of text; bold, italicize, or underline text; create a numbered or bulleted list; change paragraph indentation or align text; and create a link or insert a picture in an e-mail message.

The Internet Bookstore message window contains two toolbars. The toolbar containing buttons specific to replying to an e-mail or composing a new e-mail message are displayed below the menu bar and the Formatting toolbar is displayed below the Subject text box. The buttons on the toolbar below the menu bar are explained in Table 3-4 on page IE 153. Table 3-5 shows the buttons and boxes on the Formatting toolbar in Figure 3-16 and their functions.

Table 3-5 Formatting Toolbar Buttons / Boxes and Functions

BUTTON/BOX	FUNCTION	BUTTON/BOX	FUNCTION
Arial	Changes the font of text in the message.		Decreases the indentation of a paragraph.
10	Changes the font size of text in the message.		Increases the indentation of a paragraph.
	Changes the paragraph style in the message.		Aligns text with the left margin.
B	Bolds text in the message.		Centers text between the left and right margins.
I	Italicizes text in the message.		Aligns text with the right margin.
U	Underlines text in the message.		Aligns text with the left and right margins.
A	Changes the color of text in the message.		Adds a horizontal line to the message.
	Creates a numbered list in the message.		Inserts a link in the message.
	Creates a bulleted list in the message.		Inserts a picture in the message.

Formatting an E-Mail Message

When you select the Leaves stationery, the stationery formats the text in the e-mail message using the Arial 10-point font and brown text. In addition to selecting stationery, the Formatting toolbar allows you to add additional formatting to an e-mail message. Formatting includes changing the appearance, size, and color of text; bolding, italicizing, and underlining text; creating a numbered or bulleted list; changing paragraph indentation or aligning text; and creating a link and inserting a picture into an e-mail message.

You change the size of text by selecting a font size. A **font size** is measured in **points**. One inch contains 72 points. Thus, a font size of 36 points is approximately one-half inch in height. The steps on the next page show how to center the text, Great News!, and format the text using the 36-point font size.

To Format an E-Mail Message

1

• **Select the words, Great News!, in the first line of the e-mail message by pointing to either word (Great or News!) and then triple-click the word.**

The words, Great News!, are highlighted (Figure 3-17).

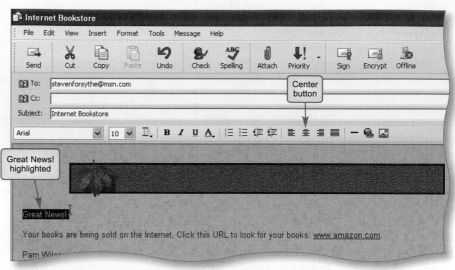

FIGURE 3-17

2

• **Click the Center button on the Formatting toolbar.**

The words, Great News!, are centered on the first line of the e-mail message and the Center button on the Formatting toolbar is active (Figure 3-18).

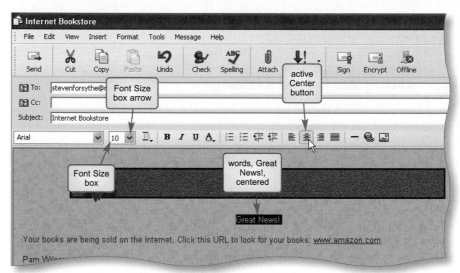

FIGURE 3-18

3

• **Click the Font Size box arrow.**

The Font Size list appears and the number 10 is highlighted in the list (Figure 3-19).

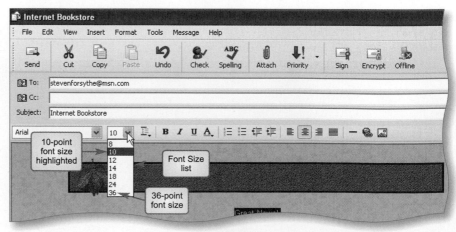

FIGURE 3-19

4

- **Click 36 in the Font Size list.**
- **Click the highlighted text to remove the highlight.**

The words, Great News!, appear in the 36-point font size, the font size 36 is displayed in the Font Size box, and the insertion point is displayed between the two words (Figure 3-20).

FIGURE 3-20

Sending an E-Mail Message

After composing and formatting an e-mail message, send the message. The following step illustrates how to send an e-mail message.

To Send an E-Mail Message

1 **Click the Send button on the toolbar below the menu bar.**

The Internet Bookstore window closes, Outlook Express stores the e-mail message in the Outbox folder temporarily while it sends the message, and then it moves the message to the Sent Items folder (Figure 3-21).

> **More About**
>
> **Abbreviations in an E-Mail Message**
>
> The use of abbreviations has become popular when composing an e-mail message. For example, you can use ASAP for As soon as possible, CU for See you later, NRN for No reply necessary, PLS for Please, and THX for Thank you.

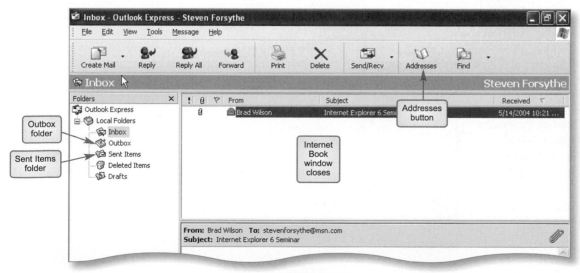

FIGURE 3-21

Address Book

The **Address Book** application included with Outlook Express allows you to store contact information including e-mail addresses, home and work addresses, telephone and fax numbers, digital IDs, conferencing information, instant messaging addresses, and personal information such as birthdays or anniversaries. The information stored in the Address Book about an individual is referred to as a **contact**.

Although most contact information is stored in the **Steven Forsythe's Contact folder**, the Address Book also allows you to create other folders in which to store groups of contacts, making it easy to send an e-mail message to a group of contacts, such as business associates, relatives, or friends. In addition, moving a contact to the **Shared Contacts folder** allows other computer users on the same computer access to the contact information.

Previously, an e-mail message was composed, formatted, and sent to one of the authors of this textbook. The author's e-mail address was typed into the To text box (see Figure 3-15 on page IE 157). The following sections show you how to add a contact for Annie Meyer to the Address Book, edit the contact information, print the contact information, send an e-mail to the contact, and delete the contact information.

Adding a Contact to the Address Book

Before using the Address Book to send an e-mail to an individual, it is a good idea to add the contact information to the Address Book. The following steps illustrate how to add the contact information (first name, last name, e-mail address, home telephone, and business telephone) for Annie Meyer.

To Add a Contact to the Address Book

1

• **Click the Addresses button on the toolbar in the Inbox - Outlook Express - Steven Forsythe window.**

• **Maximize the Address Book - Steven Forsythe window.**

The maximized Address Book - Steven Forsythe window appears (Figure 3-22). The window contains a toolbar, the Folders list contains the Shared Contacts and Steven Forsythe's Contacts folders, and the Address Book list contains a text box, four column headers, and the contact information of five contacts.

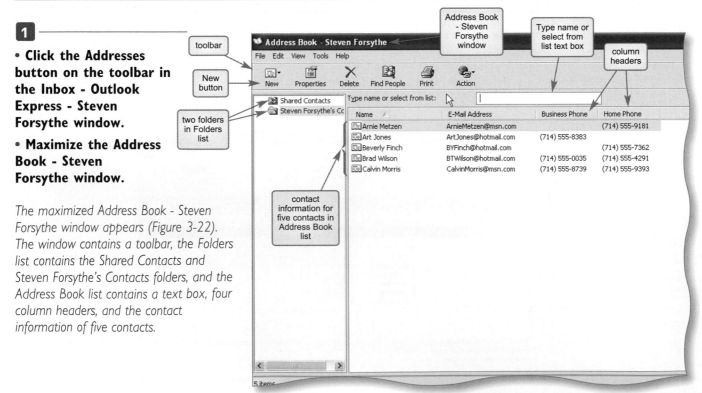

FIGURE 3-22

2

• **Click the New button on the toolbar.**

The New menu containing the New Contact, New Group, and New Folder commands appears (Figure 3-23).

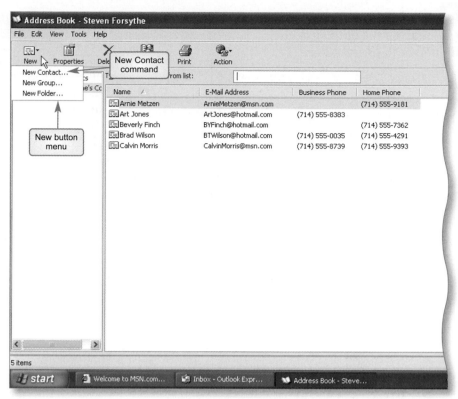

FIGURE 3-23

3

• **Click New Contact on the New button menu.**

• **Type** Annie **in the First text box.**

• **Click the Last text box and then type** Meyer **in the text box.**

• **Click the E-Mail Addresses text box and then type** agmeyer@hotmail.com **in the text box.**

The Annie Meyer Properties dialog box with the Name sheet active appears (Figure 3-24). As you type the first name (Annie) and last name (Meyer), the names appear in the Display text box and are added to the title of the dialog box. The e-mail address (agmeyer@hotmail.com) is displayed in the E-Mail Addresses text box.

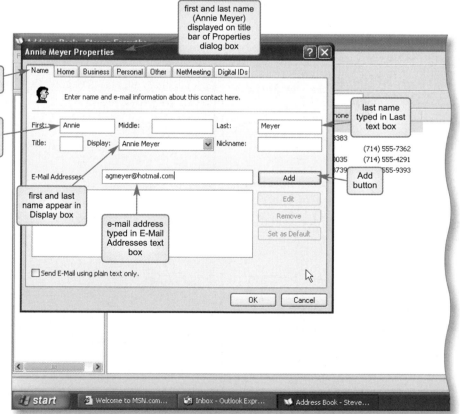

FIGURE 3-24

4

• **Click the Add button in the Name sheet.**

The e-mail address in the E-Mail Addresses text box is removed and is displayed in the E-mail list box (Figure 3-25). A letter icon precedes the e-mail address and the entry, (Default E-Mail), appears following the e-mail address.

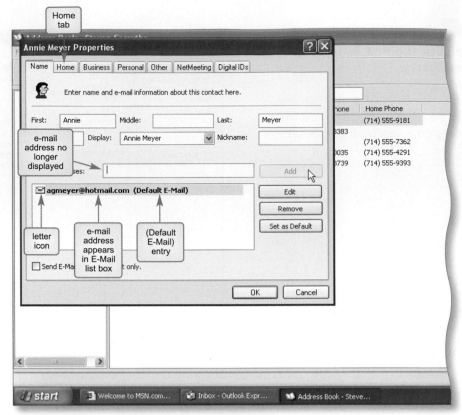

FIGURE 3-25

5

• **Click the Home tab in the Annie Meyer Properties dialog box.**

• **Type** 173 Winding Lane **in the Street Address text box.**

• **Click the City text box and then type** Brea **as the name of the city.**

• **Click the State/Province text box and then type** CA **as the name of the state.**

• **Click the Zip Code text box and then type** 92821 **as the Zip code.**

• **Click the Phone text box and then type** (714) 555-3292 **as the telephone number.**

The Home sheet appears in the dialog box and the street address, city, state, Zip code, and home telephone number are entered in the Home sheet (Figure 3-26).

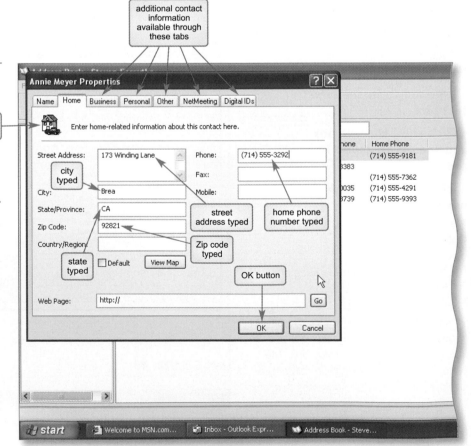

FIGURE 3-26

6

• **Click the OK button in the Annie Meyer Properties dialog box.**

The Annie Meyer Properties dialog box closes and an entry for the new contact is added to the Address Book list in the Address Book - Steven Forsythe window (Figure 3-27).

7

• **Click the Close button in the Address Book window.**

The Address Book - Steven Forsythe window closes.

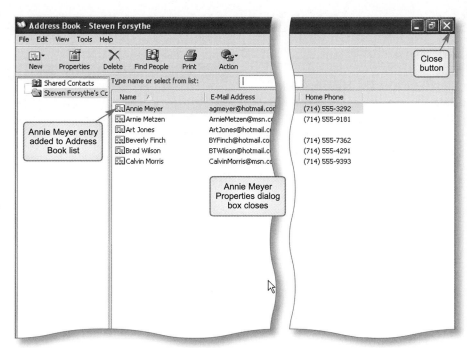

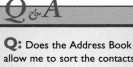

FIGURE 3-27

After entering the contact information, you can update the information, copy the contact to another folder, or delete the contact. In addition, you can use the contact information to dial a telephone number, send an e-mail message, or have an online meeting.

Clicking the Business tab shown in Figure 3-26 allows you to enter a company name, business address (street address, city, state/province, Zip code, and country/region), business information (job title, department, and office), telephone numbers (telephone, fax, pager, and IP), view the company Web page, and view a map of the business location.

Clicking the Personal tab allows you to enter personal information (spouse's name, children's names, gender, birthday, and anniversary date). Clicking the Other tab allows you to enter notes and group memberships, and view the location of the folder containing the contact information. Clicking the NetMeeting tab allows you to enter Windows NetMeeting information (conference server name and conference address) and start a video conferencing session.

Clicking the Digital IDs tab allows you to select an e-mail address and view the Digital IDs of the e-mail address. A **Digital ID** allows you to encrypt messages sent over the Internet and to prove your identity in an electronic transaction on the Internet in a manner similar to showing your driver's license when you cash a check.

Composing an E-Mail Message Using the Address Book

When you compose an e-mail message, you must know the e-mail address of the recipient of the message. Previous steps illustrated how to compose an e-mail message by typing the e-mail address in the To text box in the New Message window (see Figure 3-15 on page IE 157). In addition to entering an e-mail address by typing the e-mail address, you can enter an e-mail address using the Address Book. The steps on the next page show how to select the Clear Day stationery and compose an e-mail message to Annie Meyer using her e-mail address in the Address Book.

Q & A

Q: Does the Address Book allow me to sort the contacts in the Contacts list?

A: Yes. You can sort the contacts in the Contacts list in one of four ways: name, e-mail address, business phone, or home phone. You sort the contacts by clicking the Name, E-Mail Address, Business Phone, or Home Phone button at the top of the Contacts list.

To Compose an E-Mail Message Using the Address Book

1

• **Click the Create Mail button arrow.**

The maximized Create Mail menu, containing a list of 10 stationeries, appears (Figure 3-28).

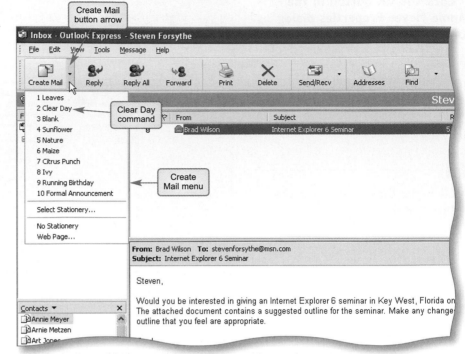

FIGURE 3-28

2

• **Click Clear Day on the Create Mail menu.**

• **Maximize the New Message window.**

The New Message window appears (Figure 3-29). The window contains a menu bar, toolbar, three text boxes, dimmed Formatting toolbar, and message area. The insertion point is located in the To text box and the Clear Day stationery is displayed in the message area.

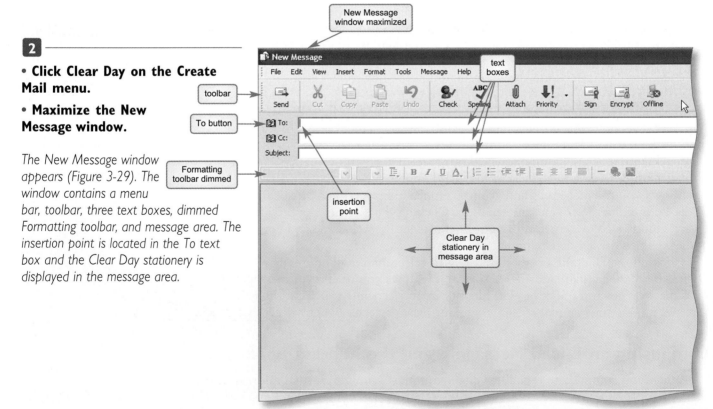

FIGURE 3-29

3

• **Click the To button in the New Message window.**

• **Click the Annie Meyer entry in the E-Mail Address list box.**

The Select Recipients dialog box appears and the Annie Meyer entry in the E-Mail Address list box is highlighted (Figure 3-30).

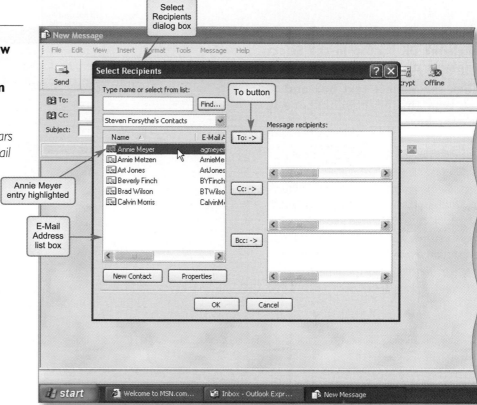

FIGURE 3-30

4

• **Click the To button in the Select Recipients dialog box.**

The Annie Meyer entry is highlighted in light gray in the E-Mail Address list box and appears in the To list box (Figure 3-31).

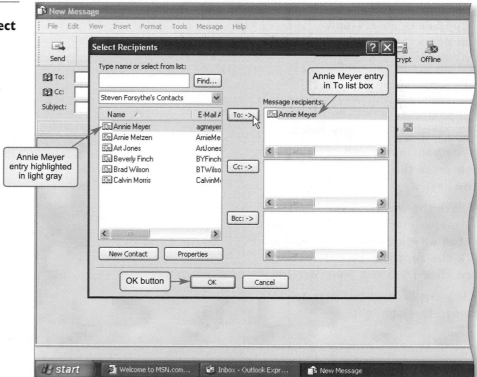

FIGURE 3-31

5

• **Click the OK button in the Select Recipients dialog box.**

• **Click the Subject text box and then type** Internet Bookstore **in the text box.**

The Select Recipient's dialog box closes, and the underlined Annie Meyer entry appears in the To text box in the Internet Bookstore window. As the subject is typed in the Subject text box, the subject appears in the Subject text box and the window title (New Message) changes to the subject of the e-mail (Internet Bookstore) (Figure 3-32).

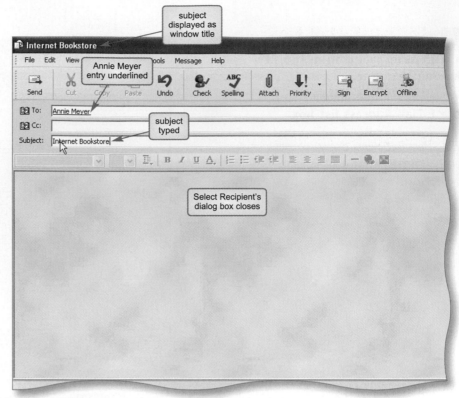

FIGURE 3-32

6

• **Press the TAB key.**

• **Type** Great News! **and then press the ENTER key twice.**

• **Type** I have learned to enter an e-mail address using the Address Book. **and then press the ENTER key twice.**

• **Type your name and then press the ENTER key.**

• **Select the words, Great News!, in the message area, click the Center button on the Formatting toolbar, click the Font size box arrow, and then click 36 in the Font Size list.**

• **Click the highlighted text to remove the highlight.**

The formatted e-mail message appears in the message area using the Arial 10-point font in blue text and the words, Great News!, are centered and displayed in the 36-point font size (Figure 3-33).

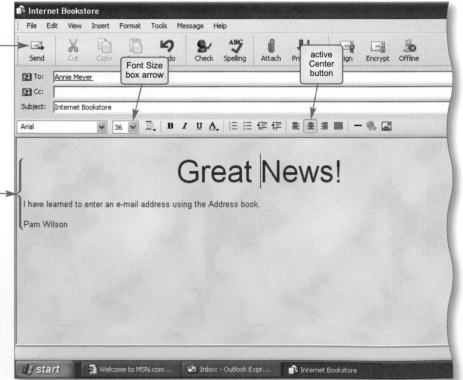

FIGURE 3-33

Sending an E-Mail Message

After retrieving an e-mail address from the Address Book and composing and formatting the e-mail message, send the message. The following step shows how to send the message.

To Send an E-Mail Message

1 Click the Send button on the toolbar.

The Internet Bookstore window closes, Outlook Express stores the e-mail message in the Outbox folder temporarily while it sends the message, and then it moves the message to the Sent Items folder (Figure 3-34). The Inbox - Outlook Express - Steven Forsythe window remains on the desktop.

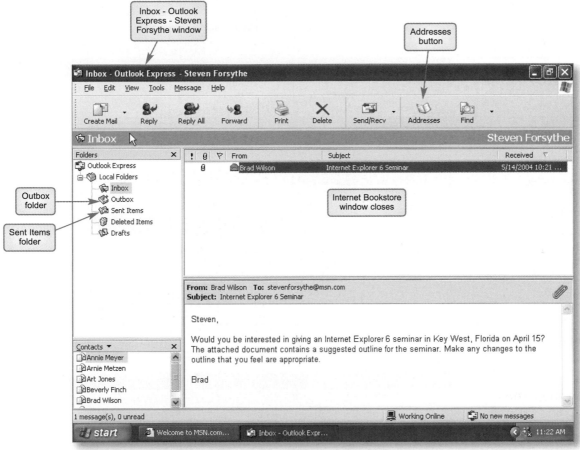

FIGURE 3-34

Deleting a Contact from the Address Book

After adding a contact to the Address Book, you may want to remove the contact. The steps on the next page illustrate how to remove the Annie Meyer contact from the Address Book.

To Delete a Contact from the Address Book

1

• **Click the Addresses button on the toolbar.**

• **Maximize the Address Book - Steven Forsythe window.**

• **Click the Annie Meyer entry in the E-Mail Address list box.**

The Address Book - Steven Forsythe window appears and the Annie Meyer entry is highlighted in the Address Book list (Figure 3-35).

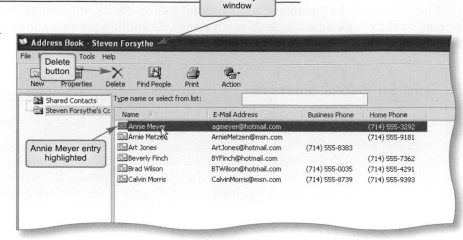

FIGURE 3-35

2

• **Click the Delete button on the toolbar.**

The Address Book - Steven Forsythe dialog box appears (Figure 3-36). A question in the dialog box asks if you want to permanently delete the selected item.

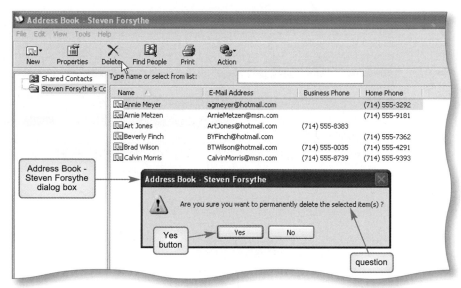

FIGURE 3-36

3

• **Click the Yes button in the Address Book - Steven Forsythe dialog box.**

The Annie Meyer entry is removed from the Address Book list in the Address Book - Steven Forsythe window (Figure 3-37). The contact information for Annie Meyer is removed from the Address Book.

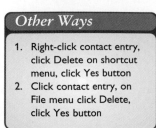

Other Ways

1. Right-click contact entry, click Delete on shortcut menu, click Yes button
2. Click contact entry, on File menu click Delete, click Yes button

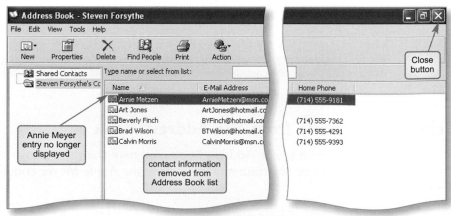

FIGURE 3-37

Quitting Address Book

Once you have finished adding a contact to the Address Book, composing and sending an e-mail message, and deleting an Address Book contact, you should quit the Address Book. The following steps show how to quit Address Book.

To Quit the Address Book

1 **Click the Close button on the Address Book - Steven Forsythe window.**

2 **Click the Close button in the Inbox - Outlook Express - Steven Forsythe window.**

The Address Book - Steven Forsythe window closes, the Inbox - Outlook Express - Steven Forsythe window closes, and the Internet Explorer window remains on the desktop.

Internet Newsgroups

Besides exchanging e-mail messages, another popular method of communicating over the Internet is to read and place messages on a **newsgroup**. A newsgroup is one of a collection of news and discussion groups that you can access via the Internet. Each newsgroup is devoted to a particular subject. A special computer, called a **news server**, contains related groups of newsgroups.

To participate in a newsgroup, you must use a program called a **newsreader**. The newsreader enables you to access a newsgroup to read a previously entered message, called an **article**, or add an article, called **posting**. A newsreader also keeps track of which articles you have and have not read. In this project, Outlook Express, which is a newsreader, is used to read and post articles.

Newsgroup members often post articles in reply to other articles - either to answer questions or to comment on material in the original articles. These replies often cause the author of the original article, or others, to post additional articles related to the original article. This process can be short-lived or go on indefinitely depending on the nature of the topic and the interest of the participants. The original article and all subsequent related replies are called a **thread**, or **thread discussion**. Figure 3-38 on the next page shows some articles and threads from a newsgroup called microsoft.public.games.ageofkings.

More About

Newsgroup Articles

Many newsgroup articles contain pictures, movies, and sound clips. Check the newsgroup name for the words, pictures, movies, or audio.

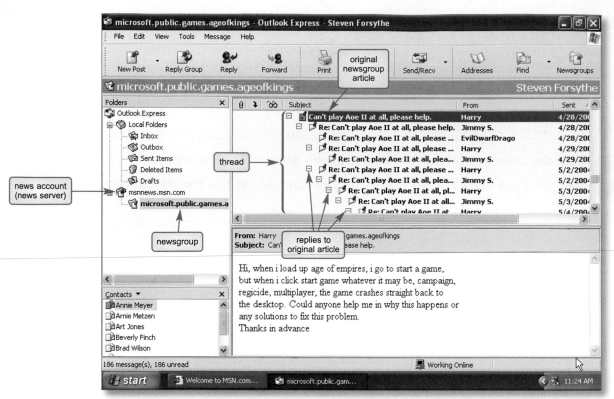

FIGURE 3-38

More About

Local Newsgroups

Many schools maintain a local newsgroup to disseminate information about school events and answer technical questions asked by students. To locate your local newsgroup, search for the school's name in the list of newsgroup names.

Newsgroups exist on products from vendors such as Microsoft and IBM; on subjects such as recipes, gardening, and music; or on just about any other topic you can imagine. A **newsgroup name** consists of a **prefix** and one or more subgroup names. For example, the comp.software newsgroup name consists of a prefix (comp), which indicates that the subject of the newsgroup is computers, a period (.), and a **subgroup name** (software), which indicates that the subject is further narrowed down to a discussion of software. A list of some prefix names and their descriptions are shown in Table 3-6.

Table 3-6 Prefix Names and Descriptions

PREFIX	DESCRIPTION
alt	Groups on alternative topics
biz	Business topics
comp	Computer topics
gnu	GNU Software Foundation topics
ieee	Electrical engineering topics
info	Information about various topics
misc	Miscellaneous topics
news	Groups pertaining to newsgroups
rec	Recreational topics
sci	Science topics
talk	Various conversation groups

The newsgroup prefixes found in Table 3-6 are not the only ones used. Innovative newsgroups are being created everyday. Many colleges and universities have their own newsgroups on topics such as administrative information, tutoring, campus organizations, and distance learning. Microsoft Corporation's newsgroup prefix is microsoft.

In addition, some newsgroups are supervised by a **moderator**, who reads each article before it is posted to the newsgroup. If the moderator thinks an article is appropriate for the newsgroup, then the moderator posts the article for all members to read.

Accessing Newsgroups Using Internet Explorer

Before accessing the articles in a newsgroup or posting an article to a newsgroup, you must establish a news account on your computer. A **news account** allows access to the news server with the same name. One news account (msnnews.msn.com) appears in the Folders list in the Outlook Express window shown in Figure 3-38. Thus, for this project, access is available to the msnnews.msn.com news server.

The msnnews.msn.com news server is available because Microsoft Network (MSN) is the Internet service provider used to connect to the Internet and is displayed in the window shown in Figure 3-38. The Microsoft Network makes access available to this account as part of their Internet services.

In this project, it is assumed that the msnnews.msn.com account has been added to your computer. If this account has not been added, use one of the news accounts in your Folders list, ask your instructor for instructions to add the account to the Folders list, or follow the instructions in Appendix B to add the account.

The following steps illustrate how to use Internet Explorer and Outlook Express to view the newsgroups on the msnnews.msn.com news server.

To Display the Newsgroups on a News Server

1

• **Click the Mail button on the Standard Buttons toolbar in the Microsoft Internet Explorer window.**

The Mail menu appears (Figure 3-39).

FIGURE 3-39

2

• **Click Read News in the Mail menu.**

• **If necessary, click the No button in the Outlook Express dialog box.**

The Outlook Express window contains a toolbar, Folder bar, Folders list, Contacts list, and Newsgroup Subscription area (Figure 3-40). The news server name appears in the window title, Folder bar, and Folders list. The news accounts in the Folders list on your computer may be different.

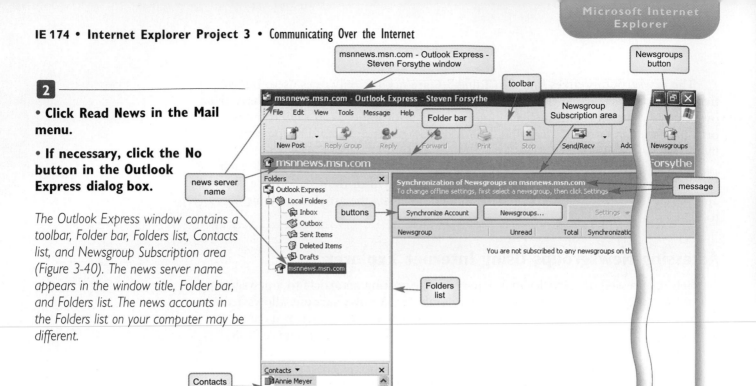

FIGURE 3-40

3

• **Click the Newsgroups button on the toolbar.**

• **If necessary, click the All tab.**

The Newsgroup Subscriptions dialog box appears (Figure 3-41). The highlighted msnnews.msn.com icon appears in the Account(s) list and the insertion point appears in the text box. A partial list of the newsgroups on the msnnews.msn.com news server appears in alphabetical order in the Newsgroup list. The list of newsgroups on your computer may be different.

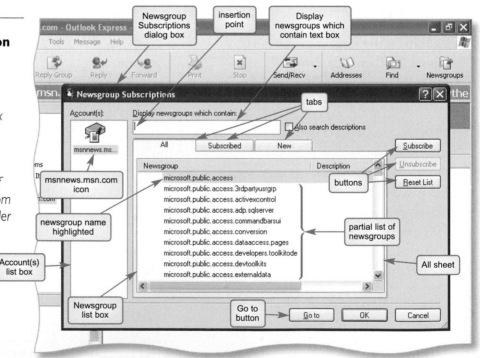

FIGURE 3-41

Other Ways

1. Click Newsgroups button in Newsgroup Subscription area
2. On Tools menu click Newsgroups
3. Press ALT+T, press W
4. Press CTRL+W

Below the menu bar shown in Figure 3-40 is a toolbar containing buttons specific to working with news messages (New Post, Reply Group, Reply, and so on). Table 3-7 contains the toolbar buttons and a brief explanation of their functions.

Table 3-7 Toolbar Buttons and Functions

BUTTON	FUNCTION
New Post	Displays a window used to post a reply to a newsgroup article.
Reply Group	Displays a window that allows you to reply to all authors of articles in newsgroup by e-mail.
Reply	Displays a window that allows you to reply to the author of an article in a newsgroup by e-mail.
Forward	Displays a window that allows you to forward an article in a newsgroup by e-mail.
Print	Prints the highlighted article in the message area.
Stop	Stops the transfer of articles from a news server to the message area.
Send/Recv	Displays the Outlook Express dialog box, contacts the news server, and displays new news messages in the message area.
Addresses	Displays the Address Book window containing a list of frequently used contacts.
Find	Displays the Find Message window that allows you to search for a newsgroup in the message area based on sender name, recipient name, subject, message, and date.
Newsgroups	Displays a dialog box that allows you to select a news server and view the newsgroups on the server.

In Figure 3-41, the All sheet contains a partial list of the newsgroups on the msnnews.msn.com news server. The first newsgroup name (microsoft.public.access) is highlighted. The buttons to the right of the Newsgroup list allow you to subscribe to a newsgroup (Subscribe), unsubscribe from a newsgroup (Unsubscribe), and redisplay the list of newsgroups (Reset List). When you **subscribe** to a newsgroup, the newsgroup name appears in the Folders list, making it easy to return to the newsgroup.

Clicking the Subscribed tab in Figure 3-41 displays a list of newsgroups to which you have subscribed and clicking the New tab allows you to view new newsgroups that have been added recently. The steps to follow to subscribe to and unsubscribe from a newsgroup are shown later in this project. The Go to button at the bottom of the dialog box allows you to view the articles in the highlighted newsgroup.

Searching for a Newsgroup

After viewing a list of the newsgroups on a news server, you can locate an interesting newsgroup and view the articles in the newsgroup. Two methods can be used to locate a newsgroup. The first method is to scroll the Newsgroup list to locate a newsgroup. The second method is to type a keyword in the Display newsgroups which contain text box and let Outlook Express search for and display a list of newsgroup names that contain the keyword.

The steps on the next page show how to search for and display the newsgroup names that contain the keywords (windows xp help). **Windows XP** is the latest version of the Microsoft Windows operating system. Select one of the newsgroups found and then display the articles in the newsgroup.

More About

Column Headers

You can change the width of columns in the message list by dragging the vertical line between two column headers. Likewise, you can drag the vertical line that separates the Folders list and Contacts list from the message list and preview pane to change the size of the two areas.

To Display the Articles in a Newsgroup

1

• **Type** windows xp help **in the Display newsgroups which contain text box.**

When you type the words, windows xp help, a list of newsgroup names that contains the words, windows xp help, appears (Figure 3-42).

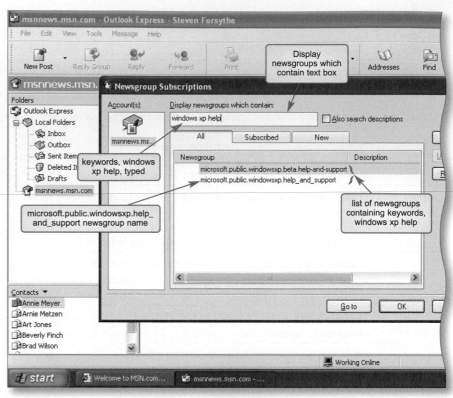

FIGURE 3-42

2

• **Click the microsoft.public .windowsxp.help_and_support newsgroup name.**

The microsoft.public.windowsxp .help_and_support newsgroup name is highlighted (Figure 3-43).

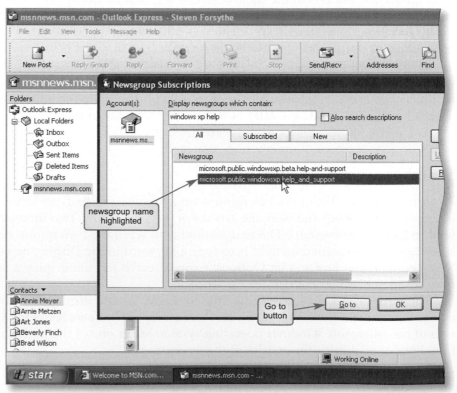

FIGURE 3-43

3

- **Click the Go to button in the dialog box.**

- **Scroll the Folders list to display the left side of the Folders list.**

The Newsgroup Subscriptions window closes, the newsgroup name is displayed in the window title and Folder bar and indented below the server name in the Folders list (Figure 3-44). The message list and preview pane appear on the right side of the window and a list of articles in the newsgroup is displayed in the message list.

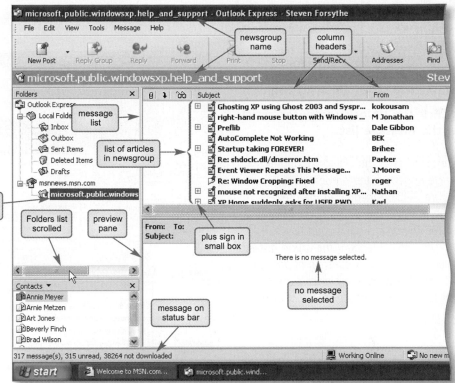

FIGURE 3-44

The message list contains column headers and a list of the original articles (postings) in the microsoft.public.windowsxp.help_and_support newsgroup. Each original article consists of the subject of the article, author name, date and time the article was sent, and file size. The date and file size are not visible in Figure 3-44.

The plus sign in a small box to the left of some of the articles indicates the article is part of a thread. Clicking the plus sign expands the thread so you can see a list of the replies to the original article. A minus sign in a small box icon to the left of an article indicates the article is expanded. Clicking the minus sign collapses the thread so you cannot see the replies to the original article.

When you select an article in the message list, the text of the article is displayed in the preview pane. In Figure 3-44, the preview pane indicates no message is selected.

The status bar at the bottom of the Outlook Express window indicates that 317 articles (messages) have been retrieved, 315 articles have not been read, and 38264 have not been downloaded.

Reading Newsgroup Articles

The entries in the Subject column in the message list allow you to look at the subject of an article before deciding to read the article. The step on the next page shows how to read the Newsgroup article.

More About

Newsgroups

Instructors use newsgroups in courses taught over the Internet. An instructor posts a question and students respond by posting an article. Students can read the articles in the thread to be aware of all responses and subscribe to the newsgroup to quickly return to it.

To Read a Newsgroup Article

1

• **Scroll the message list to display the article titled Unlock computer.**

• **Click the Unlock computer article in the message list.**

The contents of the Unlock computer article appear in the preview pane (Figure 3-45). A header in the preview pane contains the initials of the person who posted the article, newsgroup name, and subject. The contents of the article appear below the header. A question appears in the preview pane. The Unlock computer article on your computer may not display.

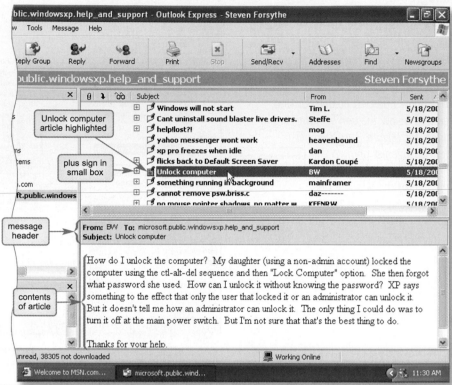

FIGURE 3-45

Other Ways

1. Press CTRL+< to read previous article
2. Press CTRL+> to read next article

Expanding a Thread

When a plus sign appears to the left of an article in the message list, the article is part of a thread and can be expanded. **Expanding the thread** displays the replies to the original article indented below the original article and changes the plus sign to a minus sign. The following step illustrates how to expand the Unlock computer thread and view the replies to the article.

To Expand a Thread

1

- **Click the plus sign in the small box to the left of the Unlock computer name.**

- **Click the reply (Re: Unlock computer) below the original article.**

- **Scroll the preview pane to view an answer to the question.**

The plus sign to the left of the original article changes to a minus sign and a reply appears in the message list (Figure 3-46). The Re: entry in the message list is highlighted and the text of the reply appears in the preview pane. The text in the preview pane contains an answer to the question asked in the original article.

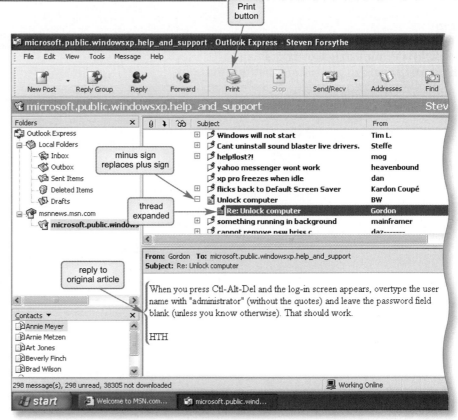

FIGURE 3-46

Other Ways

1. Press CTRL+PLUS on numeric keypad
2. Press CTRL+RIGHT ARROW

Collapsing a Thread

When you expand a thread, a minus sign replaces the plus sign to the left of the original article within the thread. Sometimes, after reading the reply within a thread, you will want to collapse the expansion. **Collapsing the thread** removes the reply from the thread, displays the original article in the preview pane, and changes the minus sign to the left of the original article to a plus sign. The step on the next page shows how to collapse the Unlock computer thread.

To Collapse a Thread

1

• **Click the minus sign in the small box to the left of the original Unlock computer article.**

The minus sign to the left of the original article changes to a plus sign and the reply to the original article no longer appears (Figure 3-47).

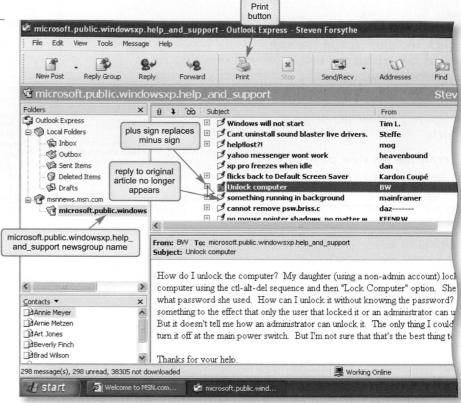

FIGURE 3-47

Other Ways

1. Press CTRL+MINUS on numeric keypad
2. Press CTRL+LEFT ARROW

Printing a Newsgroup Article

After displaying and reading an article, you may want to print the article. The printout is similar to the printout that results when you print an e-mail message (see Figure 3-6 on page IE 150). The following steps illustrate how to print the contents of the Unlock computer article.

To Print a Newsgroup Article

1 **Click the Print button on the toolbar.**

2 **Click the Print button in the Print dialog box.**

The newsgroup article is printed (Figure 3-48).

In Figure 3-48, the printed newsgroup article consists of a header at the top of the page containing the page number (Page 1 of 1), the user's name (Steven Forsythe), and a horizontal line that is heavier below the user's name. Below the header are the From, Newsgroups, Sent, and Subject entries and the body of the Unlock computer article. The Newsgroups entry contains the newsgroup name and the Subject entry contains the article name. A footer at the bottom of the page contains the current date (5/18/2005). If the article contains pictures, the pictures do not print.

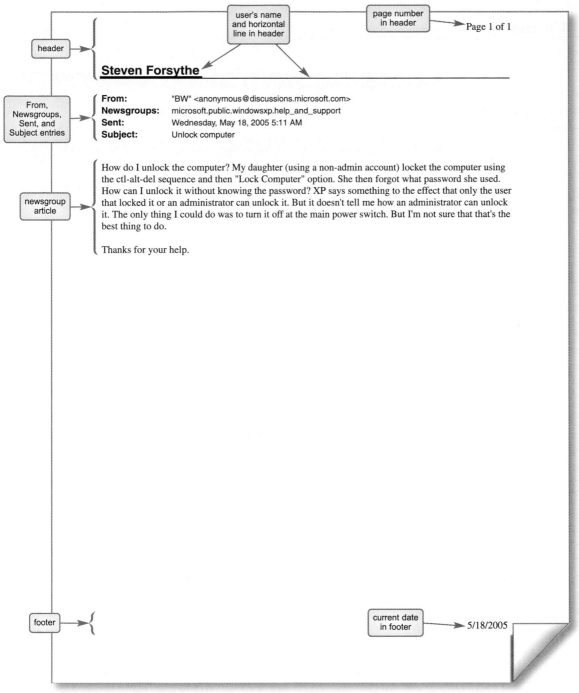

FIGURE 3-48

Subscribing to a Newsgroup

Several hundred newsgroups may be listed in the Newsgroup Subscriptions dialog box. Searching for a previously visited newsgroup or scrolling the newsgroup list to find a previously visited newsgroup can be time-consuming. To find a previously visited newsgroup quickly, Outlook Express allows you to subscribe to a newsgroup. **Subscribing to a newsgroup** permanently adds the newsgroup name to the Folders list and allows you to return to the newsgroup quickly by clicking the newsgroup name in the Folders list instead of searching or scrolling to find the newsgroup name. The steps on the next page show how to subscribe to the microsoft.public.windowsxp.help_and_support newsgroup.

To Subscribe to a Newsgroup

1

• **Right-click the microsoft
.public.windowsxp.help_and_
support newsgroup name in the
Folders list.**

*A shortcut menu, containing the Subscribe
command, appears (Figure 3-49).*

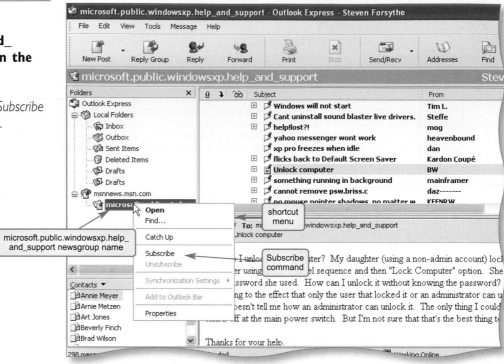

FIGURE 3-49

2

• **Click Subscribe on the
shortcut menu.**

*The folder and pushpin icon to the left of
the newsgroup name in the Folders list
changes color to indicate a subscription to
the newsgroup has been made and the
newsgroup name is added to the
subscription list (Figure 3-50).*

Other Ways

1. Select newsgroup name in
   Newsgroups Subscription
   list, click Subscribe button
2. Double-click newsgroup
   name

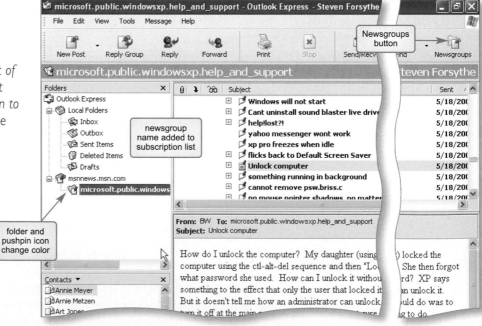

FIGURE 3-50

A subscription to the microsoft.public.windowsxp.help_and_support newsgroup
has been made.

Posting a Newsgroup Article

At some point in time you may want to post, or send, a reply to a newsgroup article. The following steps illustrate how to post a newsgroup article to the microsoft.test newsgroup. The microsoft.test newsgroup is a newsgroup just for miscellaneous purposes. Posting to this newsgroup will not disturb any other newsgroup articles.

To Display the Articles in the Microsoft.test Newsgroup

1 **Click the Newsgroups button on the toolbar.**

2 **Type** microsoft.test **in the Display newsgroups which contain text box.**

3 **Click the Go to button.**

4 **Scroll the Folders list to display the microsoft.test newsgroup.**

The Newsgroup Subscriptions dialog box appears, the keyword, microsoft.test, is displayed in the Display newsgroups which contain text box, the Go to button is clicked, and the Newsgroup Subscription dialog box closes (Figure 3-51). The articles in the microsoft.test newsgroup appear in the message list. The microsoft.test newsgroup name is indented below the microsoft.public .windowsxp.help_and_support entry in the Folders list, in the window title, and in the Folder bar. A partial list of articles in the microsoft.test newsgroup are displayed in the message list.

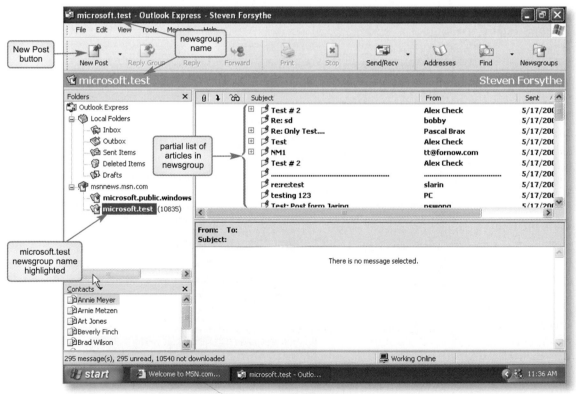

FIGURE 3-51

The steps on the next page illustrate how to post a test article to the newsgroup using the words, Test Message, as the subject of the article to indicate that the article is a test and can be disregarded by anyone browsing the newsgroup.

To Post a Newsgroup Article

1

• **Click the New Post button on the toolbar.**

• **Maximize the New Message window.**

The maximized New Message window appears (Figure 3-52). The window contains a menu bar, toolbar, three text boxes, and a message area. The Newsgroups text box contains the newsgroup name (microsoft.test) and the Subject text box contains the insertion point.

2

• **Type** Test Message **in the Subject text box and then press the TAB key.**

• **Type** Please ignore this message. I am learning to post a message to a newsgroup. **as the message.**

The subject appears in the window title and in the Subject text box and the message is displayed in the message area (Figure 3-53). The subject indicates that this is a test message and can be disregarded.

3

• **Click the Send button on the toolbar.**

The Post News dialog box appears (Figure 3-54). The dialog box contains a message to indicate the message is being sent to the news server and may not appear immediately in the message list.

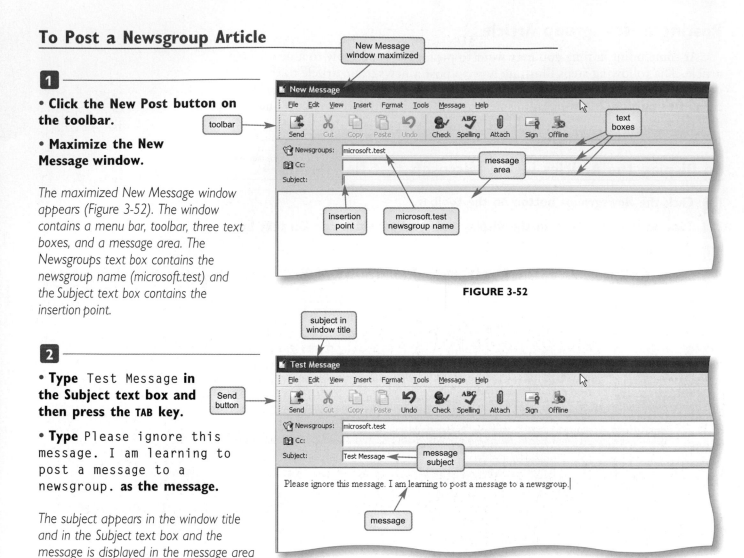

FIGURE 3-52

FIGURE 3-53

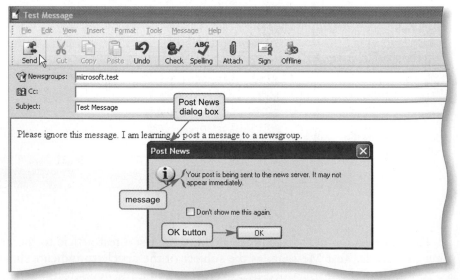

FIGURE 3-54

4

• **Click the OK button in the Post News dialog box.**

The Post News dialog box and Test Message window close, and the microsoft.test - Outlook Express - Steven Forsythe window reappears (Figure 3-55). You may have to wait several minutes for the article to be posted to the microsoft.test newsgroup.

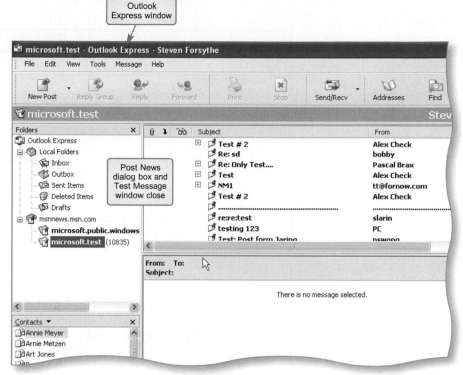

FIGURE 3-55

5

• **When the message appears in the message list, scroll the message list to view the test message and then click the test message.**

The Test Message article appears in the message list and the contents of the message are displayed in the preview pane (Figure 3-56).

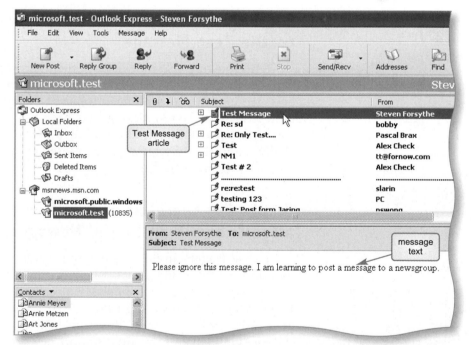

FIGURE 3-56

The buttons on the toolbar illustrated in Figure 3-54 (Send, Cut, Copy, Paste, and so on) are useful when posting a new article. Table 3-8 on the next page shows the buttons on the toolbar and their functions.

Other Ways

1. On File menu in Outlook Express window point to New, click News Message on New submenu
2. Press ALT+M, press N
3. Press CTRL+N

Table 3-8 Toolbar Buttons and Functions

BUTTON	FUNCTION
Send	Sends the article in the New Message window to a news server.
Cut	Moves a selected item in an article to the Clipboard and removes the item from the article.
Copy	Moves a selected item in an article to the Clipboard.
Paste	Copies an item from the Clipboard to an article.
Undo	Undoes the previous operation.
Check	Checks the recipient's name against the Address Book.
Spelling	Spell checks the article.
Attach	Attaches a file to the article.
Sign	Digitally signs an article, allowing the recipient to verify the sender's identity.
Offline	Allows you to work without being connected to a news server (offline).

Viewing the Automated E-Mail Response to the Test Message

After posting a test message to the microsoft.test newsgroup, you may have to wait several minutes for the message to appear. In addition, the Microsoft.test newsgroup also may send an automated e-mail message to your e-mail account indicating that the test message has been posted. To view the automated e-mail, start Microsoft Outlook Express, click the Mail button on the Standard Buttons toolbar, and then double-click the closed envelope icon to the left of the automated e-mail in the message list.

Displaying the Articles in a Newsgroup after Subscribing to the Newsgroup

Previous steps in this project, illustrated subscribing to the microsoft.public .windowsxp.help_and_support newsgroup. After subscribing to a newsgroup, you can view the articles in the newsgroup by clicking the newsgroup name in the Folders list without having to search or scroll to find the articles in the newsgroup. The following step illustrates how to view the articles in the microsoft .public.windowsxp.help_and_support newsgroup.

To Display the Articles in a Newsgroup

1

• **Click microsoft.public .windowsxp.help_and_support in the Folders list.**

• **If the Outlook Express dialog box is displayed, click the No button.**

The microsoft.public.windowsxp.help_ and_support newsgroup name is highlighted in the Folders list and the articles in the newsgroup appear in the message area (Figure 3-57).

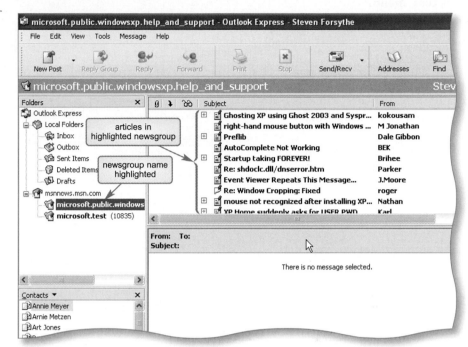

FIGURE 3-57

Unsubscribing from a Newsgroup

When you no longer need quick access to a newsgroup, you can cancel the subscription to the newsgroup, which is called **unsubscribing**, and then remove the newsgroup name from the Folders list. The next steps show how to unsubscribe from the microsoft.public.windowsxp.help_and_support newsgroup.

To Unsubscribe from a Newsgroup

1

• **Right-click the microsoft.public .windowsxp.help_and_support newsgroup name in the Folders list.**

A shortcut menu, containing the Unsubscribe command, appears (Figure 3-58).

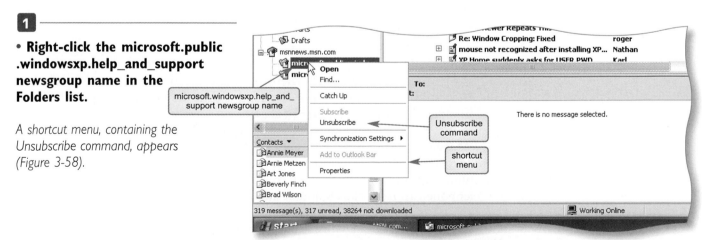

FIGURE 3-58

2

• **Click Unsubscribe on the shortcut menu.**

• **If the Outlook Express dialog box appears, click the OK button in the dialog box.**

• **If a second Outlook Express dialog box appears, click the No button in the dialog box.**

The newsgroup name is removed from the Folders list to indicate the subscription to the newsgroup has been canceled (Figure 3-59).

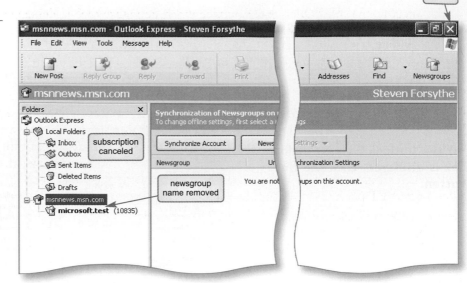

FIGURE 3-59

Quitting Outlook Express and Internet Explorer

When you have finished working with newsgroups, you should quit Outlook Express. In preparation for working with MSN Messenger, you also can close the Microsoft Internet Explorer window, as the following steps illustrate.

To Quit Outlook Express

1 Click the Close button in the Outlook Express window.

2 If necessary, click the OK button in the Outlook Express dialog box.

3 Click the Close button in the Microsoft Internet Explorer window.

The Outlook Express window and the Microsoft Internet Explorer window close.

MSN Messenger and Instant Messaging

One of the more useful communication tools available today is MSN Messenger. **MSN Messenger** allows you to communicate instantly with your online contacts. MSN Messenger is included with all Microsoft Windows operating systems. The advantage of using MSN Messenger over e-mail is that the message you send appears immediately on the computer of the person with whom you are communicating, provided that person has signed in to MSN Messenger.

MSN Messenger maintains a **contact list** of individuals with whom you can communicate. MSN Messenger allows you to add a contact to the contact list, view a list of online and offline contacts, talk to a single contact or a group of contacts, place a telephone call from the computer and talk using the microphone and headset, send files to another computer, send instant messages to a pager, and invite someone to an online meeting or to play an Internet game. The message you send appears immediately on the computer of the person with whom you are communicating and that person can respond immediately by sending a reply to you. MSN Messenger works with the **.NET Messenger Service** to deliver these services to your computer.

You connect to the .NET Messenger Service when you start MSN Messenger and sign in using a sign-in name and password. A **sign-in name** is the unique name a person uses when they log on to the .NET Messenger service.

Before using MSN Messenger, a contact must have an MSN Hotmail account or a Microsoft .NET Passport and have the MSN Messenger software installed on their computer. **MSN Hotmail** is a Microsoft service that provides free e-mail accounts to allow you to read your e-mail messages from any computer connected to the Internet. With an MSN Hotmail account you use a sign-in name and password to access your e-mail. The **Microsoft .NET Passport service** is a secure way for you to sign in to multiple Web sites using just one user name and one password. As a MSN Hotmail user, your MSN Hotmail sign-in name and password also are your Microsoft .NET passport user name and password. For more information about signing up for a free MSN Hotmail account or Microsoft .NET passport, read the More About on this page.

Before using MSN Messenger, you must start MSN Messenger and sign in to the .NET Messenger service using your sign-in name and password. The following steps illustrate how to sign in and enter the password for one of the authors of this book (Steven Forsythe). They show how to start MSN Messenger and sign in to .NET Messenger Service using your sign-in name and password.

> ### *More About*
>
> ### .NET Passports
>
> .NET Passports are available for children age 12 and under who live in the United States and use MSN Messenger. A Kids Passport requires the signature of a parent or guardian to use the service.

To Start MSN Messenger and Sign In

1

• **Double-click the Messenger icon in the notification area on the Windows taskbar.**

The MSN Messenger window appears (Figure 3-60). The Messenger icon and the Sign in button are displayed in an open area below the menu bar.

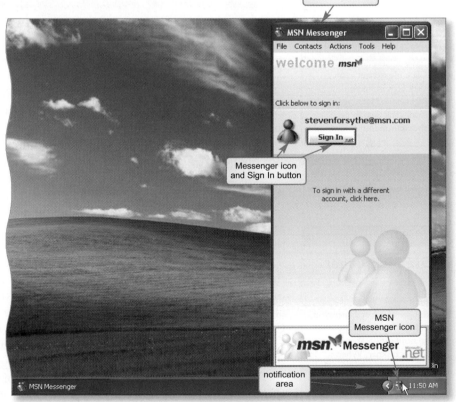

FIGURE 3-60

2

• **Click the Sign In button
in the MSN Messenger
window.**

*MSN Messenger signs you in to
the MSN Messenger service and
the contents of the MSN
Messenger window change
(Figure 3-61). The MSN
Messenger window contains a
menu bar, nine tabs along the left
side of the window, the My
Status sheet, and a message
area at the bottom of the
window.*

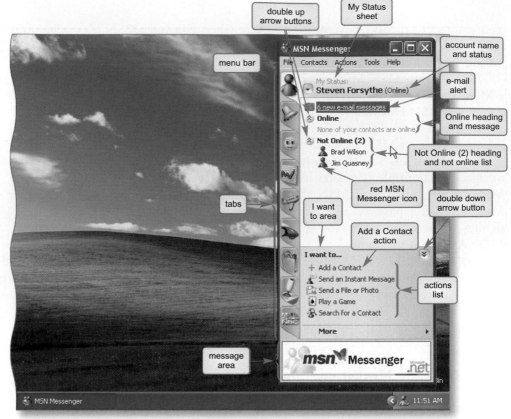

FIGURE 3-61

The My Status sheet in Figure 3-61 contains the MSN Messenger account name
(Steven Forsythe), account status (Online), e-mail alert indicating 6 new e-mail
messages, Online heading and message (None of your contacts are online), Not
Online (2) heading and Not Online list containing two contacts (Brad Wilson and
Jim Quasney), I want to area, and Add a Contact action.

The contacts in the Not Online list are identified by a red MSN Messenger icon.
Although not visible in Figure 3-61, contacts in the Online list are identified by a
green MSN Messenger icon. A double up arrow button precedes the Online heading
and Not Online (2) heading. Clicking the double up arrow button preceding either of
these headings collapses the appropriate list.

The I want to area containing the Add a Contact action appears at the bottom of
the My Status sheet. The I want to heading is preceded by a double down arrow
button to indicate the pane is expanded. Clicking the double down arrow button
closes the I want to area. The action list in the I want to area contains the Add a
Contact, Send an Instant Message, Send a File or Photo, Play a Game, and Search for
a Contact actions. The Add a Contact action, which allows you to add a contact to
the contact list, is identified by a green plus sign.

Nine tabs are displayed along the left side of the MSN Messenger window. Table 3-9
shows the tabs in the MSN Messenger window and a brief explanation of their
functions.

Table 3-9 MSN Messenger Window Tabs and Functions

TAB	FUNCTION
	Displays the account name and status, Online list, Not Online list, and I want to area in the My Status sheet.
	Sends Microsoft .NET alerts from the MSN Money, MSN Carpoint, eBay, MSN Calendar, MSN Music, and FYE Web sites to your computer, mobile device, or e-mail inbox.
	Allows downloads of movie and musician themes, pictures and emoticons, and Xpress Greetings.
	Displays stock symbols and prices from the MSN Money Central Web site.
	Displays airfare, hotels, and other travel deals from Expedia.com.
	Features live traffic updates, personalized traffic forecasts, and local gas prices.
	Features offers and bargains on MSN shopping.
	Accesses free MSN Games.
	Displays the MSNBC Web site.

Adding a Contact to the Contact List

After starting MSN Messenger, you can add a contact to the contact list if you know the e-mail address or MSN sign-in name of the contact. A contact must have an MSN Hotmail account or a Microsoft .NET Passport and have the MSN Messenger software installed on his or her computer. If you try to add a contact that does not meet these requirements, you are given the chance to send the contact an e-mail invitation that explains how to get a passport and download the MSN Messenger software.

To simplify the process of adding a contact to the contact list, MSN Messenger allows you to use the Add a Contact wizard. A **wizard** makes a difficult process easier by guiding you through the process step by step. The **Add a Contact wizard** assists you in adding a contact to the contact list. The steps on the next page illustrate how to add a contact to the contact list using the e-mail address of someone you know who has signed in to MSN Messenger.

To Add a Contact to the Contact List

1

• **Click Add a Contact on the My Status sheet.**

• **Click the Create a new contact by entering their e-mail address or sign-in name option button.**

MSN Messenger starts the Add a Contact wizard and the Add a Contact dialog box appears (Figure 3-62). The dialog box contains a question, two option buttons, a link to the Address Book, a message, and the Next button. The Create a new contact by entering their e-mail address or sign-in name option button is selected.

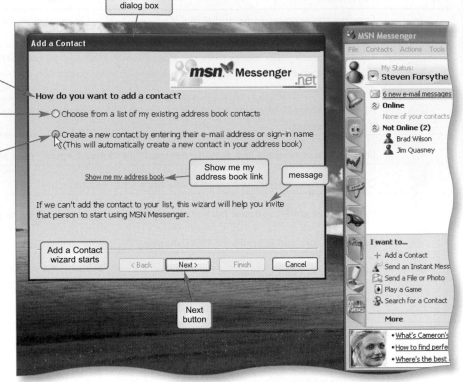

FIGURE 3-62

2

• **Click the Next button in the Add a Contact dialog box.**

• **Type** byfinch@hotmail.com **in the text box.**

The contents of the Add a Contact dialog box change (Figure 3-63). The dialog box contains a request to type an e-mail address, a text box, and three examples of e-mail addresses. The byfinch@hotmail.com e-mail address appears in the text box.

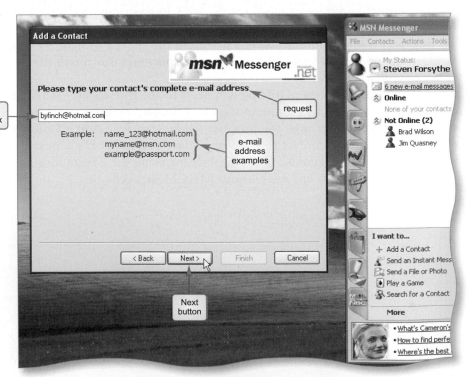

FIGURE 3-63

3

• **Click the Next button in the Add a Contact dialog box.**

The contents of the Add a Contact dialog box change (Figure 3-64). The dialog box contains a message indicating Beverly Finch was successfully added to the contact list, another message indicating that if byfinch@hotmail.com (Beverly Finch) is not using the MSN Messenger program, a custom e-mail can be sent to her explaining the MSN Messenger program and how to install the program, and the Send E-mail button.

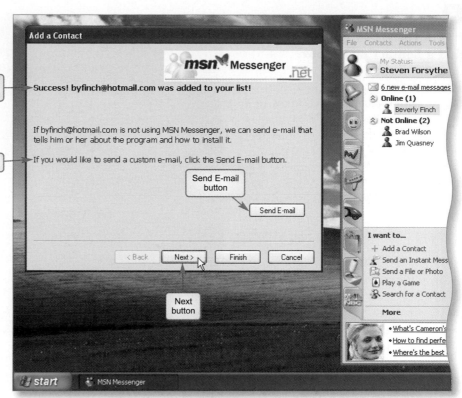

FIGURE 3-64

4

• **Click the Next button in the Add a Contact dialog box.**

The contents of the Add a Contact dialog box change (Figure 3-65). The dialog box contains a message indicating you are done adding the contact and the instructions to add another contact or stop adding contacts.

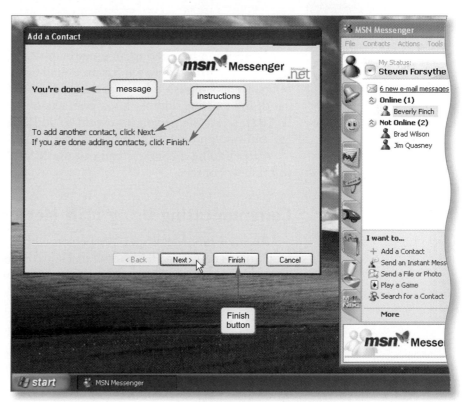

FIGURE 3-65

5

• **Click the Finish button in the Add a Contact dialog box.**

The Add a Contact wizard closes, the Beverly Finch contact is added to the contact list, the Beverly Finch icon and name appear in the Online list below the Online (1) heading, and the Online (1) heading indicates that one contact is in the Online list (Figure 3-66). The Beverly Finch icon on your computer may display in the Not Online list. In this case, read the steps to send an instant message and have an online meeting instead of performing the steps.

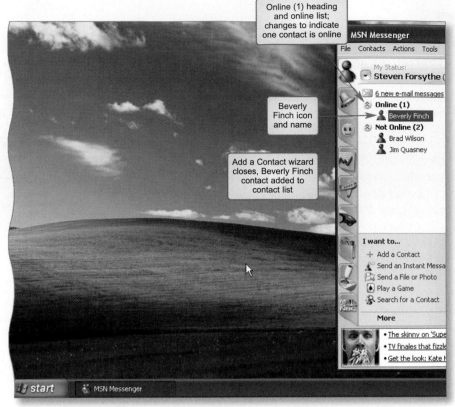

FIGURE 3-66

In addition to entering an e-mail address to add a contact in Figure 3-63 on page IE 192, you also can search for an e-mail address in the Address Book on your computer. To accomplish this, start the Add a Contact wizard, click the Choose from a list of my existing address book contacts option button (see Figure 3-62 on page IE 192), select the person you want to add, and then click the Next button to search for and find an e-mail address.

After adding a contact, you can use MSN Messenger to send an instant message to the new contact.

Communicating Using MSN Messenger

To use MSN Messenger, the person with whom you want to communicate must be online. The Online list shown in Figure 3-66 indicates Beverly Finch is online. The following steps illustrate how to send an instant message to someone you know is online.

To Send an Instant Message

1

• **Double-click the Beverly Finch icon in the Online list.**

• **Maximize the Beverly Finch - Conversation window.**

• **Type** I understand you bought a Web camera and headset for your computer. Do you want to use our cameras to exchange video images? **in the Send text box.**

The Beverly Finch - Conversation window is displayed maximized (Figure 3-67). The window contains a toolbar containing eight buttons, conversation area, and message area. The conversation area contains the To entry and a blank area to view typed messages. The message area contains a toolbar containing three buttons, a message to Beverly Finch, and the Send button. Two video image areas display to the right of the conversation area. Clicking the Webcam icon allows you to display video images for online meetings.

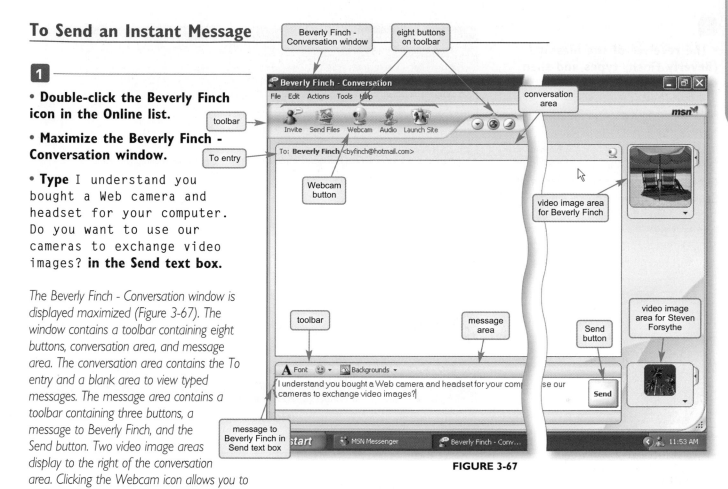

FIGURE 3-67

2

• **Click the Send button in the Beverly Finch - Conversation window.**

MSN Messenger removes the message from the message area, the sender's name and message appear in the conversation area, and the status of the receiver at the bottom of the Conversation window is displayed (Figure 3-68). The status indicates the receiver (Beverly Finch) is writing a message.

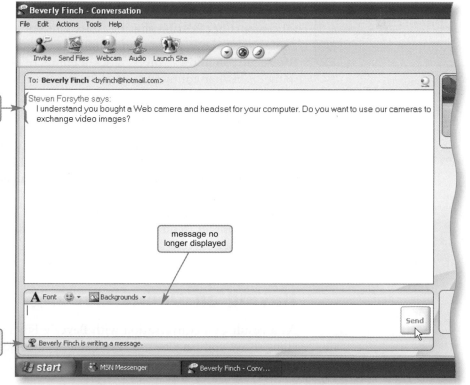

FIGURE 3-68

3

• **The receiver of the message (Beverly Finch) types and then sends a response.**

MSN Messenger displays the receiver's name (Beverly Finch) and message in the conversation area and changes the message at the bottom of the Conversation window to indicate the date and time the message was sent (Figure 3-69).

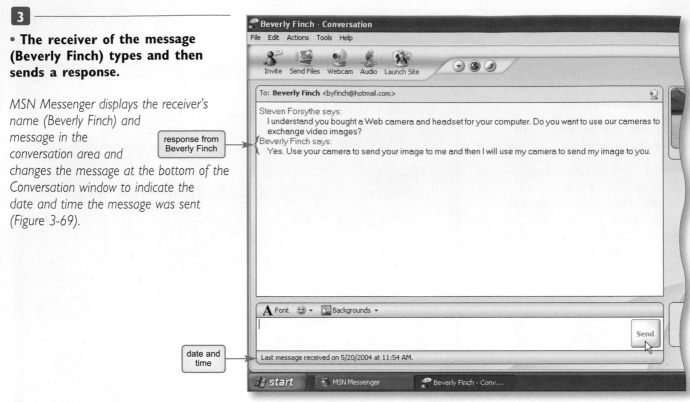

FIGURE 3-69

You can continue conversing in this manner, reading what the other user has to say, and then typing your response.

In Figure 3-67 on the previous page, three buttons are displayed on the toolbar. The **See More Actions button** allows you to send an e-mail, ask for remote assistance, start application sharing, start whiteboard, make a telephone call, start a video conference, play a game, and connect small groups (family and friends) online. The **Block button** allows you to block a contact. The contact will not be able to see your name in his/her contact list or contact you. The **Color Scheme button** allows you to change the color scheme.

Three buttons are displayed in the Send area. The **Font button** allows you to select a font, font style, font size, and apply special effects to the text in a message. The **Emoticons button** allows you to insert icons in a message that convey an emotion or a feeling. Among the icons available are icons that convey happiness, surprise, confusion, and disappointment. The **Backgrounds button** allows you to change the background.

The items in the I want to area shown in Figure 3-61 on page IE 190 allow you to add a contact, send an instant message, send a file or photo, play a game, and search for a contact.

Having an Online Meeting

As a result of a conversation with Beverly Finch in the previous steps, the following steps show you how to use Web cameras and headsets attached to each computer to have an online meeting.

If your computer has a sound card, speakers, and a microphone, you can talk and listen to other users without the usual costs associated with long-distance telephone calls. If your computer has a video camera, you can engage in online meetings by exchanging live video images. If your computer has a sound card, speakers, a microphone, and a camera, the following steps show how to have an online meeting.

More About

Audio Quality

Current Internet capabilities cause the quality of the audio connection to be less than you have with a typical telephone conversation. The quality will improve as the technology progresses.

To Have an Online Meeting

1

• **Click the Webcam button on the toolbar.**

An invitation to start viewing webcam appears in the conversation area and the image of the sender (Steven Forsythe) appears in the smaller video image area (Figure 3-70).

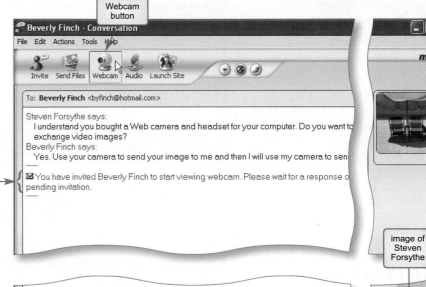

FIGURE 3-70

2

• **Beverly Finch responds by clicking the Accept link in the conversation area on her desktop.**

An acceptance message appears in the conversation area (Figure 3-71). Although not visible, Steven Forsythe's image appears in the larger video image area on Beverly Finch's computer.

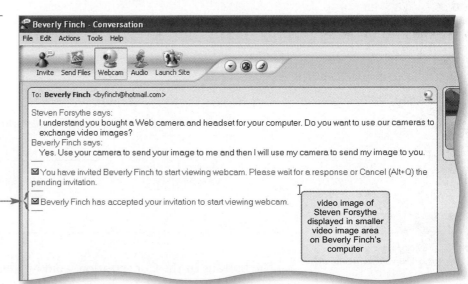

FIGURE 3-71

3

• **Beverly Finch receives the video image and then clicks the Webcam button on the toolbar on her computer.**

An invitation to start viewing webcam appears in the conversation area (Figure 3-72). Although not visible, the image of the sender (Beverly Finch) appears in the smaller video image area on Beverly Finch's computer.

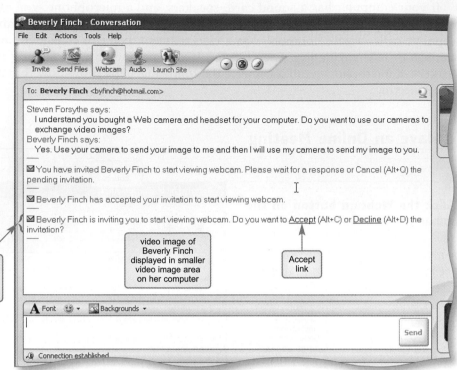

FIGURE 3-72

4

• **Click the Accept link in the conversation area.**

An acceptance message appears in the conversation area and Beverly Finch's image appears in the larger video image area (Figure 3-73).

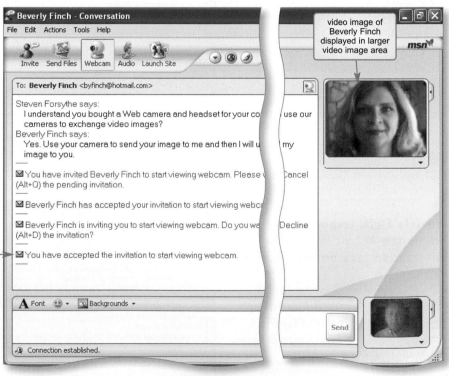

FIGURE 3-73

Other Ways

1. On Actions menu click Video Conference, select contact, click OK button
2. Press ALT+A, press Y

The buttons in the Conversation window illustrated in Figure 3-73 are displayed in various places. Table 3-10 shows the buttons and briefly describes their functions.

Table 3-10 Conversation Area Buttons and Functions

BUTTON	FUNCTION
Invite	Invite another person to the conversation.
Send Files	Send a file or photo.
Webcam	Start or stop webcam.
Audio	Start or stop an audio conversation.
Launch Site	View a list of games or activities.
(arrow down button)	Send an e-mail, ask for remote assistance, start application sharing, start whiteboard, make a telephone call, start a video conference, play a game, and connect small groups (family and friends) online.
(block button)	Block a person from seeing or contacting you.
(color button)	Change the color scheme of the window.
A Font	Change the font or text color.
(emoticon button)	Select a emoticon icon.
Backgrounds	Select a background for the conversation window.

Closing the Conversation Window

When you have finished having a conversation, you should close the Conversation window to end the conversation. The next step illustrates how to close the Conversation window.

To Close the Conversation Window

1 **Click the Close button in the Beverly Finch - Conversation window.**

The online meeting ends and the Conversation window closes.

Deleting a Contact on the Contact List

The Beverly Finch contact remains on the contact list and the Beverly Finch icon appears below the Online heading in the My Status sheet in the MSN Messenger window. In many cases after you have added a contact, you will want to delete the contact. The steps on the next page illustrate how to delete the Beverly Finch contact and remove her entry from the Online list.

To Delete a Contact on the Contact List

1

• **Right-click the Beverly Finch icon in the Online list.**

The shortcut menu is displayed (Figure 3-74).

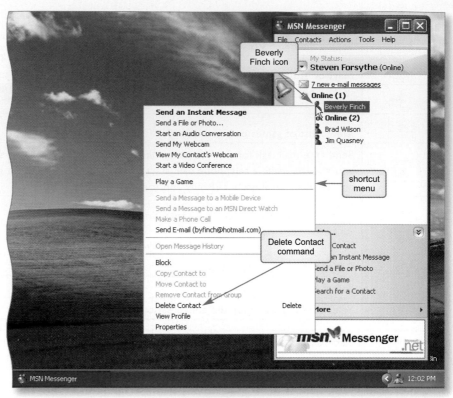

FIGURE 3-74

2

• **Click Delete Contact on the shortcut menu.**

The shortcut menu closes and the MSN Messenger dialog box appears (Figure 3-75). The dialog box contains a message, check box, question, and the Yes button.

FIGURE 3-75

3

• **Click the Yes button in the MSN Messenger dialog box.**

The Beverly Finch name is removed from the contact list and no longer appears below the Online heading (Figure 3-76).

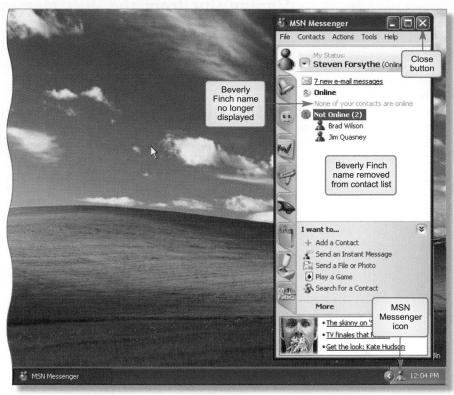

FIGURE 3-76

Quitting MSN Messenger

When you have finished using MSN Messenger, close the MSN Messenger window. The following step shows how to close the MSN Messenger window.

To Close the MSN Messenger Window

1 Click the Close button in the MSN Messenger window.

The MSN Messenger window closes.

Although the MSN Messenger window closes, the MSN Messenger program continues to run and the MSN Messenger icon appears in the notification area on the Windows taskbar to allow you to continue receiving Microsoft .NET alerts and instant messages.

Other Ways

1. On Contacts menu point to Manage Contacts, click Delete a Contact on Manage Contacts submenu, select contact, click OK button, click Yes button
2. Press ALT+C, press M, press D, select contact, press ENTER, press Y

Signing Out from the .NET Messenger Service

After closing the MSN Messenger window, you may want to quit the MSN Messenger program and then sign off from the .NET Messenger Service. The following steps show how to sign out from the .NET Messenger Service.

To Sign Out from the .NET Messenger Service

1 Click the MSN Messenger icon in the notification area on the Windows taskbar.

2 Click the Sign Out command on the shortcut menu.

You are signed out from the .NET Messenger Service. The MSN Messenger icon in the notification area appears with a red circle containing an X to indicate you are signed out.

The Media Bar

As shown in Project 1, an **Explorer Bar** allows you to personalize the Microsoft Internet Explorer window so that information you use most frequently is easy to locate. Internet Explorer displays a list of the five Explorer Bars (Search, Favorites, Media, History, and Folders) when you click View on the menu bar and point to the Explorer Bar command. Four Explorer Bars (Search, Favorites, Media, and History) have buttons on the Standard Buttons toolbar.

In Project 1, the Favorites bar and History bar were used to search for and display Web pages. In Project 2, the Search bar was used to search for Web pages, e-mail addresses, maps, definitions, and pictures. In the following sections, the Media bar will be used to play music from an Internet radio station.

Starting Internet Explorer

In preparation for displaying the Media bar and listening to an Internet radio station, the following step starts Internet Explorer.

To Start Internet Explorer

1 Click the Start button on the Windows taskbar, point to All Programs on the Start menu, and then click Internet Explorer on the All Programs submenu.

Internet Explorer starts and the Microsoft Internet Explorer window appears on the desktop.

Displaying the Media Bar

The **Media bar** allows you to play media files (music, video, and multimedia), listen to Internet radio stations, and access the WindowsMedia.com Web site. In this project, you will use the Media bar to listen to an Internet radio station. The following step shows how to display the Media bar.

To Display the Media Bar

1

• **Click the Media button on the Standard Buttons toolbar.**

The Media bar appears in the Welcome to MSN.com - Microsoft Internet Explorer window (Figure 3-77). A link to the WindowsMedia.com Web site, Today pane, and Media Player toolbar are displayed on the Media bar. Links to today's music videos and movie previews appear in the Today pane. The contents of the Today pane on your computer may be different.

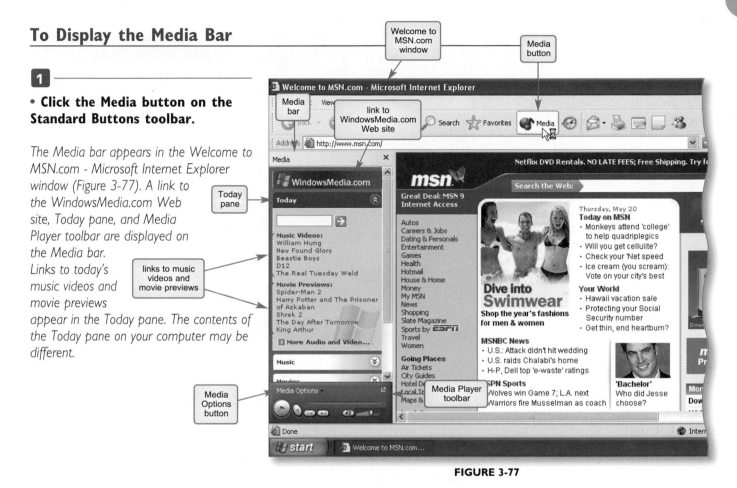

FIGURE 3-77

Clicking the WindowsMedia.com link in Figure 3-77 displays the WindowsMedia.com Media Guide home page containing links to music, movies, entertainment, radio, current events, and the Site index. Clicking the double up arrow button to the right of the Today heading closes the Today pane and displays the Today, Music, Movies, and Radio headings on the Media bar. The **Media Player toolbar** appears at the bottom of the Media bar and contains buttons to play media files and change media options.

Displaying the Radio Guide

The **Radio Guide**, located on the Media Options menu in the Media bar, allows you to select an Internet radio station from a list of previously selected radio stations. The steps on the next page illustrate how to display the Radio Guide.

To Display the Radio Guide

1

• **Click the Media Options button in the Media bar.**

The Media Options menu is displayed (Figure 3-78).

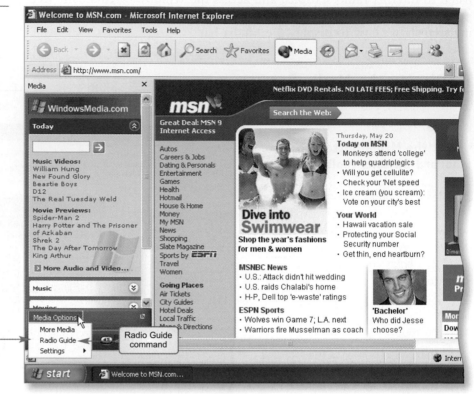

FIGURE 3-78

2

• **Click Radio Guide on the Media Options menu.**

Although not visible in Figure 3-79, the window title changes to contain the words, My Radio - WindowsMedia.com Radio Tuner (Figure 3-79). The window contains three headings, Find More Stations area, and Search Keyword box.

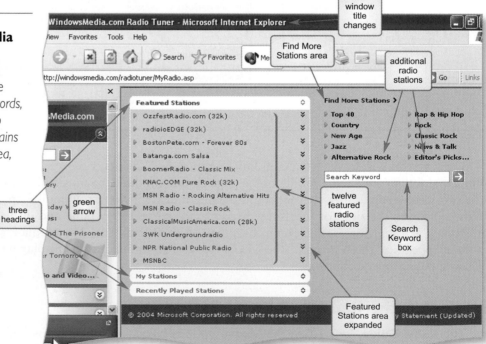

FIGURE 3-79

The Featured Stations heading, My Stations heading, and Recently Played Stations heading are displayed in Figure 3-79. Clicking a heading expands the heading and displays a list of radio stations. The **Featured Stations heading** is expanded and a list of 12 featured stations are displayed. An additional list of radio stations is displayed to the right of the Featured Stations list.

Selecting a Radio Station

Currently, 12 radio stations are displayed in the Featured Stations list. To listen to one of these radio stations, click the radio station name in the Featured Stations list and then click the Play button in the Media Player toolbar. The following step illustrates how to listen to the MSN Radio - Classic Rock station.

To Listen to a Radio Station

1

• **Click the green arrow to the left of MSN Radio - Classic Rock station in the Featured Stations list (Figure 3-80).**

A window containing the MSN Entertainment Web site opens, a second window (MSN Radio window) containing the song title (Message in a Bottle), artist name (The Police), and album title (Every Breath You Take: The Singles) opens, and the currently advertised song plays (Figure 3-80).

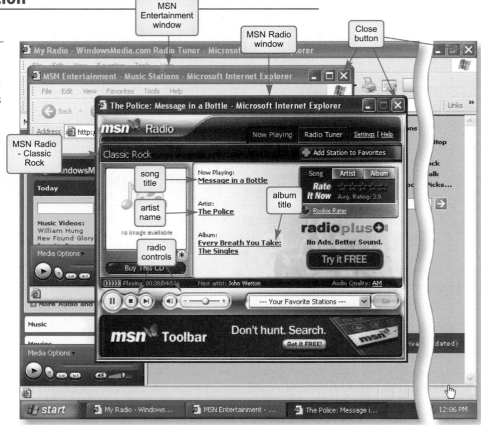

FIGURE 3-80

While listening to a radio station, you may want to play a song, pause the music, stop the music, skip to another song, or adjust the volume. To do so, use the controls in the MSN Radio window.

Closing all Open Windows

When you are finished listening to radio stations, you should close the MSN Radio window, close the MSN Entertainment window, and then close the Media bar. The following steps show how to close the windows and Media bar.

To Close Open Windows and the Media Bar

1 Click Close button in the MSN Radio window.

2 Click the OK button in the Microsoft Internet Explorer window.

3 Click the Close button on the Media bar.

The MSN Radio window closes, MSN Entertainment window closes, and the Media bar closes. The Internet Explorer window remains on the desktop.

Quitting Internet Explorer

When you have finished using Internet Explorer, you should quit Internet Explorer. The following step closes Internet Explorer.

To Quit Internet Explorer

1 Click the Close button in the Microsoft Internet Explorer window.

Internet Explorer quits, the Microsoft Internet Explorer window closes, and the Windows desktop is displayed.

Project Summary

In this project, you learned to use Outlook Express to open, read, print, reply to, delete, compose, send, format e-mail messages, and view file attachments. You added and deleted contacts in an Address Book. You also used Outlook Express to search for and display newsgroups, read and post newsgroup articles, print newsgroup articles, expand and collapse a thread, and subscribe and unsubscribe to a newsgroup. You started MSN Messenger, signed in to MSN Messenger, added and removed a contact on the contact list, and sent an instant message. You had an online meeting, and sent and received video images. Finally, you displayed the Media bar and used the Radio Guide to select and listen to an Internet radio station.

What You Should Know

Having completed the project, you now should be able to perform the tasks below. The tasks are listed in the same order they were presented in this project. For a list of the buttons, menus, toolbars, and commands introduced in this project, see the Quick Reference Summary at the back of this book and refer to the Page Number column.

1. Start Internet Explorer (IE 143)
2. Start Microsoft Outlook Express (IE 144)
3. Open (Read) an E-Mail Message (IE 148)
4. Print an Opened E-Mail Message (IE 149)
5. Close an E-Mail Message (IE 151)
6. Reply to an E-Mail Message (IE 152)
7. Delete an E-Mail Message (IE 154)
8. View a File Attachment (IE 155)
9. Compose an E-Mail Message Using Stationery (IE 156)
10. Format an E-Mail Message (IE 160)
11. Send an E-Mail Message (IE 161)
12. Add a Contact to the Address Book (IE 162)
13. Compose an E-Mail Message Using the Address Book (IE 166)
14. Send an E-Mail Message (IE 169)
15. Delete a Contact from the Address Book (IE 170)
16. Quit the Address Book (IE 171)
17. Display the Newsgroups on a News Server (IE 173)
18. Display the Articles in a Newsgroup (IE 176)
19. Read a Newsgroup Article (IE 178)
20. Expand a Thread (IE 179)
21. Collapse a Thread (IE 180)
22. Print a Newsgroup Article (IE 180)
23. Subscribe to a Newsgroup (IE 182)
24. Display the Articles in the Microsoft.test Newsgroup (IE 183)
25. Post a Newsgroup Article (IE 184)
26. Display the Articles in a Newsgroup (IE 187)
27. Unsubscribe from a Newsgroup (IE 187)
28. Quit Outlook Express (IE 188)
29. Start MSN Messenger and Sign In (IE 189)
30. Add a Contact to the Contact List (IE 192)
31. Send an Instant Message (IE 195)
32. Have an Online Meeting (IE 197)
33. Close the Conversation Window (IE 199)
34. Delete a Contact on the Contact List (IE 200)
35. Close the MSN Messenger Window (IE 201)
36. Sign Out from the .NET Messenger Service (IE 202)
37. Display the Media Bar (IE 203)
38. Display the Radio Guide (IE 204)
39. Listen to a Radio Station (IE 205)
40. Close Open Windows and the Media Bar (IE 206)
41. Quit Internet Explorer (IE 206)

Learn It Online

Instructions: To complete the Learn It Online exercises, start your browser, click the Address box, enter scsite.com/ie6winxp/learn, and then click the Go button. When the Internet Explorer Learn It Online page is displayed, follow the instructions in the exercises below. Each exercise has instructions for printing your results, either for your own records or for submission to your instructor.

1 Project Reinforcement TF, MC, and SA

Below Internet Explorer Project 3, click the Project Reinforcement link. Print the quiz by clicking Print on the File menu for each page. Answer each question.

2 Flash Cards

Below Internet Explorer Project 3, click the Flash Cards link and read the instructions. Type 20 (or a number specified by your instructor) in the Number of playing cards text box, type your name in the Enter your name text box, and then click the Flip Card button. When the flash card is displayed, read the question and then click the ANSWER box arrow to select an answer. Flip through Flash Cards. If your score is 15 (75%) correct or greater, click Print on the File menu to print your results. If your score is less than 15 (75%) correct, then redo this exercise by clicking the Replay button.

3 Practice Test

Below Internet Explorer Project 3, click the Practice Test link. Answer each question, enter your first and last name at the bottom of the page, and then click the Grade Test button. When the graded practice test is displayed on your screen, click Print on the File menu to print a hard copy. Continue to take practice tests until you score 80% or better.

4 Who Wants To Be a Computer Genius?

Below Internet Explorer Project 3, click the Computer Genius link. Read the instructions, enter your first and last name at the bottom of the page, and then click the PLAY button. When your score is displayed, click the PRINT RESULTS link to print a hard copy.

5 Wheel of Terms

Below Internet Explorer Project 3, click the Wheel of Terms link. Read the instructions, and then enter your first and last name and your school name. Click the PLAY button. When your score is displayed, right-click the scores and then click Print on the shortcut menu to print a hard copy.

6 Crossword Puzzle Challenge

Below Internet Explorer Project 3, click the Crossword Puzzle Challenge link. Read the instructions, and then enter your first and last name. Click the SUBMIT button. Work the crossword puzzle. When you are finished, click the Submit button. When the crossword puzzle is displayed, click the Print Puzzle button to print a hard copy.

7 Tips and Tricks

Below Internet Explorer Project 3, click the Tips and Tricks link. Click a topic that pertains to Project 3. Right-click the information and then click Print on the shortcut menu. Construct a brief example of what the information relates to in Internet Explorer to confirm you understand how to use the tip or trick.

8 Newsgroups

Below Internet Explorer Project 3, click the Newsgroups link. Click a topic that pertains to Project 3. Print three comments.

9 Expanding Your Horizons

Below Internet Explorer Project 3, click the Expanding Your Horizons link. Click a topic that pertains to Project 3. Print the information. Construct a brief example of what the information relates to in Internet Explorer to confirm you understand the contents of the article.

10 Search Sleuth

Below Internet Explorer Project 3, click the Search Sleuth link. To search for a term that pertains to this project, select a term below the Project 3 title and then use the Google search engine at google.com (or any major search engine) to display and print two Web pages that present information on the term.

11 Internet Explorer How-To Article

Below Internet Explorer Project 3, click the Internet Explorer How-To Articles link. When your browser displays the Internet Explorer How-to Articles Web page, scroll down and click one of the links that covers one or more of the objectives listed at the beginning of the project on page IE 142. Print the first page of the how-to article before stepping through it.

12 Getting More From the Web

Below Internet Explorer Project 3, click the Getting More from the Web link. When your browser displays the Getting More from the Web with Internet Explorer 6 Web page, click one of the Top Stories or Featured Contents links. Print the first page.

In the Lab

1 Sending E-Mail Messages

Problem: You are enrolled in two courses at the local college. You want to send the same e-mail to the instructor of each course stating what you like best about his or her class. You decide to use Internet Explorer, Outlook Express, and the carbon copy feature to send the e-mails.

Instructions: Use Internet Explorer and a computer to perform the following tasks.

1. If necessary, connect to the Internet and then start Internet Explorer.
2. Search for the home page for your school. Figure 3-81 shows the home page for Rio Hondo College located in Whittier, California.

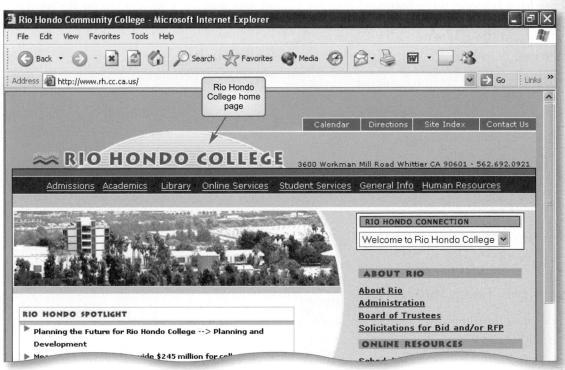

FIGURE 3-81

3. Find and write down on a piece of paper the e-mail address of your instructor.
4. Find and write down on a piece of paper the e-mail address of an instructor from your school that teaches another course that you are enrolled in.
5. Click the Mail button on the Standard Buttons toolbar and then click Read Mail on the Mail menu.
6. Click the Create Mail button on the toolbar to open the New Message window.
7. Using the e-mail address of the instructor you obtained in step 4, compose a mail message to this instructor stating what you like best about his or her class.
8. Using the e-mail address of your instructor obtained in step 3, type the e-mail address in the Cc text box to send a carbon copy of the message to your instructor.
9. Print a copy of the mail message, write your name on the printout, and then hand it in to the instructor.
10. Close all open windows.

In the Lab

2 Adding Contacts to the Address Book

Problem: You want to use the Address Book to keep track of the names, e-mail addresses, home addresses, and home telephone numbers of your favorite school friends. You use Internet Explorer, Outlook Express, and Address Book to create a group containing the information for your friends. You name the group, School Buddies.

Instructions: Use Internet Explorer and a computer to perform the following tasks.

Part 1: *Display the Address Book*

1. If necessary, connect to the Internet and then start Internet Explorer.
2. Click the Mail button on the Standard Buttons toolbar and then click Read Mail on the Mail menu.
3. Click the Addresses button on the toolbar to open the Address Book window. Maximize the window (Figure 3-82).

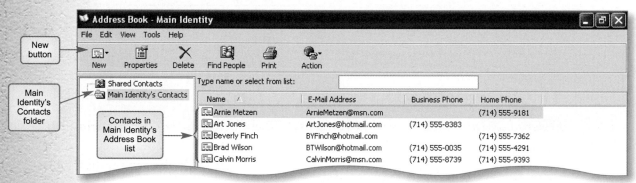

FIGURE 3-82

Part 2: *Add a New Group and Contacts to the Group*

1. Click the New button on the toolbar and then click New Group to display the Properties dialog box.
2. Type School Buddies in the Group Name text box and then click the OK button.
3. Use the New button on the toolbar and the New Contact command to add the contacts listed in Table 3-11 to the School Buddies group.

In the Lab

Table 3-11 Contact List for School Buddies Group

NAME	E-MAIL ADDRESS	ADDRESS	HOME PHONE
Barbara Clark	bclark@isp.com	8451 Colony Brea, CA 92821	(714) 555-7384
Javier Cortez	jcortez@isp.com	3581 Clayton Placentia, CA 92871	(714) 555-2982
Allen Goldberg	agoldberg@isp.com	5689 State Fullerton, CA 92834	(714) 555-3938
Frank Springer	fspringer@isp.com	7812 Bennington Atwood, CA 92811	(714) 555-9832
Carol Thomas	cthomas@isp.com	257 W. Wilson Yorba Linda, CA 92885	(714) 555-0393
Julie Price	jprice@isp.com	648 Flower Brea, CA 92821	(714) 555-3730

4. Print an Address Card for each contact by selecting a contact name, clicking the Print button on the toolbar, and then clicking the Print button in the Print dialog box. Write your name on each printout.

Part 3: *Delete the Contacts and School Buddies Group*

1. Delete each contact by selecting the contact name, clicking the Delete button on the toolbar, and then clicking the Yes button in the Address Book dialog box.
2. Delete the School Buddies group by selecting the group name, clicking the Delete button on the toolbar, and then clicking the Yes button in the Address Book dialog box.
3. Close all open windows.

3 Reading Newsgroup Articles

Problem: You want to display the list of all newsgroups on the default news server, search for a newsgroup of interest to you, select a thread that contains at least three replies, and then print each article in the thread.

Instructions: Use Internet Explorer and a computer to perform the following tasks.

1. If necessary, connect to the Internet and then start Internet Explorer.
2. Click the Mail button on the Standard Buttons toolbar, click Read News on the Mail menu, and then click the No button in the Outlook Express dialog box.
3. Click the Newsgroups button on the toolbar to display the list of all the newsgroups on the default news server (Figure 3-83 on the next page).

(continued)

Reading Newsgroup Articles *(continued)*

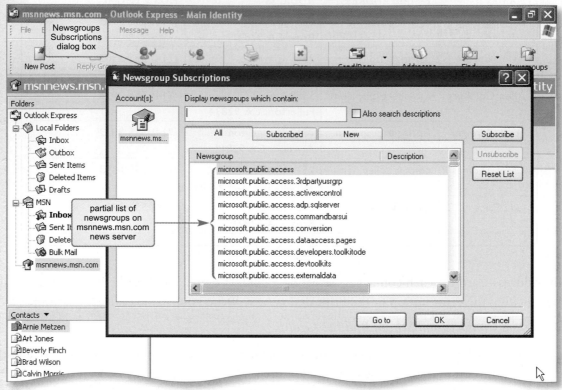

FIGURE 3-83

4. Search for or scroll to find a newsgroup of interest to you, click the newsgroup, and then click the Go to button.
5. Find a thread that contains the original article and at least three replies.
6. Read and then print each article in the thread. Write your name on each printout and then hand them in to your instructor.
7. Close all open windows.

4 Posting Newsgroup Articles

Problem: You want to display the list of all newsgroups on the default news server, search for and display a newsgroup of interest to you, use the New Post button to compose and send a message to the newsgroup, find your message in the message pane, and then print the message.

Instructions: Use Internet Explorer and a computer to perform the following tasks.

1. If necessary, connect to the Internet and then start Internet Explorer.
2. Click the Mail button on the Standard Buttons toolbar, click Read News on the Mail menu, and then click the No button in the Outlook Express dialog box.
3. Click the Newsgroups button on the toolbar to display the list of all the newsgroups on the default news server.
4. Search for or scroll to find a newsgroup of interest to you, click the newsgroup, and then click the Go to button.
5. Click the New Post button to display the New Message window (Figure 3-84).

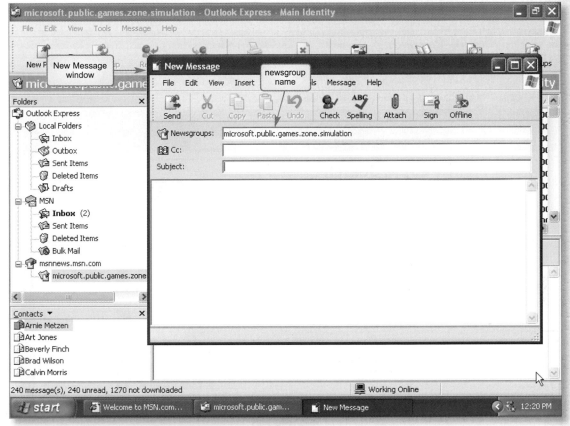

FIGURE 3-84

6. Compose and then send a message to the newsgroup.
7. Find your message in the message list. Print the message, write your name on the printout, and then hand it in to your instructor.
8. Close all open windows.

5 Finding E-Mail Addresses

Problem: You want to use the White Pages link on the MSN home page to search for and print information about yourself, a friend, and a famous person whom you admire.

Instructions: Use Internet Explorer and a computer to perform the following tasks.

1. If necessary, connect to the Internet and then start Internet Explorer.
2. Click the Address bar in the Microsoft Internet Explorer window, type www.msn.com, and then click the Go button.
3. Find and then click the White Pages link on the MSN home page. The White Pages - MSN.com search page appears (Figure 3-85 on the next page).

(continued)

Finding E-Mail Addresses *(continued)*

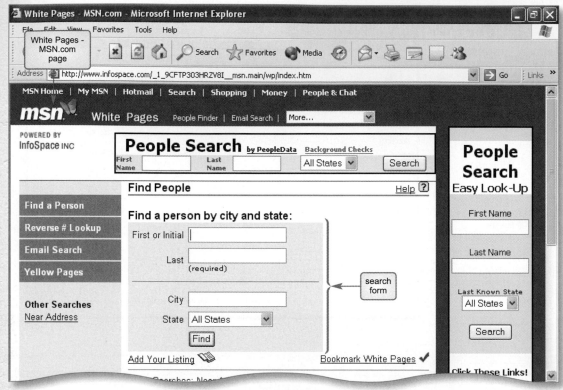

FIGURE 3-85

4. Use the search form on the MSN search page to search for your name. Print the resulting page and then write your name on the printout.
5. Use the search form to search for one of your friends. Print the resulting page and then write your name on the printout.
6. Use the search form to search for someone famous or someone whom you admire. Print the resulting page and then write your name on the printout.
7. Hand in all printouts to your instructor.
8. Close all open windows.

6 Using MSN Messenger

Problem: You want to add a new contact using MSN Messenger and the Add a Contact wizard. After adding the contact, you want to converse with the new contact by sending instant messages to each other, and then save and print the entire conversation.

Instructions: Use Internet Explorer and a computer to perform the following tasks.

Part 1: Start MSN Messenger and Sign In

1. If necessary, connect to the Internet.
2. Double-click the MSN Messenger icon in the notification area on the Windows taskbar and then click the Sign In button.

Part 2: *Add a Contact to the Contact List*

1. Click Add a Contact on the My Status sheet.
2. Click Create a new contact by entering their e-mail address or sign-in name option button.
3. Click the Next button in the Add a Contact dialog box, type the e-mail address of a friend in the text box, and then click the Next button.
4. If the Success! message is displayed, click the Next button, and then go to step 6 below.
5. If the Sorry! message is displayed, the e-mail address is incorrect and you should click the Cancel button, and then go to Step 1 above.
6. When the You're done! message displays, click the Finish button.

Part 3: *Send an Instant Message*

1. Double-click the icon of the contact you added in the Online list.
2. Type each message below in the Send text box, click the Send button, wait for the response, and then write the response in the space provided. A sample conversation is shown in Figure 3-86.

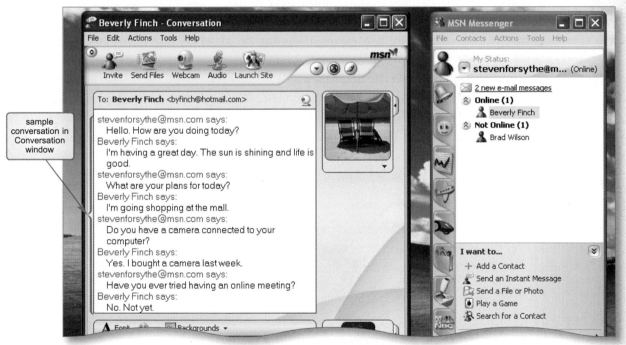

FIGURE 3-86

a. **Message 1:** Hello. How are you doing today?
   Response: _____
   _____

b. **Message 2:** What are your plans for today?
   Response: _____
   _____

(continued)

In the Lab

Using MSN Messenger *(continued)*

    c. **Message 3:** Do you have a camera connected to your computer?
    Response: _____

    _____

    d. **Message 4:** Have you ever tried having an online meeting?
    Response: _____

    _____

3. Continue conversing in this manner until you want to end the conversation.

Part 4: *Save and Print the Conversation*

1. Click File on the menu bar in the Conversation window and then click Save as on the File menu.
2. If necessary, click the OK button in the MSN Messenger window.
3. Type My Conversation in the File name text box in the Save As dialog box.
4. If necessary, click the OK button in the MSN Messenger window.
5. Click the Save in box arrow and then click Desktop in the Save in list.
6. Click the Save button in the Save As dialog box.
7. Move the Conversation window and/or MSN Messenger window to make the My Conversation icon visible on the desktop.
8. Double-click the My Conversation icon on the desktop.
9. Click File on the menu bar and then click Print on the File menu. Write your name on the printout.
10. Click the Close button in the My Conversation - Notepad window.
11. Right-click the My Conversation icon on the desktop, click Delete on the shortcut menu, and then click Yes in the Confirm File Delete dialog box.
12. Click the Close button in the Conversation window.

Part 5: *Delete a Contact on the Contact List*

1. Right-click the friend's name in the MSN Messenger window you want to delete.
2. Click Delete Contact on the shortcut menu.
3. Click the Yes button in the MSN Messenger dialog box.

Part 6: *Close the MSN Messenger Window and Sign Out from the .NET Messenger Service*

1. Click the Close button in the MSN Messenger window.
2. Click the MSN Messenger icon in the notification area on the Windows taskbar.
3. Click Sign Out on the shortcut menu.
4. If necessary, click the OK button in the MSN Messenger dialog box.
5. Hand in all printouts to your instructor.

In the Lab

7 Using MSN Messenger to Have an Online Meeting

Problem: You want to use MSN Messenger to have an online meeting with a friend. After having the conversation, you want to print a copy of the conversation.

Instructions: Use Internet Explorer and a computer to perform the following tasks.

Part 1: Start MSN Messenger and Sign In

1. If necessary, connect to the Internet.
2. Double-click the MSN Messenger icon in the notification area on the Windows taskbar.
3. Click the Sign In button in the MSN Messenger window.

Part 2: Start an Online Meeting

1. Double-click the icon of a contact in the Online list.
2. Type the following messages in the Send text box, click the Send button, wait for the response, and then write the response in the space provided (Figure 3-87).

FIGURE 3-87

 a. **Message 1:** Do you want to have an online meeting?
   Response: _____
 b. **Message 2:** I will show you how to have an online meeting.
   Response: _____

3. Click the Webcam icon on the toolbar.
4. Wait for the other user to respond and then click the Webcam icon on the toolbar.
5. Click the Accept link in the conversation area.

Part 3: Printing a Copy of the Desktop

1. Click the PRINT SCREEN key on the keyboard to place an image of the desktop on the Clipboard. The Clipboard is a temporary Windows storage area.
2. Click the Start button on the Windows taskbar, point to All Programs on the Start menu, point to Accessories on the All Programs submenu, and then click Paint on the Accessories submenu to start the Paint program and display the Paint window.

(continued)

In the Lab

Using MSN Messenger to Have an Online Meeting *(continued)*

3. Click Edit on the menu bar and then click Paste to copy the image of the desktop from the Clipboard to the Paint window.
4. Click File on the menu bar, click Print on the File menu, and then click the Print button in the Print dialog box to print the image of the desktop.
5. Write your name on the printout.
6. Click the Close button in the Paint window and then click the No button in the Paint dialog box to close the Paint window.

Part 4: *Close All Open Windows and Sign Out from the .NET Messenger Service*

1. Click the Close button in the Conversation window.
2. Click the Close button in the MSN Messenger window.
3. Click the MSN Messenger icon in the notification area on the Windows taskbar.
4. Click Sign Out on the shortcut menu.

8 Using the Media Bar and Radio Guide to Listen to Internet Radio Stations

Problem: You want to use the Media Bar and Radio Guide to listen to several Internet radio stations. You would like to record the station name, type of music, and your impressions of the three radio stations you like the most.

Instructions: Use Internet Explorer and a computer to perform the following tasks.

Part 1: *Display the Media Bar*

1. If necessary, connect to the Internet and then start Internet Explorer.
2. Click the Media button on the Standard Buttons toolbar.

Part 2: *Displaying the Radio Guide and Listening to Radio Stations*

1. Click the Media Options button in the Media bar.
2. Click Radio Guide on the Media Options menu (Figure 3-88).
3. Listen to three radio stations by clicking the radio station name and clicking the Play button. In the space provided below, record the following information about each radio station.

Station 1: Station Name _____
Type of Music _____
Give Your Impressions of the Music _____
_____

Station 2: Station Name _____
Type of Music _____
Give Your Impressions of the Music _____
_____

Station 3: Station Name _____
Type of Music _____
Give Your Impressions of the Music _____
_____

FIGURE 3-88

Part 3: *Closing the Media Bar and All Open Windows*

1. Click Close button in the MSN Radio window.
2. Click the OK button in the Microsoft Internet Explorer dialog box.
3. Click the Close button in the MSN Entertainment window.
4. Click the Close button in the Media bar.

Part 4: *Quitting Internet Explorer*

1. Click the Close button in the Microsoft Internet Explorer window.

Cases and Places

The difficulty of these case studies varies:
■ are the least difficult and ■■ are more difficult. The last exercise is a group exercise.

1 ■ Several Web sites are available that allow you to enter a person's name and search for information about the individual. Using a search engine, locate three of these sites. Use your name, a friend's name, and a relative's name to search for information using all three sites you find. Print the information you find, write your name on the printouts, and then hand them in to your instructor.

2 ■ Many software products such as Microsoft Word contain a library of images, graphics, pictures, and other clip art. Libraries of clip art also are available for you to download on the Web. Using the Web search engine of your choice, search for five sites that offer clip art for use on Web pages. Print a few of the images from each site.

3 ■■ Using computer magazines, advertising brochures, the Internet, or other resources, compile information about the latest version of Microsoft Outlook. In a brief report, compare Microsoft Outlook and Microsoft Outlook Express. Include the differences and similarities, how to obtain the software, the function and features of each program, and so forth. If possible, test Microsoft Outlook and add your personal comments.

4 ■■ Using Address Book, create a new group to contain a list of your family, friends, and colleagues. Include their names, addresses, telephone numbers, and e-mail addresses, if any. Enter the name of the organization each one works for, if appropriate. For family, list their birthdays and wedding anniversaries using the Other tab. Submit a printout of each contact to your instructor.

5 ■■ Microsoft owns and operates several news servers. Conservative users have expressed concerns that some users try to disguise their identities by displaying false information when signing up for a Hotmail account or a .NET Passport. In a brief report, summarize the reasons for correctly identifying yourself on the Internet, problems that result when users disguise their identities, who you think is responsible, and how to prevent this problem.

6 ■■ Using computer magazines, advertising brochures, the Internet, or other resources, compile information about two other e-mail programs. In a brief report, compare the two programs and the e-mail program included with Internet Explorer. Include the differences and similarities, how to obtain the software, the functions and features of each program, and so forth. Submit the report to your instructor.

Cases and Places

7 ■■ **Working Together** Many colleges and universities maintain their own news servers containing school-related newsgroups. Have each member of your group locate a school that has a news server. Each member should explore the news server, determine how many newsgroups are on the server, locate at least two newsgroups of interest, determine the number of articles in each newsgroup, and then read several articles in each newsgroup. Instruct each member to write a brief report summarizing their findings and then present the findings to your class.

Appendix A

Internet Options

Internet Options Dialog Box

When you use Internet Explorer to browse the World Wide Web, learn about Web resources techniques, and communicate over the Internet, default Internet Explorer settings control your interaction with Internet Explorer. You can view and modify many of these settings by using the **Internet Options dialog box** shown in Figure A-1.

The Internet Options dialog box contains seven tabs (General, Security, Privacy, Content, Connections, Programs, and Advanced) that allow you to view and modify the Internet Explorer default settings. Using these settings, you can change the home page that is displayed when you start Internet Explorer; delete cookies and temporary Internet files; specify a privacy setting when using the Internet; assign a Web site to a security zone; control the Internet content to which a computer can gain access; set up an Internet connection; and select the programs to send and receive e-mail, read and post articles to a newsgroup, and place Internet calls.

To display the Internet Options dialog box, click Tools on the Microsoft Internet Explorer menu bar and then click Internet Options on the Tools menu. The remainder of this appendix explains the contents of the seven sheets in the Internet Options dialog box.

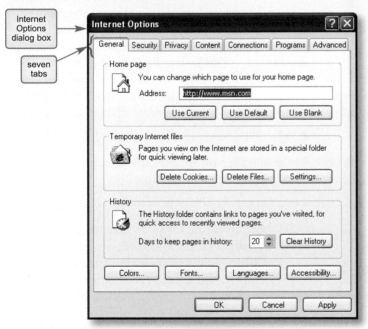

FIGURE A-1

The General Sheet

The **General sheet** illustrated in Figure A-2 on the next page contains the Home page area, Temporary Internet files area, and History area. The **Home page area** allows you to change the home page, which is the Web page that is displayed when you launch Internet Explorer. The home page should be the Web page that contains the information you use most frequently. The Address box in the Home page area contains the URL for the current home page. The three buttons below the Address box allow you to use the Web page that is currently displayed in the Microsoft Internet Explorer window as the home page (Use Current), use the default Web page (Use Default), or display no Web page (Use Blank).

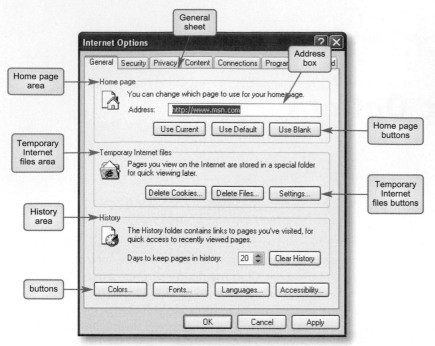

FIGURE A-2

The **Temporary Internet files area** permits you to delete the files in the Temporary Internet Files folder on the hard drive or change the settings of the folder. The Temporary Internet Files folder contains cookies and temporary Internet files. A **cookie** is a file created by a Web site that stores information on your computer, such as your preferences when visiting that site. The Delete Cookies button in the Temporary Internet files area allows you to delete all cookies in the Temporary Internet Files folder.

When you display a Web page in the Microsoft Internet Explorer window, a file called a **temporary Internet file** is stored in the Temporary Internet Files folder. The next time you display that Web page, the page appears quickly because Internet Explorer retrieves the page from the Temporary Internet Files folder instead of the Internet.

The Delete Files button in the Temporary Internet files area allows you to delete all files in the Temporary Internet Files folder. The Settings button allows you to view a list of the temporary Internet files, check for newer versions of the files, change the amount of disk space reserved to store the files, and move the Temporary Internet Files folder to another location on the hard drive.

The **History area** lets you control the number of days the Web pages in the History list are kept before being automatically deleted. It also allows you to delete the contents of the History list.

You can use the four buttons at the bottom of the General sheet to change the default text, background, and link colors (Colors); change the default fonts used to display a Web page (Fonts); specify the language to use when displaying Web pages (Languages); and cause the color and font settings you select to override the settings specified by a Web page (Accessibility).

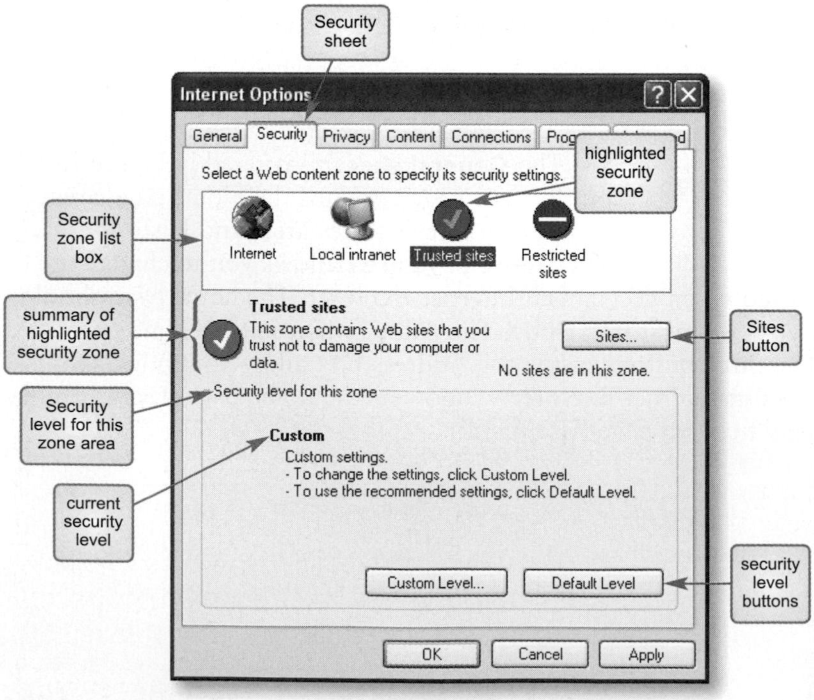

The Security Sheet

The **Security sheet** shown in Figure A-3 contains a security zone list box that contains an icon for each security zone available on the computer (Internet, Local intranet, Trusted sites, and Restricted sites), a summary of the highlighted security zone, the Sites button, and the Security level for this zone area. The Trusted sites icon is highlighted; a summary of the Trusted sites zone is displayed below

FIGURE A-3

the list box; and the **Security level for this zone area**, which indicates the security level of the zone, appears at the bottom of the Security sheet. The Security level can be changed as needed.

Internet Explorer divides the Internet into four zones of content to which you can assign a security setting. These zones are called **security zones** (Internet, Local intranet, Trusted sites, and Restricted sites), and Internet Explorer allows you to assign a Web site to a zone with a suitable security level. An explanation of the four security zones appears below:

- **Internet**: This zone contains all Web pages that you have not placed in other zones. The default security level for this zone is Medium.
- **Local intranet**: This zone contains all Web sites that are on an organization's intranet, including sites specified on the Connections sheet in the Internet Options dialog box, network paths, and local intranet sites. The default security level for this zone is Medium-low.
- **Trusted sites**: This zone contains Web sites that are trusted not to damage the computer or the data on the computer. The default security level for this zone is Low.
- **Restricted sites**: This zone contains Web sites that you do not trust because they could possibly damage the computer or the data on the computer. The default security level for this zone is High.

To assign a Web site to a security zone, click the appropriate icon in the security zone list box, click the Sites button, and then follow the instructions to assign a security zone. After assigning a Web page to a security zone, the icon of the security zone to which the Web site is assigned appears at the right side of the status bar in the Microsoft Internet Explorer window. Each time you attempt to open or download content from that Web site, Internet Explorer checks the security settings and responds appropriately.

The two buttons at the bottom of the Security sheet allow you to customize the settings for a security zone (Custom Level) and set the security level or reset the security level to the default level for the security zone (Default Level).

To change the security level of the highlighted security zone, click the Default Level button in the Security level for this zone area and then move the slider along the slide to display the different security levels.

The Privacy Sheet

The **Privacy sheet** illustrated in Figure A-4 contains the Settings area and Web Sites area. The **Settings area** displays the privacy setting (Medium) and allows you to change the privacy setting for the four security zones (Internet, Local intranet, Trusted sites, and Restricted sites) by moving the slider along the slide.

The three buttons at the bottom of the Settings area allow you to customize privacy settings and override the default setting for cookies. The Import button allows you to import a file containing customized privacy settings. The Advanced button allows you to override the default settings for cookies, select the settings for first-party cookies and third-party cookies, or choose to always accept

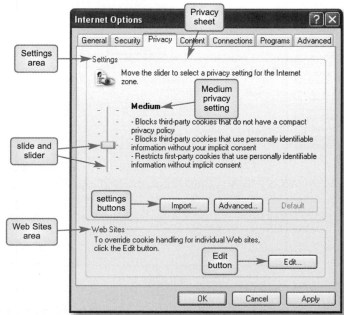

FIGURE A-4

cookies. A **first-party cookie** is a cookie that either originates on or is sent to a Web site you currently are viewing. A **third-party cookie** is a cookie that either originates on or is sent to a Web site other than the one you are viewing. The Default button resets the privacy setting to the default level and displays a slide you can use to select a privacy setting (Accept All Cookies, Low, Medium, Medium High, High, and Block All Cookies). The **Web Sites area** allows you to override cookie handling for an individual Web site and choose to allow or block cookies from the Web site.

The Content Sheet

The **Content sheet** illustrated in Figure A-5 contains three areas: Content Advisor area, Certificates area, and Personal information area. The **Content Advisor area** permits you to control the types of content (violent content, sexual content, and so on) that a computer can access on the Internet. The **Certificates area** allows you to positively identify yourself, agencies that grant certificates, and certificate publishers. In the **Personal information area**, you can modify the AutoComplete settings and your personal information (name, e-mail address, telephone numbers, and so on).

Content Advisor provides a way to help you control the types of content that your computer can access on the Internet. After turning on Content Advisor, content that does not meet or exceed the chosen criteria will not be displayed. Initially, Content Advisor is set to the most conservative (least likely to offend) setting. The two buttons in the Content Advisor area allow you to turn on Content Advisor (Enable) and modify the Content Advisor ratings for Internet sites (Settings).

A **certificate** is a statement guaranteeing the identity of a person or the security of a Web site. The **Personal certificate** guarantees your identity to Web sites that require certification. The **Web site certificate** guarantees that a Web site is secure and no other Web site has falsely assumed the identity of the Web site. The Clear SSL State button allows you to remove all client authentication certificates from the SSL cache. The **SSL cache** is a memory location that stores all certificates until you restart your computer. The Certificates button in the Certificates area allows you to require a Web site to send a security certificate to you before sending them information, and the Publishers button displays a list of trusted software publishers whose software can safely be placed on the computer.

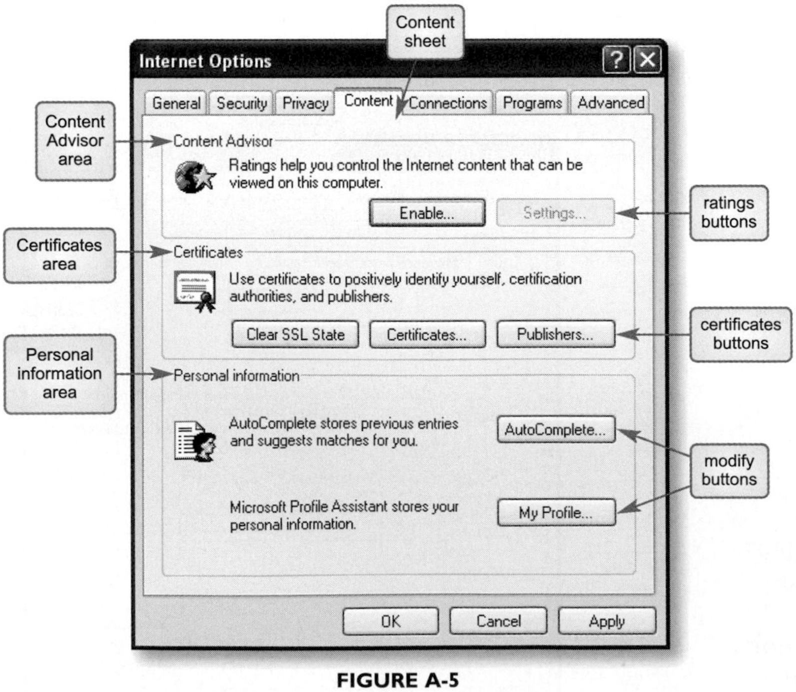

The two buttons in the Personal information area permit you to modify the settings of the AutoComplete feature and modify a user profile. The AutoComplete button lets you use AutoComplete to display Web addresses, forms, and user names and passwords. You can use the My Profile button to modify the personal information stored on the computer (name, e-mail address, home and business addresses, birthdays, NetMeeting settings, and Digital IDs).

FIGURE A-5

The Connections Sheet

The **Connections sheet** shown in Figure A-6 allows you to use the Internet Connection wizard to create a new Internet connection, control dial-up networking connections, and modify local area network (LAN) settings. The Setup button at the top of the sheet lets you create a new Internet connection. The **Dial-up and Virtual Private Network settings area** contains a list box displaying the current dial-up settings. The buttons in the area allow you to add, remove, and modify connections. The three options buttons control the method to connect to the Internet and allow you to select the default dial-up networking connection. The **Local Area Network (LAN) settings area** permits you to edit the local area network (LAN) settings if the computer is connected to a local area network.

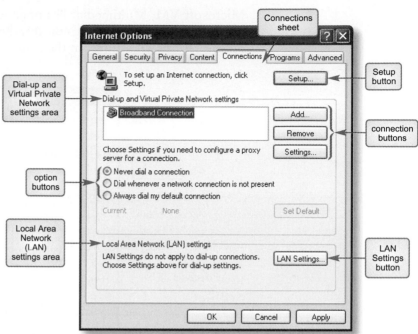

FIGURE A-6

The Programs Sheet

In Figure A-7, the **Programs sheet** allows you to select the Microsoft Windows program to use to edit Web pages, send and receive e-mail, read and post articles to a newsgroup, place an Internet call, manage appointments and tasks, and maintain contact information. The **Internet programs area** contains six boxes that contain the default program for each of the following Internet services: HTML editor, E-mail, Newsgroups, Internet call, Calendar, and Contact list.

The Reset Web Settings button below the Internet programs area lets you restore the default settings for the six Internet services listed in the Internet programs area. You can use the check box below the button to select Internet Explorer as the default Web browser.

The Advanced Sheet

The **Advanced sheet** illustrated in Figure A-8 on the next page contains the Settings list box and the Restore Defaults button. The **Settings list box** contains check boxes for each Internet Explorer setting. The settings are organized into categories: Accessibility, Browsing, HTTP 1.1 settings,

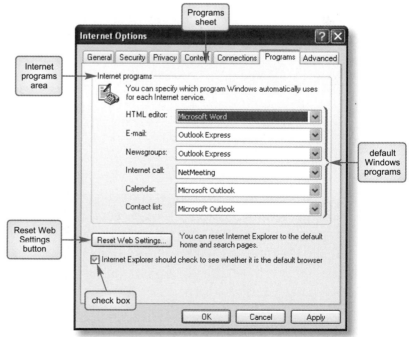

FIGURE A-7

Microsoft VM, Multimedia, Printing, Search from the Address bar, and Security. A check mark in a check box indicates the setting is selected. The Restore Defaults button returns all settings in the Settings list box to their original (default) settings.

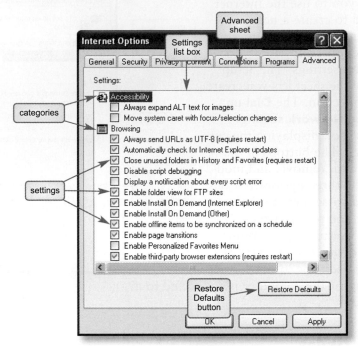

FIGURE A-8

Appendix B

Adding News Accounts

The msnnews.msn.com News Account

In Project 3, it is assumed that the msnnews.msn.com news account has been added to your computer and the msnnews.msn.com entry appears in the Folders list in the Outlook Express window. If the msnnews.msn.com news account is not displayed in the Folders list, it will be necessary to add the account. The following steps show how to add the news account to your computer.

1. Start Internet Explorer.
2. Click the Mail button on the Standard Buttons toolbar in the Microsoft Internet Explorer window.
3. Click Read News on the Mail menu.
4. If the Internet Connection Wizard dialog box is displayed (Figure B-1), go to step 9.

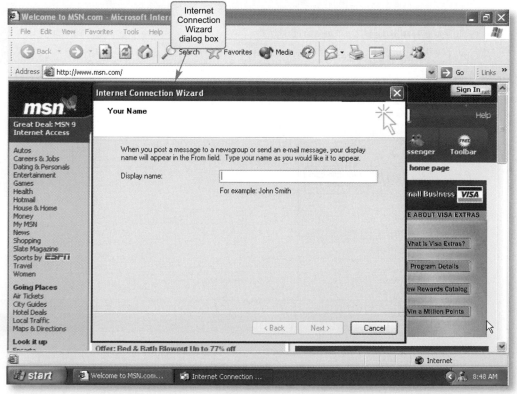

FIGURE B-1

5. Click the No button in the Outlook Express dialog box to close the dialog box.

6. Click Accounts on the Tools menu.

7. Click the Add button in the Internet Accounts dialog box.

8. Click News on the Add menu.

9. Type your name in the Display name text box in the Internet Connection Wizard dialog box and then click the Next button.

10. Type your e-mail address in the E-mail address text box in the Internet Connection Wizard dialog box and then click the Next button.

11. Type msnnews.msn.com in the News (NNTP) server text box and then click the Next button.

12. Click the Finish button in the Internet Connection Wizard dialog box.

13. If the Internet Accounts dialog box is displayed, click the Close button in the dialog box.

14. Click the No button in the Outlook Express dialog box.

15. The msnnews.msn.com account has been added and the msnnews.msn.com entry appears in the Folders list in the Outlook Express window (Figure B-2).

16. Close Outlook Express and Internet Explorer.

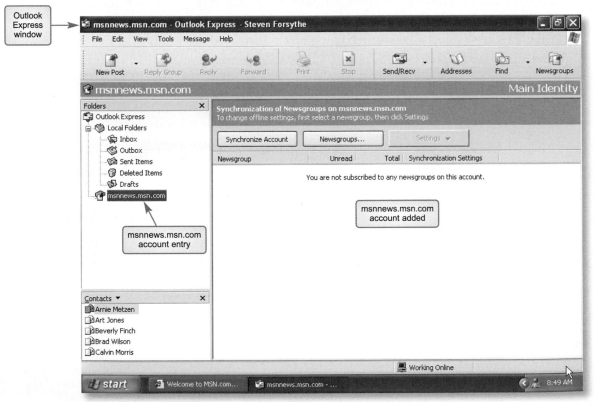

FIGURE B-2

Index